LibreOffice Base 4.0

A catalogue record for this book is available from the Hong Kong Public Libraries.

Published by Samurai Media Limited.

Email: info@samuraimedia.org

ISBN 978-988-14435-7-1

Contents

Copyright...2
   Contributors...2
   Feedback..2
   Acknowledgments...2
   Publication date and software version..2

Preface...7
  Who is this book for?..8
  What's in this book?...8
  Where to get more help..8
   Help system..8
   Free online support...8
   Paid support and training..9
  What you see may be different..9
   Illustrations...9
   Icons...10
  Using LibreOffice on a Mac...10
  What are all these things called?..10
  Who wrote this book?..11
  Frequently asked questions..12

Chapter 1
Introduction to Base..13
  Introduction...14
  Base – a container for database content...14
  Data input using forms..15
  Data input directly into a table..16
  Queries – getting information on data in tables..17
  Reports – presentation of data..17

Chapter 2
Creating a Database...21
  General notes on the creation of a database...22
  New database using the internal HSQL engine..22
  Accessing external databases...22
  MySQL databases...23
  dBase databases...30
  Spreadsheets...31
  Thunderbird address book..32

Chapter 3
Tables...33
  General information on tables..34
  Relationships between tables...34
   Relationships for tables in databases..34
   Tables and relationships for the example database...37
  Creating tables...40
   Creation using the graphical user interface...41
   Direct entry of SQL commands...43

Linking tables...48
Entering data into tables..52
    Entry using the Base GUI...52
    Direct entry using SQL..57
    Problems with these data entry methods..................................59

Chapter 4
Forms..61
Forms make data entry easier...62
Creating forms..62
    A simple form..62
    Toolbars for form design...63
Form properties..66
    Properties of controls..69
    A simple form completed..95
Main forms and subforms...103
One view – many forms..115

Chapter 5
Queries..121
General information on queries..122
Entering queries..122
    Creating queries using the Query Design dialog.......................122
    Query enhancement using SQL Mode...134
Using an alias in a query..141
Queries for the creation of list box fields.......................................142
Queries as a basis for additional information in forms..................143
Data entry possibilities within queries...143
Use of parameters in queries..144
Subqueries...144
Correlated subqueries..145
Queries as source tables for queries...145
Summarizing data with queries...146
More rapid access to queries using table views.............................147

Chapter 6
Reports...149
Creating reports using the Report Builder.......................................150
The user interface of the Report Builder..150
    General properties of fields...157
    Data properties of fields...161
Functions in the Report Builder...162
    Entering formulas...162
    User-defined functions..168
    Formula entry for a field..169
    Conditional print...169
    Conditional formatting...169

Chapter 7
Linking to Databases...171
General notes on database linkage...172

Registration of databases..172
Data source browser..172
    Data to Text...174
    Data to Fields...177
Mail merge...178
    Data source of current document...178
    Explorer on/off...178
Creating mail merge documents..178
Label printing..185
Direct creation of mail merge and label documents.......................................188
    Mail merge using the mouse..188
    Creating form letters by selecting fields...189
External forms..190
Database use in Calc..191
    Entering data into Calc...191
    Exporting data from Calc into a database..193
Converting data from one database to another...196

Chapter 8
Database tasks..197
General remarks on database tasks...198
Data filtering..198
Searching for data...200
Code snippets..201
    Getting someone's current age..201
    Getting a running balance by categories...202
    Line numbering...203
    Getting a line break through a query...205
    Grouping and summarizing..205

Chapter 9
Macros...207
General remarks on macros..208
Improving usability..209
    Automatic updating of forms..209
    Filtering records..210
    Searching data records...213
    Comboboxes as listboxes with an entry option.......................................215
    Navigation from one form to another..225
    Removing distracting elements from forms...226
Database tasks expanded using macros..226
    Making a connection to a database...226
    Securing your database...227
    Database compaction..228
    Decreasing the table index for autovalue fields.....................................228
Dialogs...229

Chapter 10
Database Maintenance..239
General remarks on maintaining databases...240
Compacting a database..240
Resetting autovalues..240

Querying database properties..240
Testing tables for unnecessary entries..241
    Testing entries using relationship definition..241
    Editing entries using forms and subforms...242
    Queries for finding orphan entries..243
Database search speed...243
    Effect of queries..243
    Effect of listboxes and comboboxes...244

Appendix **245**
Barcodes..246
Data types for the table editor...246
    Integers...246
    Floating-point numbers..246
    Text..247
    Time...247
    Other..247
Built-in functions and stored procedures...248
    Numeric..248
    Text..249
    Date/Time..250
    Database connection..251
    System...251
Information tables for HSQLDB..252
Database repair for *.odb files..253
Connecting a database to an external HSQLDB...255
Changing the database connection to external HSQLDB..257
    Changing the database connection for multi-user access..................................257
    Auto-incrementing values with external HSQLDB...259

Preface

Who is this book for?

Anyone who wants to get up to speed quickly with LibreOffice Base will find this book valuable. You may wish to first read Chapter 8, Getting Started with Base, in the *Getting Started* guide.

What's in this book?

This book introduces Base, the database component of LibreOffice. Base uses the HSQLDB database engine to create database documents. It can access databases created by many database programs, including Microsoft Access, MySQL, Oracle, and PostgreSQL. Base includes additional functionality that allows you to create full data-driven applications.

This book introduces the features and functions of Base, using two example databases.

- Creating a database
- Accessing external databases
- Creating and using tables in relational databases
- Creating and using forms for data entry
- Using queries to bring together data from different tables, calculate results where necessary, and quickly filter a specific record from a mass of data
- Creating reports using the Report Builder
- Linking databases to other documents and external forms, including use in mail merge
- Filtering and searching data
- Using macros to prevent input errors, simplify tasks, and improve usability of forms
- Maintaining databases

Where to get more help

This book, the other LibreOffice user guides, the built-in Help system, and user support systems assume that you are familiar with your computer and basic functions such as starting a program, opening and saving files.

Help system

LibreOffice comes with an extensive Help system. This is your first line of support for using LibreOffice. To display the full Help system, press *F1* or select **LibreOffice Help** from the Help menu. In addition, you can choose whether to activate Tips, Extended Tips, and the Help Agent (using **Tools > Options > LibreOffice > General**).

If Tips are enabled, place the mouse pointer over any of the icons to see a small box ("tooltip") with a brief explanation of the icon's function. For a more detailed explanation, select **Help > What's This?** and hold the pointer over the icon.

Free online support

The LibreOffice community not only develops software, but provides free, volunteer-based support. See Table 1 and this web page: http://www.libreoffice.org/get-help/

You can get comprehensive online support from the community through mailing lists and the Ask LibreOffice website. Other websites run by users also offer free tips and tutorials. This forum provides community support for LibreOffice: http://en.libreofficeforum.org/

This site provides support for LibreOffice, among other programs:
http://forum.openoffice.org/en/forum/

Table 1: Free support for LibreOffice users

Free LibreOffice support	
Ask LibreOffice	Questions and answers from the LibreOffice community http://ask.libreoffice.org/en/questions/
Documentation	User guides, how-tos, and other documentation. http://www.libreoffice.org/get-help/documentation/ https://wiki.documentfoundation.org/Documentation/Publications
FAQs	Answers to frequently asked questions http://wiki.documentfoundation.org/Faq
Mailing lists	Free community support is provided by a network of experienced users http://www.libreoffice.org/get-help/mailing-lists/
International support	The LibreOffice website in your language. http://www.libreoffice.org/international-sites/ International mailing lists http://wiki.documentfoundation.org/Local_Mailing_Lists
Accessibility options	Information about available accessibility options. http://www.libreoffice.org/get-help/accessibility/

Paid support and training

Alternatively, you can pay for support services. Service contracts can be purchased from a vendor or consulting firm specializing in LibreOffice.

What you see may be different

Illustrations

LibreOffice runs on Windows, Linux, and Mac OS X operating systems, each of which has several versions and can be customized by users (fonts, colors, themes, window managers). The illustrations in this guide were taken from a variety of computers and operating systems. Therefore, some illustrations will not look exactly like what you see on your computer display.

Also, some of the dialogs may be differ because of the settings selected in LibreOffice. You can either use dialogs from your computer system (default) or dialogs provided by LibreOffice. To change to using LibreOffice dialogs:

1) On Linux and Windows operating systems, go to **Tools > Options >LibreOffice > General** on the main menu bar to open the dialog for general options.

2) On a Mac operating system, go to **LibreOffice > Preferences > General** on the main menu bar to open the dialog for general options.

3) Select *Use LibreOffice dialogs* in *Open/Save dialogs* and, in Linux and Mac OS X operating systems only, *Print dialogs* to display the LibreOffice dialogs on your computer display.

4) Click **OK** to save your settings and close the dialog.

Icons

The icons used to illustrate some of the many tools available in LibreOffice may differ from the ones used in this guide. The icons in this guide have been taken from a LibreOffice installation that has been set to display the Galaxy set of icons.

If you wish, you can change your LibreOffice software package to display Galaxy icons as follows:

1) On Linux and Windows operating systems, go to **Tools > Options >LibreOffice > View** on the main menu bar to open the dialog for view options.

2) On a Mac operating system, go to **LibreOffice > Preferences > View** on the main menu bar to open the dialog for view options.

3) In *User interface > Icon size and style* select *Galaxy* from the options available in the drop-down list.

4) Click **OK** to save your settings and close the dialog.

Note	Some Linux operating systems, for example Ubuntu, include LibreOffice as part of the installation and may not include the Galaxy set of icons. You should be able to download the Galaxy icon set from the software repository for your Linux operating system.

Using LibreOffice on a Mac

Some keystrokes and menu items are different on a Mac from those used in Windows and Linux. The table below gives some common substitutions for the instructions in this chapter. For a more detailed list, see the application Help.

Windows or Linux	Mac equivalent	Effect
Tools > Options menu selection	**LibreOffice > Preferences**	Access setup options
Right-click	*Control+click* and/or *right-click* depending on computer setup	Open a context menu
Ctrl (Control)	⌘ *(Command)*	Used with other keys
F5	*Shift+⌘+F5*	Open the Navigator
F11	⌘*+T*	Open the Styles and Formatting window

What are all these things called?

The terms used in LibreOffice for most parts of the *user interface* (the parts of the program you see and use, in contrast to the behind-the-scenes code that actually makes it work) are the same as for most other programs.

A *dialog* is a special type of window. Its purpose is to inform you of something, or request input from you, or both. It provides controls for you to use to specify how to carry out an action. The technical names for common controls are shown in Figure 1. In most cases we do not use the technical terms in this book, but it is useful to know them because the Help and other sources of information often use them.

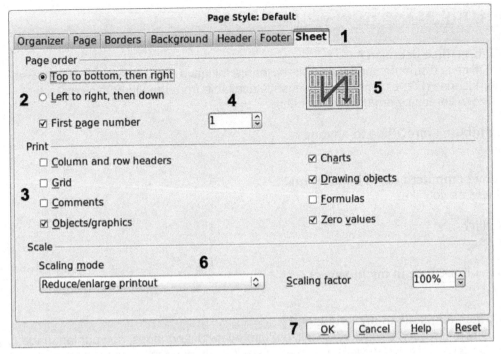

Figure 1: Dialog showing common controls

1) Tabbed page (not strictly speaking a control).
2) Radio buttons (only one can be selected at a time).
3) Checkbox (more than one can be selected at a time).
4) Spin box (click the up and down arrows to change the number shown in the text box next to it, or type in the text box).
5) Thumbnail or preview.
6) Drop-down list from which to select an item.
7) Push buttons.

In most cases, you can interact only with the dialog (not the document itself) as long as the dialog remains open. When you close the dialog after use (usually, clicking **OK** or another button saves your changes and closes the dialog), then you can again work with your document.

Some dialogs can be left open as you work, so you can switch back and forth between the dialog and your document. An example of this type is the Find & Replace dialog.

Who wrote this book?

This book was written by volunteers from the LibreOffice community. Profits from sales of the printed edition will be used to benefit the community.

How is LibreOffice licensed?

LibreOffice is distributed under the Open Source Initiative (OSI) approved Lesser General Public License (LGPL). The LGPL license is available from the LibreOffice website: http://www.libreoffice.org/download/license/

May I distribute LibreOffice to anyone?

Yes.

How many computers may I install it on?

As many as you like.

May I sell it?

Yes.

May I use LibreOffice in my business?

Yes.

Is LibreOffice available in my language?

LibreOffice has been translated (localized) into over 40 languages, so your language probably is supported. Additionally, there are over 70 *spelling*, *hyphenation*, and *thesaurus* dictionaries available for languages, and dialects that do not have a localized program interface. The dictionaries are available from the LibreOffice website at: www.libreoffice.org.

How can you make it for free?

LibreOffice is developed and maintained by volunteers and has the backing of several organizations.

I am writing a software application. May I use programming code from LibreOffice in my program?

You may, within the parameters set in the LGPL. Read the license: http://www.libreoffice.org/download/license/

Why do I need Java to run LibreOffice? Is it written in Java?

LibreOffice is not written in Java; it is written in the C++ language. Java is one of several languages that can be used to extend the software. The Java JDK/JRE is only required for some features; the most notable one is the HSQLDB relational database engine.

How can I contribute to LibreOffice?

You can help with the development and user support of LibreOffice in many ways, and you do not need to be a programmer. To start, check out this webpage: http://www.documentfoundation.org/contribution/

May I distribute the PDF of this book, or print and sell copies?

Yes, as long as you meet the requirements of one of the licenses in the copyright statement at the beginning of this book. You do not have to request special permission. In addition, we request that you share with the project some of the profits you make from sales of books, in consideration of all the work we have put into producing them.

Chapter 1
Introduction to Base

Introduction

In everyday office operation, spreadsheets are regularly used to aggregate sets of data and to perform some kind of analyses on them. As the data in a spreadsheet is laid out in a table view, plainly visible and able to be edited or added to, many users ask why they should use a database instead of a spreadsheet. This handbook explains the differences between the two, beginning with a short section on what can be done with a database.

This chapter introduces two database examples and the entire Handbook is built around these. One database is named Media_without_macros.odb and the other, extended with the inclusion of macros, is named Media_with_macros.odb.

Base – a container for database content

A Base file is a compressed folder that contains information for the different work areas of Base. In daily use, Base initially opens with the following view.

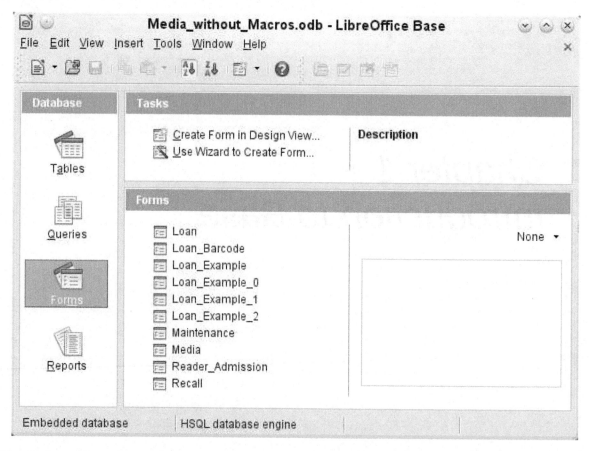

The Base environment contains four work areas: Tables, Queries, Forms, and Reports. Depending on the work area selected, various tasks—creating new content or calling up existing elements—may be carried out.

Base starts with the Form view, because forms are the elements most commonly used when working with databases.

Data input using forms

Simple forms show just one table as in the upper part of the *Loan* form.

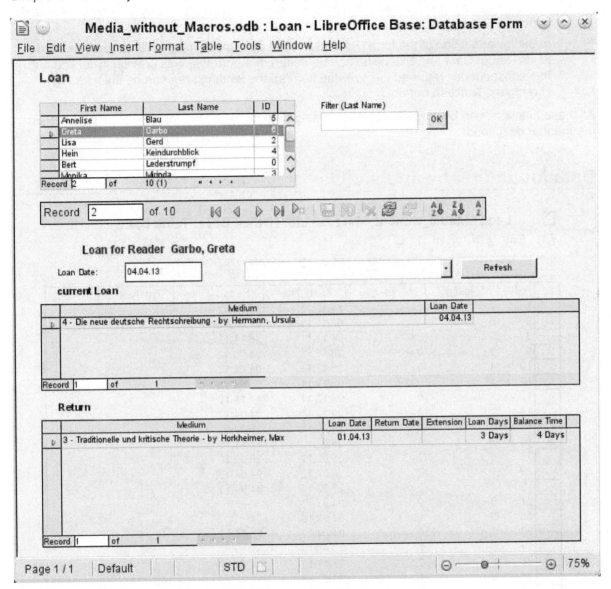

The Loan form has been extended to show additional information:

- The range of persons shown can be filtered on last name to limit the detail shown. If a user inputs the letter "G" in the Filter (Last Name) field at the right of the Loan table, only persons whose last name begins with "G" will be shown.

- New borrower information can be input directly into the table fields of the form.

- Details of items to be borrowed are input and shown in the area in the middle of the form. If a previously borrowed item is overdue and must be returned this area is blocked (no input possible) and the title will indicate "Loan temporary locked!".

- Items on loan are shown in the lower area of the form. The date for returning each borrowed item is compared with the current date and the remaining loan duration shown.

- The borrowing date is set as the current date. In the pull-down field at the right of the Loan Date are the media items which can be borrowed. Items which are already on loan to the selected borrower are not available for selection.

- Media items selected for loan are added to the current loan details by clicking the **Refresh** button.

- In the lower section of the form (Return) it is not possible to delete a data row. Only the fields Return Date and Extension can be edited. If a borrower was previously locked and has subsequently returned the overdue item(s), the lending area can be unlocked by clicking the **Refresh** button.

All these functions can be carried out without using macros, when the form is set up and filled in the manner described.

Data input directly into a table

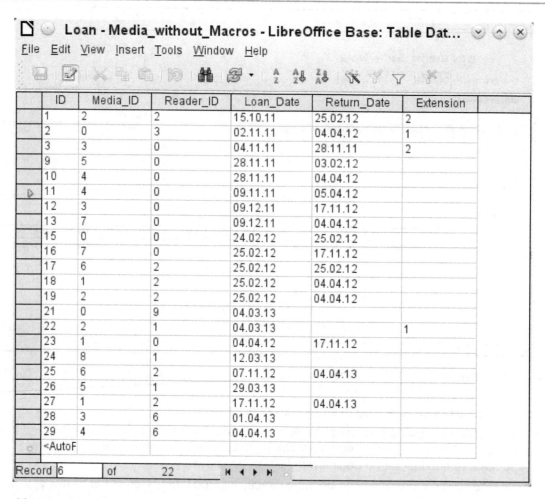

The table structure for such a form is relatively basic and easy to set up. In the table shown above, the same data can be directly input in the rows and columns of the table as when using the form.

- The first field shows a primary key ("ID") which is automatically generated. More on this topic can be found in the chapter on Tables.

- The second field, Media_ID, stores the primary key of the Media table, a number which refers to the Media. In the form the media id, title and author are shown in the drop-down menu.

- The third field, Reader_ID, stores the primary key of the Reader table. This key is a number which refers to the reader. In the form the Last name and First name of the reader are shown.
- The fourth field stores the loan date. If this date is present and is later than the current date, the corresponding data set for the reader is shown in the bottom table of the form under Return.
- The field marked Extension contains information about extensions of the loan for an item. The meaning of the values 1, 2 and so on is explained later. The database contains a special table called Settings for this type of information.

The input of this data permits the management of a simple library.

Queries – getting information on data in tables

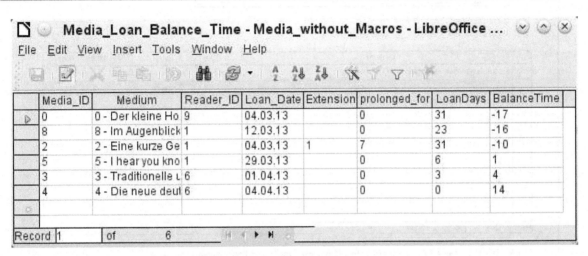

The query shown above lists all media which are currently out on loan. It calculates for each item how long it has been on loan and the balance of the loan period.

- All media for which the Return_Date field is empty is listed. As an additional overview, the medium name is included in the query together with the Media_ID.
- The reference to the Reader is established with the primary key of the Reader table.
- The value of the LoanDays field is calculated as the difference between the Loan_Date and the current date.
- The number of LoanDays is subtracted from the Loan Time to give the remaining number of days in the loan period. The Loan Time can vary with different media types.
- In the Settings table a value of '1' for Extension corresponds to an extension of the loan period of 7 days. In the data set above, the line with Media_ID '2' shows an extension of 7 days.

Reports – presentation of data

Before an actual report in the form of a recall notice can be printed, the recall information must be entered into the Recall form. The table in the form shows all persons who have borrowed items with a negative remaining loan time.

For each media item to be recalled, the recall date and recall notice number is entered. The recall date defaults to the current date. The recall number is an integer incremented by 1 with each successive recall notice for a particular lender/media.

This form, in the current database example without macros, requires user input to create recall notices. In the macro version, the date is automatically entered and the recall notice printed.

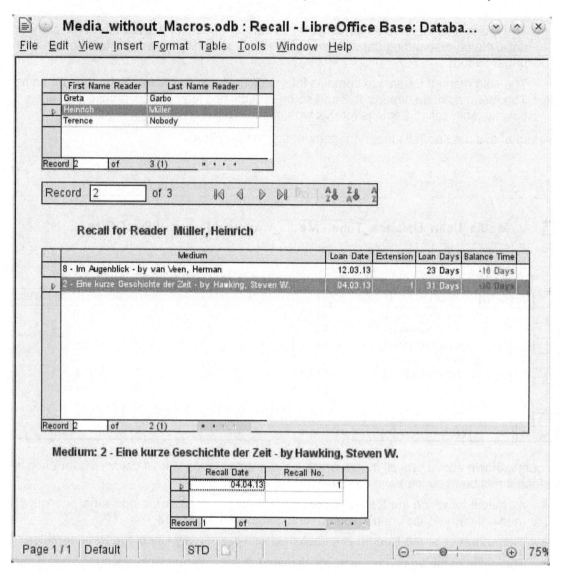

The recall notice is generated by means of a query from the previously input data. The user of the database needs only to choose the Recall report and a recall letter can be printed out and sent to all persons who have a recall entry made in the form on the previous page.

In such a report there may be multiple entries (overdue items) for a particular person. If the table containing the items for this person exceeds the space on a page, it is extended to cover a succeeding page.

Such a report is more encompassing than a mail merge letter produced with Writer. It automatically gathers together the data sets for printing and arranges the necessary accompanying text accordingly.

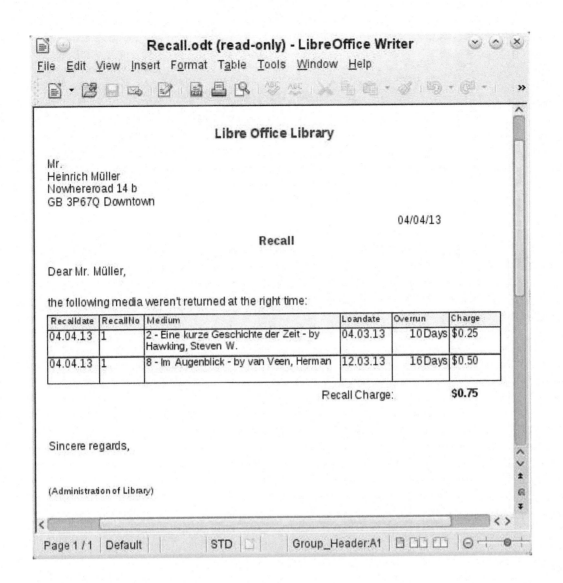

Recall.odt (read-only) - LibreOffice Writer

File   Edit   View   Insert   Format   Table   Tools   Window   Help

Libre Office Library

Mr.
Heinrich Müller
Nowhereroad 14 b
GB 3P67Q Downtown

04/04/13

Recall

Dear Mr. Müller,

the following media weren't returned at the right time:

Recalldate	RecallNo	Medium	Loandate	Overrun	Charge
04.04.13	1	2 - Eine kurze Geschichte der Zeit - by Hawking, Steven W.	04.03.13	10 Days	$0.25
04.04.13	1	8 - Im Augenblick - by van Veen, Herman	12.03.13	16 Days	$0.50

Recall Charge: **$0.75**

Sincere regards,

(Administration of Library)

Page 1 / 1   Default   STD   Group_Header:A1

Chapter 2
Creating a Database

How to create a new database

General notes on the creation of a database

The basics of creating a database in LibreOffice are described in Chapter 8 of the *Getting Started* guide, Getting Started with Base.

The database component of LibreOffice, called Base, provides a graphical interface for working with databases. In addition, LibreOffice contains a version of the HSQL database engine. This HSQLDB database can only be used by a single user. The entire data set is stored in an ODB file which has no file locking mechanism when opened by a user.

New database using the internal HSQL engine

If a database with multiple users is not planned, or the user wishes to gain some initial experience with a database, the internal database engine will suffice. It is possible at some later stage to transfer the database to an external HSQLDB environment, where multiple users can have concurrent access to the database on the HSQLDB server. This is described in the Appendix to this Handbook.

The creation of a new internal database is described in detail in Getting Started with Base.

A database which is registered in LibreOffice can be accessed by other program components as a data source (for example, mail merge). This registration process can be carried out at a later stage if desired.

Accessing external databases

An external database must exist before it can be accessed. Assuming that access to a database is desired, the database must be set up to allow network connections with a specific user name and password before external programs can connect to it.

When such a database is properly set up, a user may, depending on the available connection software (the database driver), create tables, input data, and query data.

Click on **File > New > Database** to open the Database Wizard and allow a connection to an existing database to be made. The list of available database types varies according to operating system and user interface, but the following should always be available:

- dBase
- JDBC
- MySQL
- ODBC
- Oracle JDBC
- PostgreSQL
- Spreadsheet
- Text
- as well as various types of address books.

The connection options will vary according to the type of database selected. These can in any case be corrected later, after the *.odb file is created.

Some database types (for example spreadsheets) do not allow new data to be entered. These are used only to search for or report on existing data.

MySQL databases

There was an extension for MySQL, the MySQL Native Connector, which should allow Base to connect directly to a MySQL database. The extension was in the LibreOffice Extensions center under the Base Category but is not being developed at present.

General access to MySQL for versions of LibreOffice from 3.5 onwads is via JDBC or ODBC. To be able to use JDBC, it is necessary to install mysql-connector-java.jar. This Java Archive file is best copied into the same folder where the current java version used in LibreOffice is located. This is likely to be a subfolder like ...javapath.../lib/ext for a Linux installation.

Alternatively the appropriate folder containing the Java archive can be set through **Tools > Options > Java > ClassPath**.

The method of access to an existing MySQL database is shown in the following steps.

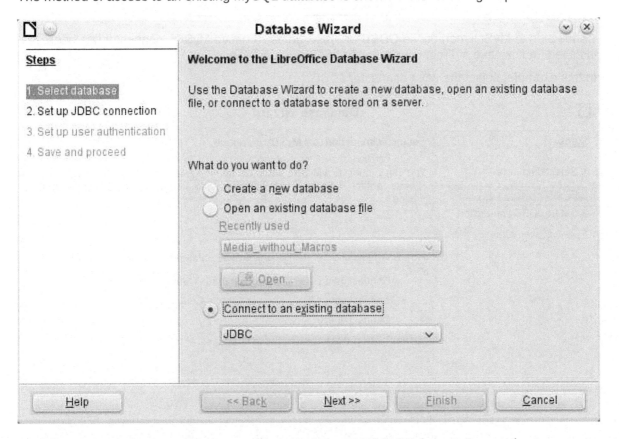

Creation of a new database is only possible in the internal HSQLDB format. Connection to an external database is only possible when the database already exists.

Select the *Connect to an existing database* option. A list of database formats is contained on the pull-down menu. Select MySQL.

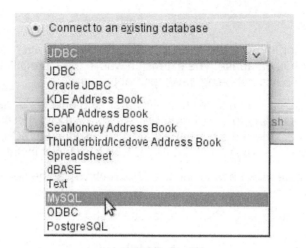

Connection to MySQL can be via ODBC or JDBC unless a native MySQL connector has been installed. In this case a direct connection to MySQL is possible.

In this example, select the Java connector JDBC.

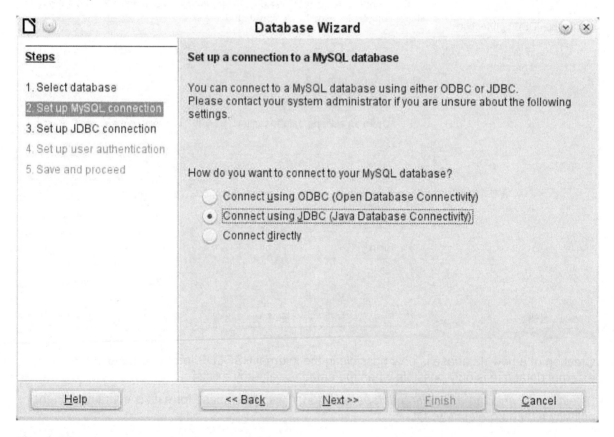

The database name must be known and input.

If the MySQL server is on the same computer as LibreOffice, then the Server name can be set as localhost. Otherwise the IP address of the server or its hostname on the network or internet must be input. It is also possible to access a database with Base where the database is located on the website of an Internet Service Provider.

The default port number will usually be correct.

Type in the JDBC driver class and click the **Test class** button. A dialog should pop up confirming that the connector is loaded and accessible using Java. The mysql-connector-java.jar file must either be in the same path as the version of Java in use in LibreOffice or directly linked in to LibreOffice.

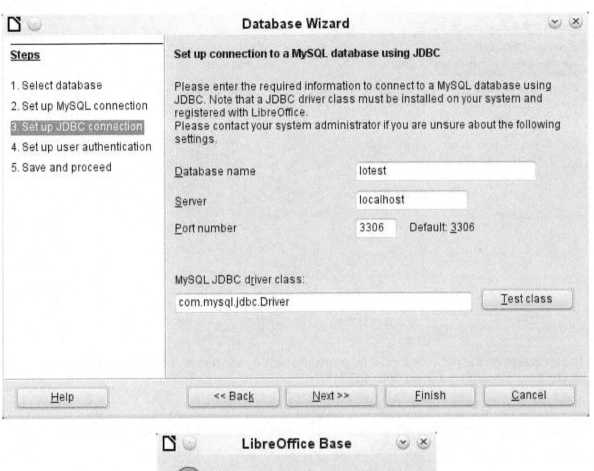

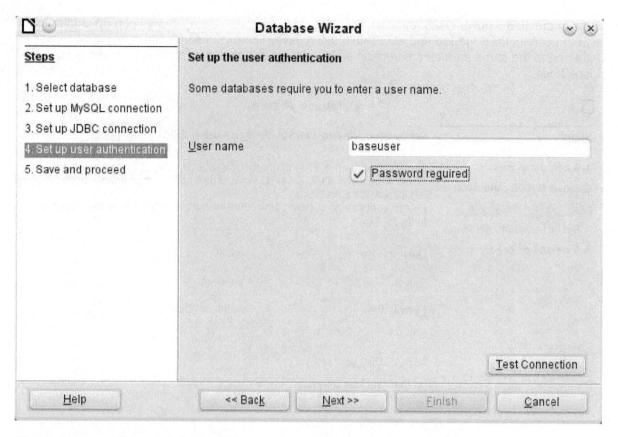

The database on the network should be protected with a user name and password. Again a connection test may be carried out.

Note	If a direct connection was selected, this test will generate error messages. Without testing, Base will, at the end of the Assistant, open the database window and connection to MySQL.

The connection test starts the authentication process using the user name previously input. After the correct password is input, a dialog announces the result of the test. If MySQL is not running at this time, an error message is shown.

The final step is registering the database. The database can, if necessary, be registered at a later time to allow its use with Writer or Calc.

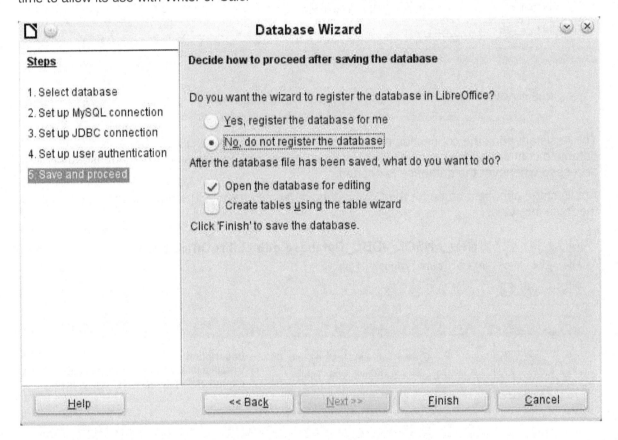

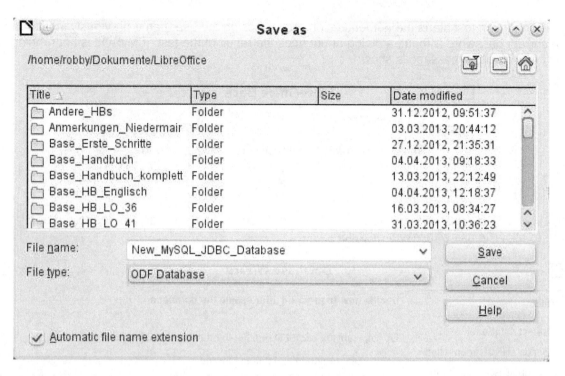

The Assistant ends the connection process with the storage of the ODB database. The ODB database contains all the connection information needed to allow tables in the database to be accessed whenever the database is opened.

At this stage choose a name for the ODB database file and save it. The next picture is a view of the Base interface.

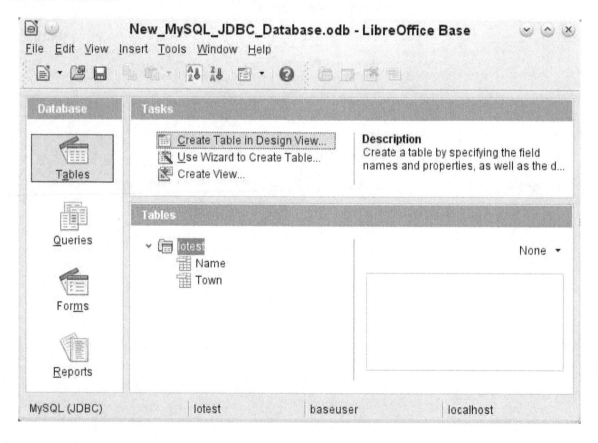

The tables in the database are contained in the tree under the name of the database.

The view of the table tree can be closed by clicking on the database name. For a single database connection this does not make much sense, but it does give a visible indication of the direct connection.

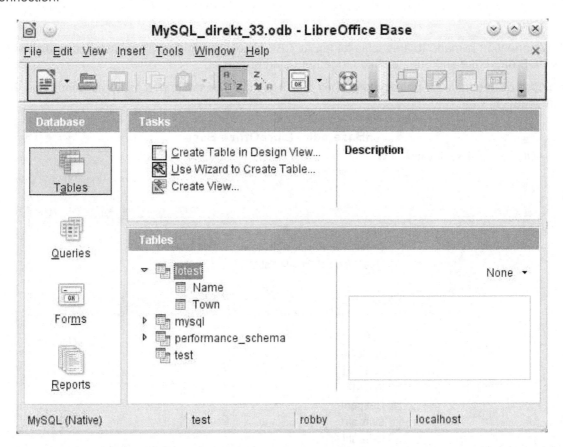

Instead of only the database input in Step 3 of the Wizard (see lower status bar), LibreOffice opens all databases that are available in MySQL to the user "robby".

Queries must include in the MySQL syntax not only the table name but also the database which contains, for example, the following code:

```
… FROM "myphplib"."ASB" AS "ASB", "myphplib"."Kategorien" AS "Kategorien"
```

It is also possible in every such case to specify an alias, made up from the database and table names. More details are given in the chapter on Queries.

Tables can be created and deleted in a database. Fields with auto values may be created when setting up the structure of tables. In MySQL the starting value of such fields defaults to 1.

dBase databases

dBase databases have a format where all data is contained in separate, previously initialized tables. Links between the tables must be made in program code. Relations are not supported.

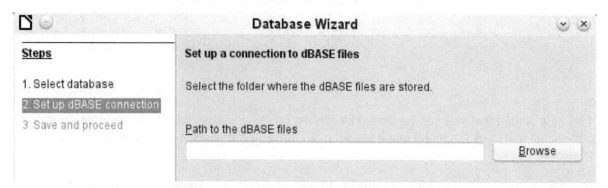

The connection is made to a specific folder. All DBF files in this folder will be included and shown in the ODB database and can be linked together using queries.

Tables in dBase have no primary key. They can in principle be described as corresponding to the worksheets in Calc.

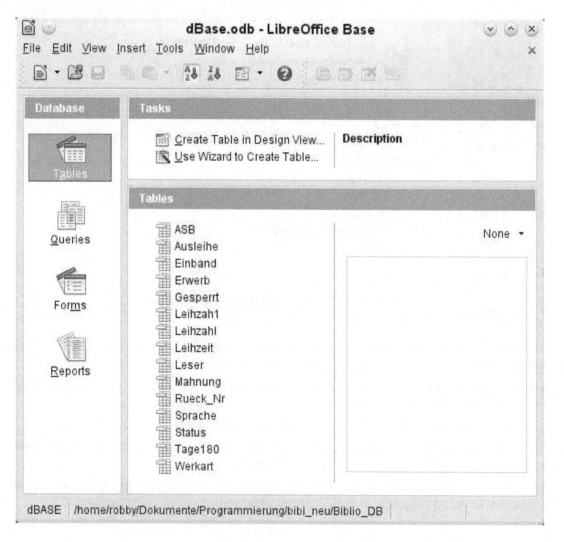

Tables can be created and will then be copied as new files in the folder previously selected.

The number of different field types for a new dBase table is clearly less than when the internal HSQLDB format is used. In the following figure there are still some field types with the same type name.

	Field Name	Field Type
	ID	Integer [INTEGER]
	FirstName	Text [VARCHAR]
▷	LastName	Text [VARCHAR] ⌄
		Yes/No [BOOLEAN]
		Memo [LONGVARCHAR]
		Decimal [DECIMAL]
		Decimal [NUMERIC]
		Integer [INTEGER]
		Double [DOUBLE]
		Double [DOUBLE]
		Text [VARCHAR]
		Date [DATE]
		Date/Time [TIMESTAMP]

The dBase format is especially suitable for the exchange and extensive editing of data. In addition, spreadsheet calculations can directly access dBase tables. It may be better to manipulate the data in Base because Calc requires the input of the type of character encoding, whereas Base simply takes the appropriate encoding provided by the operating system. Old dBase files may exhibit small decoding errors where special characters have been used.

Spreadsheets

Calc or Excel spreadsheets can also be used as the table source for databases. If, however, a Calc spreadsheet is used, no editing of the table data will be possible. If the Calc document is still open, it will be write protected.

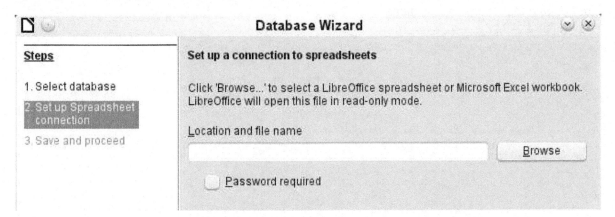

The only questions to be answered are the location of the spreadsheet file and whether or not it is password protected. Base then opens the spreadsheet and includes all worksheets in the document. The first row is used for the field names and the worksheet names become the table names.

Relationships between spreadsheets cannot be set up in Base, as Calc is not suitable for use as a relational database.

Thunderbird address book

The Assistant will automatically seek a connection to an address book, for example as used in Thunderbird. The assistant will prompt for the location of the ODB file that will be produced.

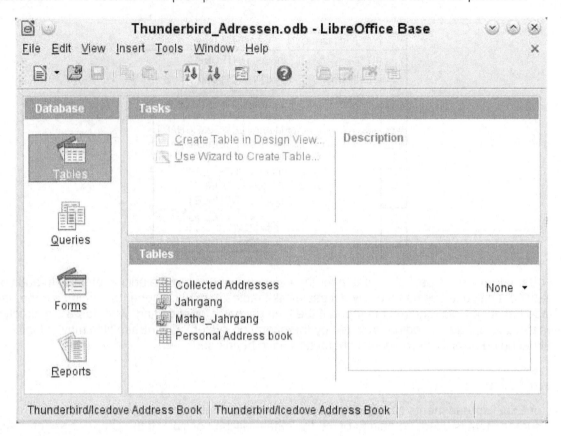

All tables are shown. As in Calc, the tables are not editable. Base uses the table data only for queries and mail merge applications.

Chapter 3
Tables

General information on tables

Databases store data in tables. The main difference from the tables in a simple spreadsheet is that the fields into which the data is written must be clearly defined beforehand. For example, a database does not allow a text field to contain numbers for use in calculations. Such numbers are displayed, but only as strings, whose actual numerical value is zero. Similarly, images cannot be included in all types of fields.

Details of which data types are available can be obtained from the Table Design window in Base. They are shown in the Appendix to this handbook.

Simple databases are based on only one table. All data elements are entered independently, which can lead to multiple entry of the same data. A simple address book for private use can be created in this way. However, the address book of a school or a sports association could contain so much repetition of postcodes and locations that these fields are better placed in one or even two separate tables.

Storing data in separate tables helps:

- Reduce repeated input of the same content
- Prevent spelling errors due to repeated input
- Improve filtering of data in the displayed tables

When creating a table, you should always consider whether multiple repetitions, especially of text or images (which consume a lot of storage) may occur in the table. If so, you need to export them into another table. How to do this in principle is described in Chapter 8, Getting Started with Base, in the *Getting Started with LibreOffice* book.

Relationships between tables

This chapter explains many of these steps in detail, using an example database for a library: media_without_macros. Constructing the tables for this database is an extensive job, as it covers not only the addition of items into a media library but also the subsequent loan of them.

Relationships for tables in databases

The more relationships there are between tables, the more complex is the design task. Figure 2 shows the overall table structure of this example database as an overview, scaled to fit the page size of this document. To read the content, zoom the page to 200%.

therefore leads to fields being exported which will be filled with content for only some of the records.

Tables and relationships for the example database

The example database (media_without_macros) must satisfy three requirements: media additions and removals, loans, and user administration.

Media addition table

First, media must be added into the database so that a library can work with them. However, for a simple summary of a media collection at home, you could create easier databases with the wizard; that might be sufficient for home use.

The central table for Media addition is the *Media* table (see Figure 5).

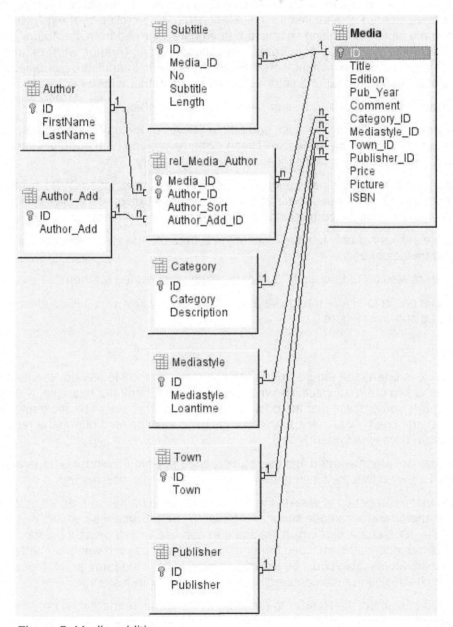

Figure 5: Media addition

In this table all fields that are directly entered are assumed not to be also in use for other media with the same content. Duplication should therefore be avoided.

For this reason, planned fields in the table include the title, the ISBN, an image of the cover, and the year of publication. The list of fields can be extended if required. So, for instance, librarians might want to include fields for the size (number of pages), the series title, and so on.

The *Subtitle* table contains the detailed content of CDs. As a CD can contain several pieces of music, a record of the individual pieces in the main table would require a lot of additional fields (Subtitle 1, Subtitle 2, etc.) or the same item would have to be entered many times. The *Subtitle* table therefore stands in a n:1 relationship to the *Media* table.

The fields of the *Subtitle* table are (in addition to the subtitle itself) the sequence number of the subtitle and the duration of the track. The *Length* field must first be defined as a time field. In this way, the total duration of the CD can be calculated and displayed in a summary if necessary.

The authors have a n:m relationship to the media. One item can have several authors, and one author might have created several items. This relationship is controlled by the *rel_Media_Author* table. The primary key of this linking table is the foreign key, formed from the *Author* and *Media* tables. The *rel_Media_Author* table includes an additional sorting (Author_Sort) of authors, for example by the sequence in which they are named in the book. In addition, a supplementary label such as Producer, Photographer and so on is added to the author where necessary.

Category, Mediastyle, Town and Publisher have a 1:n relationship.

For the **Category,** a small library can use something like Art or Biology. For larger libraries, general systems for libraries are available. These systems provide both abbreviations and complete descriptions. Hence both fields appear under Category.

The **Mediastyle** is linked to the loan period *Loantime*. For example, video DVDs might on principle have a loan period of 7 days, but books might be loaned for 21 days. If the loan period is linked to any other criteria, there will be corresponding changes in your methodology.

The **Town** table serves not only to store location data from the media but also to store the locations used in the addresses of users.

Since **Publishers** also recur frequently, a separate table is provided for them.

The *Media* table has in total four foreign keys and one primary key, which is used as a foreign key in two tables, as shown in Figure 5.

Loan table

The central table is **Loan** (see Figure 6). It is the link between the Media and Reader tables. In case you need to find out retrospectively who has taken out a book (for example, if someone notices during the loan process that the book is damaged, or if you wish to make a list of the most popular media), the *Loan_Date* in the loan record is not simply deleted during the return process. Instead a *Return_Date* is recorded.

Similarly, Reminders are integrated into the loan procedure. Each reminder is separately entered into the **Recall** table so that the total number of reminders can be determined.

As well as an extension period in weeks, there is an extra field in the loan record that enables media to be loaned using a barcode scanner (*Media_ID_BC*). Barcodes contain, in addition to the individual Media_ID, a check digit which the scanner can use to determine if the value scanned in is correct. This barcode field is included here only for test purposes. It would be better if the primary key of the Media table could be directly entered in barcode form, or if a macro were used to remove the check digit from the entered barcode number before storage.

Finally we need to connect the **Reader** to the loan. In the actual reader table, only the name, an optional lock, and a foreign key linking to the Gender table are included in the plan.

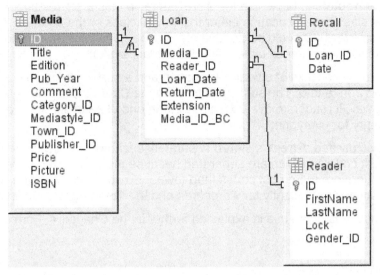

Figure 6: Loan

User administration table

For this table design, two scenarios are envisaged. The chain of tables shown in Figure 6 is designed for school libraries. Here there is no need for addresses, as the pupils can be contacted through the school. Reminders do not need to be sent out by post but can be distributed internally.

The Address chain is necessary in the case of public libraries. Here you need to enter data that will be needed for the creation of reminder letters. See Figure 7.

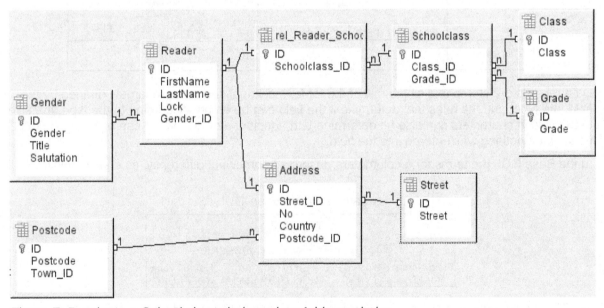

Figure 7: Readers - a School class chain and an Address chain

The **Gender** table ensures that the correct *Salutation* is used in reminders. The writing of reminders can then be automated as far as possible. In addition, some given names can be equally masculine or feminine. Therefore the separate listing of gender is required even when reminders are written out by hand.

The **rel_Reader_Schoolclass** table, like the **Address** table, has a 1:1 relationship with the **Reader** table. This was chosen because either the school class or the address might be required. Otherwise the *Schoolclass_ID* could be put directly into the pupil table; the same would be true of the complete content of the address table in a public library system.

A **School class** usually consists of a year designation and a stream suffix. In a 4-stream school, this suffix might run from **a** to **d**. The suffix is entered in the **Class** table. The year is in a separate **Grade** table. That way, if readers move up a class at the end of each school year, you can simply change the year entry for everyone.

The **Address** is also divided. **Street** is stored separately because street names within an area are often repeated. Post code and town are separated because there are often several post codes for a single area and therefore more post codes than towns. So compared with the **Address** table, the **Postcode** table contains significantly fewer records and the **Town** table even fewer.

How this table structure is put to use is explained further in the Chapter 4, Forms, in this handbook.

Creating tables

Most LibreOffice users will generally use the graphical user interface (GUI) exclusively to create tables. Direct entry of SQL commands becomes necessary when, for example, a field must subsequently be inserted at a particular position, or a standard value must be set after the table has been saved.

Table terminology: The picture below shows the standard division of tables into columns and rows.

TABLE								
		COLUMN				COLUMN		
		Field Name (FIELD)	Field Type (TYPE)	NULL	DEFAULT	Field Name (FIELD)	Field Type (TYPE)	NULL	DEFAULT
ROW		Record →						

Data records are stored in a single row of the table. Individual columns are largely defined by the field, the type, and the rules that determine if the field can be empty. According to the type, the size of the field in characters can also be determined. In addition, a default value can be specified to be used when nothing was entered into the field.

In the Base GUI, the terms for a column are described somewhat differently, as shown below.

Notations of the Base-GUI			
COLUMN			
		Field properties	
Field Name (FIELD)	Field Type (TYPE)	Entry required (NULL/NOT NULL)	Default value (DEFAULT)

Field becomes *Field Name*, *Type* becomes *Field Type*. Field Name and Field Type are entered into the upper area of the Table Design window. In the lower area you have the opportunity to set, under the Field properties the other column properties, in so far as they can be set using the GUI. Limitations include setting the default value of a date field to the actual date of entry. This is possible only by using the appropriate SQL command (see "Direct entry of SQL commands" on page 43).

Note	Default values: The term "Default value" in the GUI does not mean what the database user generally understands as a default value. The GUI displays a certain value visibly, which is saved with the data.
	The default value in a database is stored in the table definition. It is then written into the field whenever this is empty in a new data record. SQL default values do **not** appear *when editing table properties*.

Creation using the graphical user interface

Database creation using the graphical user interface is described in detail in Chapter 8, Getting Started with Base, in the *Getting Started with LibreOffice* book. Therefore only the main sources of error are described here.

When a table design is saved, you may be asked if a primary key should be created. This signifies that a necessary field is missing from the table. Without a primary key, the database cannot access the tables. Usually this field is given the abbreviation *ID* and the data type INTEGER and allowed to run as an AutoValue. You can make it the primary key with a right-click on the corresponding field.

If information from another table is to be pulled through into this one (for example, an address database with separate post codes and locations), you must include in the table a field of the same data type as the primary key of the other table. If the **Postcode** table has as its primary key the field *ID*, of data type *Tiny Integer*, the **Address** table must have a field *Postcode_ID* with the data type *Tiny Integer*. In other words, the **Address** table will always contain only the number that serves as the primary key in the **Postcode** table. This means that the **Address** table now has a foreign key in addition to its own primary key.

Basic rules for naming fields in the table: no two fields may have the same name. Therefore you cannot have a second field with the name *ID* as a foreign key in the Address table.

There are limits to the changes you can make in the field type. An upgrade (longer text field, larger numeric range) is unproblematic as all the values already entered will fit the new type. A downgrade creates problems and may cause loss of data.

Creating an index

Sometimes it is useful to index other fields or a combination of other fields in addition to the primary key. An index speeds up searching and can also be used to prevent duplicate entries.

Each index has a defined sort order. If a table is displayed without sorting, the sort order will be according to the content of the fields specified in the index.

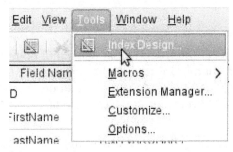

Figure 8: Access to Index Design

Open the table for editing by right-clicking and using the context menu. Then you can access index creation with **Tools > Index Design**.

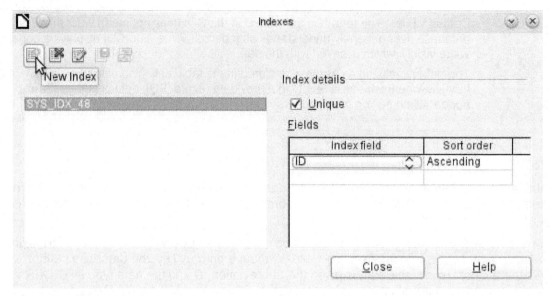

Figure 9: Creating a new Index

On the Indexes dialog (Figure 9), click **New Index** to create an index in addition to the primary key.

The new index is automatically given the name *index1*. The **Index field** specifies which field or fields are to be used for this index. At the same time you can choose the Sort order.

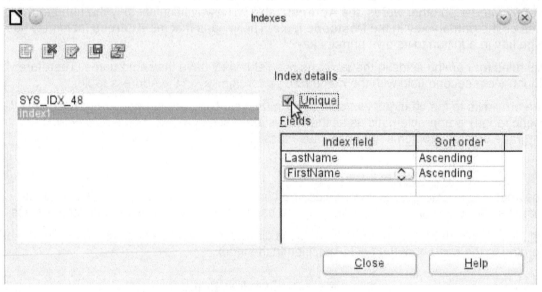

Figure 10: The Index is defined as Unique.

In principle, an index can also be created from table fields that do not contain unique values. However in Figure 10, the Index detail **Unique** has been checked, so that the *LastName* field together with the *FirstName* field can only have entries that do not already occur in that combination. So, for example, Robert Müller and Robert Maier are possible, and likewise Robert Müller and Eva Müller.

If an index is created for one field only, the uniqueness applies to that field. Such an index is usually the primary key. In this field each value may occur only once. Additionally, in the case of primary keys, the field cannot be NULL under any circumstances.

An exceptional circumstance for a unique index is when there is no entry into a field (the field is NULL). Since NULL can have any arbitrary value, an index using two fields is always allowed to have the same entry repeatedly in one of the fields as long as there is no entry in the other.

Note	**NULL** is used in databases to designate an empty cell, one that contains nothing. No calculation is possible using a NULL field. This contrasts with spreadsheets, in which empty fields automatically contain the value 0 (zero).

Example: In a media database, the media number and the loan date are entered when the item is loaned out. When the item is returned, a return date is entered. In theory, an index using the fields Media_ID and ReturnDate could easily prevent the same item from being loaned out repeatedly without the return date being noted. Unfortunately this will not work because the return date initially has no value. The index will prevent an item from being marked as returned twice with the same date but it will do nothing else.

Limitations of graphical table design

The sequence of fields in a table cannot be changed after the database has been saved. To display a different sequence requires a query.

Only the entry of direct SQL commands can insert a field into a specific position in the table. However, fields already created cannot be moved by this method either.

The properties of the tables must be set at the beginning: for example which fields must not be NULL and which must contain a standard value (Default). These properties cannot subsequently be changed using the GUI.

The default values set here have nothing to do with the default values within the database itself. For example, you cannot define the default for a date field as being the date of entry. That is only possible with directly entered SQL commands.

Direct entry of SQL commands

To enter SQL commands directly, go to **Tools > SQL**.

You can then enter commands into the upper area of the window (shown in Figure 11). The lower area shows the result or, if appropriate, the reason why the command failed.

Queries cannot be created here. For these, the Query Design window offers an extra possibility of editing the query in SQL Mode.

Figure 11: Dialog for direct entry of SQL commands

A summary of the possible commands for the built-in HSQLDB engine can be found at http://www.hsqldb.org/doc/1.8/guide/ch09.html. The contents are described in the following sections. Some commands only make sense when dealing with an external HSQLDB database (Specify User, etc.). Where necessary, these are dealt with in the section "Working with external HSQLDB" in the Appendix to this handbook.

Note	LibreOffice is based on Version 1.8.0 of HSQLDB. The currently available server version is 2.2. The functions of the new version are more extensive. A further description is given in the installation packages for HSQLDB, which can be downloaded from http://sourceforge.net/projects/hsqldb/files/hsqldb/.

Table creation

A simple command to create a usable table is:

```
CREATE TABLE "Test" ("ID" INT PRIMARY KEY, "Text" VARCHAR(50));
```

CREATE TABLE "Test": Create a table with the name "Test".
( ): with the specified field names, field types and options.
"ID" INT PRIMARY KEY, "Text" VARCHAR(50): Field name "ID" with the numeric type integer as the primary key, field name "Text" with the text type variable text length and the text size limited to 50 characters.

```
CREATE [MEMORY | CACHED | [GLOBAL] TEMPORARY | TEMP | TEXT] TABLE
"Table name" ( <Field definition> [, ...] [,
<Constraint Definition>...] ) [ON COMMIT {DELETE | PRESERVE} ROWS];
```

[MEMORY | CACHED | [GLOBAL] TEMPORARY | TEMP | TEXT]:

The default setting is **MEMORY**: HSQLDB creates all tables in core memory. This setting also applies to the tables that are written into the embedded database by LibreOffice Base. Another possibility would be to write the tables to the hard drive and use memory only to buffer access to the hard drive (**CACHED**). Tables in **TEXT** format (such as CSV) are not writable in internal databases that are set up purely in **MEMORY**, while Base cannot access **TEMPORARY** or **TEMP** tables. The SQL commands are carried out in this case but the tables are not displayed (and therefore cannot be deleted) using the GUI, and data entered via SQL is likewise not visible to the query module of the GUI, unless the automatic deletion of the contents after the final commit is prevented. Any request in this case shows a table without any contents.

Tables built directly with SQL are not immediately displayed. You must either use **View > Refresh Tables** or simply close the database and then reopen it.

<Field definition>:

```
"Field name" Data type [(Number of characters[,Decimal places])]
[{DEFAULT "Default value" | GENERATED BY DEFAULT AS IDENTITY (START
WITH <n>[, INCREMENT BY <m>])}] | [[NOT] NULL] [IDENTITY] [PRIMARY
KEY]
```

Allows default values to be included in the field definition.

For text fields, you can enter text in single quotes or **NULL**. The only SQL function allowed is **CURRENT_USER**. This only makes sense if HSQLDB is being used as an external Server database with several users.

For date and time fields, a date, a time, or a combination of the two can be entered in single quotes or else NULL. You must ensure that the date follows the American conventions (yyyy-mm-dd), that time has the format hh:mm:ss, and that a combined date/time value has the format yyyy-mm-dd hh:mm:ss.

Allowed SQL functions:
for the current date	**CURRENT_DATE, TODAY, CURDATE()**
for the current time	**CURRENT_TIME, NOW, CURTIME()**
for the current data time stamp	**CURRENT_TIMESTAMP, NOW**.

For boolean Fields (yes/no) the expressions **FALSE, TRUE, NULL** can be entered. These must be entered without single quotes.

For numeric fields, any valid number in the range, or NULL is possible. Here too, if you enter **NULL**, do not use quotes. When entering decimals, make sure that the decimal point is a dot (period) and not a comma.

For binary fields (images, etc.) any valid hexadecimal string in single quotes or **NULL** is possible. A hexadecimal example string is: '0004ff', which represents 3 bytes, first 0, then 4 and finally 255 (0xff). As binary fields in practice need only be entered for images, you need to know the binary code of the image that is to serve as a default.

NOT NULL: The field value cannot be NULL. This condition can only be given in the field definition.

Note	Hexadecimal system: Numbers are based on 16. A mixed system consisting of the numbers 0 to 9 and the letters a to f provides 16 possible digits for each column. With two columns, you can have 16*16=256 possible values. This corresponds to 1 Byte (2^8).

<Constraint definition>:
```
[CONSTRAINT "Name"]
UNIQUE ( "Field_name 1" [,"Field_name 2"...] ) |
PRIMARY KEY ( "Field_name 1" [,"Field_name 2"...] ) |
FOREIGN KEY ( "Field_name 1" [,"Field_name 2"...] )
REFERENCES "other_table_name" ( "Field_name_1" [,"Field_name 2"...])
[ON {DELETE | UPDATE}
{CASCADE | SET DEFAULT | SET NULL}] |
CHECK(<Search_condition>)
```

Constraints define conditions that must be fulfilled when data is entered. Constraints can be given a name.

UNIQUE ("Field_name"): the field value must be unique within that field

PRIMARY KEY ("Field_name"): the field value must be unique and cannot be **NULL** (primary key)

FOREIGN KEY ("Field_name") REFERENCES <"other_table_name">
("Field_name"): The specified fields of this table are linked to the fields of another table. The field value must be tested for referential integrity as foreign keys; that is, there must be a corresponding primary key in the other table, if a value is entered here.

[ON {DELETE | UPDATE} {CASCADE | SET DEFAULT | SET NULL}]: In the case of a foreign key, this specifies what is to happen if, for example, the foreign record is deleted. It makes no sense, in a loan table for a library, to have a user number for which the user no longer exists. The corresponding record must be modified so that the relationship between the tables remains valid. Usually the record is simply deleted. This happens if you select **ON DELETE CASCADE**.

CHECK(<Search_condition>): Formulated as a **WHERE** condition, but only for the current record.

You need constraints when the relationship between tables or the index for certain fields must be defined.

[ON COMMIT {DELETE | PRESERVE} ROWS]:

The content of tables of the type **TEMPORARY** or **TEMP** is erased by default when you have finished working with a particular record (**ON COMMIT DELETE ROWS**). This allows you to create temporary records, which contain information for other actions to be carried out at the same time.

If you want a table of this type to contain data available for a whole session (from opening a database to closing it), choose **ON COMMIT PRESERVE ROWS**.

Table modification

Sometimes you might wish to insert an additional field into a particular position in the table. Suppose you have a table called **Addresses** with fields *ID*, *Name*, *Street*, and so on. You realize that perhaps it would be sensible to distinguish first names and last names.

```
ALTER TABLE "Addresses" ADD "First Name" VARCHAR(25) BEFORE "Name";
```

ALTER TABLE "Addresses": Alter the table with the name "Addresses".
ADD "First Name" VARCHAR(25): insert the field "FirstName" with a length of 25 characters.
BEFORE "Name": before the field "Name".

The possibility of specifying the position of additional fields after the creation of the table is not available in the GUI.

```
ALTER TABLE "Table_name" ADD [COLUMN] <Field_definition> [BEFORE
"already_existing_field_name"];
```

The additional designation **COLUMN** is not necessary in cases where no alternative choices are available.

```
ALTER TABLE "Table_name" DROP [COLUMN] "Field_name";
```
The field "Field name" is erased from the table *Table_name*. However this does not take place if the field is involved in a view or as a foreign key in another table.
```
ALTER TABLE "Table_name" ALTER COLUMN "Field_name" RENAME TO
"New_field_name"
```
Changes the name of a field.
```
ALTER TABLE "Table_name" ALTER COLUMN "Field_name" SET DEFAULT
<Standard value>};
```
Sets a specific default value for the field. **NULL** removes an existing default value.
```
ALTER TABLE "Table_name" ALTER COLUMN "Field_name" SET [NOT] NULL
```
Sets or removes a **NOT NULL** condition for a field.
```
ALTER TABLE "Table_name" ALTER COLUMN <Field definition>;
```
The field definition corresponds to the one from the Table creation with the following restrictions:

- The field must already be a primary key field to accept the property **IDENTITY**. **IDENTITY** means, that the field has the property AutoValue. This is possible only for **INTEGER** or **BIGINT** fields. For these field type descriptions, see the Appendix to this handbook.

- If the field already has the property **IDENTITY** but it is not repeated in the field definition, the existing **IDENTITY** property is removed.

- The default value will become that specified in the new field definition. If the definition of the default value is left blank, any default already defined is removed.

- The property **NOT NULL** continues into the new definition, if not otherwise defined. This is in contrast to the default value.

- In some cases, depending on the type of modification, the table must be empty in order for the change to occur. In all cases the change will have effect only if it is possible in principle (for example a change from **NOT NULL** to **NULL**) and the existing values can all be translated (for example a change from **TINYINT** to **INTEGER**).

```
ALTER TABLE "Table_name" ALTER COLUMN "Field_name" RESTART WITH
<New_field_value>
```
This command is used exclusively for an **IDENTITY** field. It determines the next value for a field with the Autovalue function set. It can be used, for example, when a database is initially used with test data, and subsequently provided with real data. This requires the contents of the tables to be deleted and a new value such as "1" to be set for the field.
```
ALTER TABLE "Table_name"
ADD [CONSTRAINT "Condition_name"] CHECK (<Search_condition>);
```
This adds a search condition introduced by the word **CHECK**. Such a condition will not apply retrospectively to existing records, but it will apply to all subsequent changes and newly entered records. If a constraint name is not defined, one will be assigned automatically.

Example:
```
ALTER TABLE "Loan" ADD CHECK
(IFNULL("Return_Date","Loan_Date")>="Loan_Date")
```
The **Loan** table needs to be protected from input errors. For example, you must prevent a return date being given that is earlier than the loan date. Now if this error occurs during the return process, you will get an error message **Check constraint violation** …
```
ALTER TABLE "Table_name"
ADD [CONSTRAINT "Constraint_name"] UNIQUE ("Field_name1",
"Field_name2" ...);
```

Here a condition is added that forces the named fields to have different values in each record. If several fields are named, this condition applies to the combination rather than the individual fields. **NULL** does not count here. A field can therefore have the same value repeatedly without causing any problems, if the other field in each of the records is **NULL**.

This command will not work if there is already a **UNIQUE** condition for the same field combination.

```
ALTER TABLE "Table_name"
ADD [CONSTRAINT "Constraint_name"] PRIMARY KEY ("Field_name1",
"Field_name2" ...);
```

Adds a primary key, optionally with a constraint, to a table. The syntax of the constraint is the same as when a table is created.

```
ALTER TABLE "Table_name"
ADD [CONSTRAINT "Constraint_name"] FOREIGN KEY ("Field_name1",
"Field_name2" ...)
REFERENCES "Table_name_of_another_table" ("Field_name1_other_table",
"Field_name2_other_table" ...)
[ON {DELETE | UPDATE} {CASCADE | SET DEFAULT | SET NULL}];
```

This adds a foreign key (**FOREIGN KEY**) to the table. The syntax is the same as when a table is created.

The operation will terminate with an error message, if any value in the table does not have a corresponding value in the table containing that primary key.

Example: The **Name** and **Address** tables are to be linked. The **Name** table contains a field with the name *Address_ID*. The value of this should be linked to the field *ID* in the **Address** table. If the value "1" is found in *Address_ID* but not in the *ID* field of the **Address** table, the link will not work. It will not work either if the two fields are of different types.

```
ALTER TABLE "Table_name" DROP CONSTRAINT "Constraint_name";
```

This command removes the named constraint (**UNIQUE**, **CHECK**, **FOREIGN KEY**) from a table.

```
ALTER TABLE "Table_name" RENAME TO "new_table_name";
```

Finally this command changes only the name of a table.

Deleting tables

```
DROP TABLE "Table name" [IF EXISTS] [RESTRICT | CASCADE];
```

Deletes the table "Table name".

IF EXISTS prevents an error occurring if this table does not exist.

RESTRICT is the default arrangement and need not be explicitly chosen; it means that deletion does not occur if the table is linked to another table by the use of a foreign key or there is an active view of this table. Queries are not affected as they are not stored within HSQLDB.

If instead you choose **CASCADE**, all links to the table "Table_name" are deleted. In the linked tables, all foreign keys are set to NULL. All views referring to the named table are also completely deleted.

Linking tables

In principle you can have a database without links between tables. The user must then ensure during data entry, that the relationships between the tables remain correct. This usually occurs through the use of suitable input forms that manage this.

Deleting records in linked tables is not a simple matter. Suppose you wish to delete a particular street from the *Street* table in Figure 7, where this field is linked with the *Address* table as a foreign key in that table. The references in the *Address* table would disappear. The database does not allow this, once the relationship has been created. In order to delete the *Street*, the precondition must be fulfilled, that it is no longer referenced in the *Address* table.

Basic links are made using **Tools > Relationships**. This creates a connection line from the primary key in one table to the defined foreign key in the other.

You may receive the following error message when creating such a link:

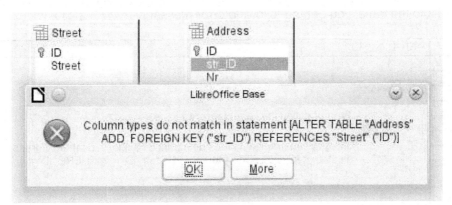

This message shows some text in English and the internal SQL command that caused the error.

Column types do not match in statement—As the SQL command is displayed as well, the reference is clearly to the columns *Address.str_ID* and *Street.ID*. For test purposes one of these fields was defined as an Integer, the other as Tiny Integer. Therefore no link could be created since the one field cannot have the same value as the other.

In this case the column types match. The SQL statement is the same as in the first example. But again there is an error:

Integrity constraint violation – no parent 1, table: Address ... —The integrity of the relationship is not ensured. In the field of the Address table, *Address.str_ID*, there is a number 1, which is not present in *Street.ID*. The parent table here is *Street*, since its primary key is the one that must exist. This error is very common, when two tables are to be linked and some fields in the table with the prospective foreign key already contain data. If the foreign key field contains an entry that is not present in the parent table (the table containing the primary key), this is an invalid entry.

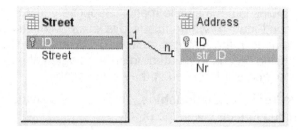

If the linking is carried out successfully and subsequently there is an attempt to enter a similarly invalid record into the table, you get the following error message:

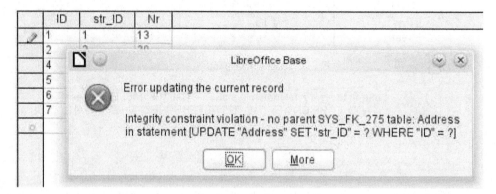

Again this is an integrity violation. Base refuses to accept the value 1 for the field *str_ID* after the link has been made because the *Street* table contains no such value in the ID field.

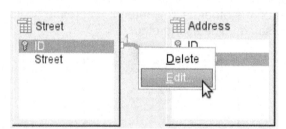

Figure 12: Links can be edited with a right-click

The properties of a link can be edited so that the deletion of a record from the *Street* table will simultaneously set to NULL the corresponding entries in the *Address* table.

The properties shown in Figure 12 always relate to an action linked to the change in a record from the table containing the corresponding primary key. In our case this is the *Street* table. If the **primary key of a record** in this table is **altered (Update)**, the following actions might take place.

No action
Changing the primary key *Street.ID* is not allowed in this case, as it would break the relationship between the tables.

Update cascade
If the primary key *Street.ID* is changed, the foreign key is automatically changed to its new value. This ensures that the linkage is not damaged. For example, if a value is changed from 3 to 4, all records from the *Address* table that contain the foreign key *Address.Street_ID* with the value 3, have it changed to 4.

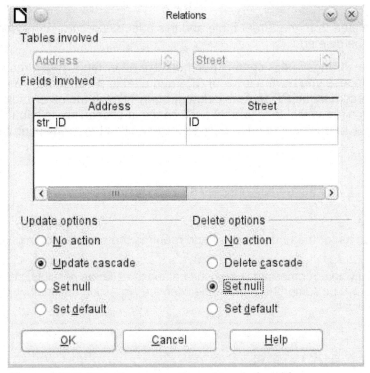

Figure 13: Editing the properties of a relationship

Set null

All records which contain this particular primary key will now have no entry in the foreign key field *Address.Street_ID;* the field will be NULL.

Set default

If the primary key *Street_ID* is changed, the value of *Address.Street_ID* originally linked to it is set to the previously defined default value. For this purpose we need an unambiguous definition of a default value. The LibreOffice Base GUI up to Version 3.5 does not seem to provide this. If the default is set using the SQL statement:

```
ALTER TABLE "Address" ALTER COLUMN "Street_ID" SET DEFAULT 1;
```

the link definition ensures that the field will return to this value in the case of an Update. So if the primary key in the *Street* table is changed, the corresponding foreign key in the *Address* table will be set to 1. This is useful when a record is required to have a street field, in other words this field cannot be NULL. But be careful! If 1 is not in use, you will have created a link to a non-existent value. In this case HSQLDB seems to have been designed without due thought. It is therefore possible to destroy the integrity of the relationship.

Attention	If the default value in a foreign key field is not linked to a primary key of the foreign table, a link to a value would be created, that isn't possible. The referential integrity of the database would be destroyed.

It would be better not to use the possibility to set the value to default.

If a record is **deleted** from the *Street* table, the following options are available.

No Action

No action takes place. If the requested deletion affects a record in the Address table, the request will be refused.

Cascading Delete

If a record is deleted from the *Street* table and this affects a record in the *Address* table, that record will also be deleted.

That might seem strange in this context but there are other table structures in which it makes a lot of sense. Suppose you have a table of CDs and a table which stores the titles on these CDs. Now if a record in the CD table is deleted, many titles in the other table have no meaning as they are no longer available to you. In such cases, a cascading deletion makes sense. It means that the user does not need to delete all these titles before deleting the CD from the database.

Set to Null

This is the same as for the update option.

Set to Default

This is the same as for the update option and requires the same precautions.

Tip	To avoid error messages from the database as far as possible, since these may not always be comprehensible to the user, the *No Action* option should definitely be avoided.

Entering data into tables

Databases that consist of only a single table usually do not require an input form unless they contain a field for images. However as soon as a table contains foreign keys from other tables, users must either remember which key numbers to enter or they must be able to look at the other tables simultaneously. In such cases, a form is useful.

Entry using the Base GUI

Tables in the table container are opened by double-clicking them. If the primary key is an automatically incrementing field, one of the visible fields will contain the text *AutoValue*. No entry is possible into the *AutoValue* field. Its assigned value can be altered if required, but only after the record has been committed.

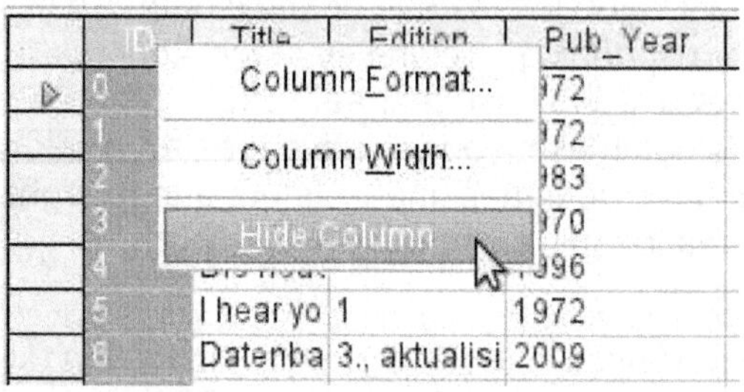

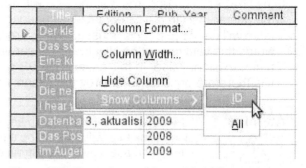

Figure 14: Entry into tables – Hiding columns

Figure 15: Entry into tables – Unhiding columns

Individual columns in the Table Data View can be hidden. For example, if the primary key field does not need to be visible, this can be specified in the table in data entry view by right-clicking on the column header. This setting is stored with the GUI. The column continues to exist in the table and can always be made visible again.

Entry into the table usually takes place from left to right using the keyboard with the *Tab or Enter* keys. You can also use the mouse.

When you reach the last field of a record, the cursor automatically jumps to the next record. The previous entry is committed to storage. Additional storage using **File > Save** is not necessary and indeed not possible. The data is already in the database.

Caution ⚠	For the HSQLDB, data is in working memory. It will only be transferred to the hard drive when Base is closed (unfortunately from the viewpoint of data security). If Base for some reason does not close down in an orderly fashion, this can lead to loss of data.

If no data is entered into a field that has been previously defined during table design as mandatory (**NOT NULL**), the appropriate error message is displayed:

`Attempt to insert null into a non-nullable column …`

The corresponding column, the table and the SQL command (as translated by the GUI) are also displayed.

Changing a record is easy: find the field, enter a different value, and leave the row again.

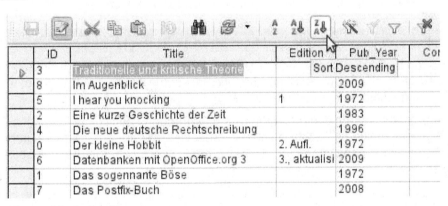

To delete a record, select the row by clicking its header (the grey area to the left), right-click and choose **Delete Rows**.

The Sort, Search, and Filter functions are very useful for retrieving particular records.

Sorting tables

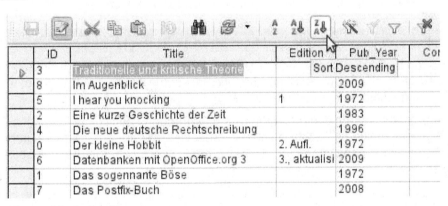

Figure 16: Quick Sort

The quick sort option hides behind the **A → Z** and **Z → A b**uttons. One field is selected, one click on the button, and the data is sorted by that column. The figure shows a descending sort by the *Title* field.

Quick sort sorts only by one column. To sort by several columns simultaneously, a further sort function is provided.

The field name of the column and the current sort order are selected. If a previous quick sort has been carried out, the first row will already contain the corresponding field name and sort order.

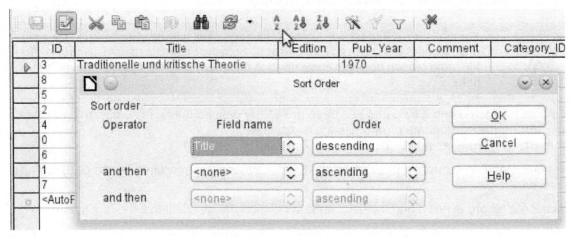

Figure 17: Sorting by more than one column

Searching tables

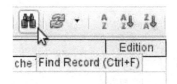

Functions for searching records are extensive and perhaps not the first choice for locating a particular record for users accustomed to search engines.

Tip	Before you search, make sure the columns you will be searching are wide enough to show correctly the records that you will find. The search window remains in the foreground and you will not be able to correct the settings for column width in the underlying table. To reach the table, you must break off the search.

The search takes over terms from the field from which it was invoked.

To make the search effective, the search area should be limited as far as possible. It would be pointless to search for the above text from the *Title* field in the *Author* field. Instead, the field name *Title* is already suggested as the single Field name.

Further settings for the search can make things easier through specific combinations. You can use the normal SQL placeholders ("**_**" for a variable character, "**%**" for an arbitrary number of variable characters, "****" as an escape character, to enable these special characters themselves to be searched for).

Regular expressions are described in detail in LibreOffice Help. Apart from that, the Help available for this module is rather sparse.

Title	Edition	Pub_Year	Comment	Category_ID	Mediastyle_I
Traditionelle und kritische Theorie		1970		1	

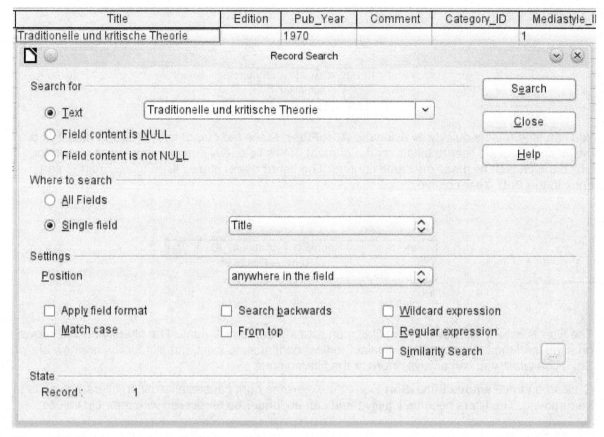

Figure 18: Entry mask for a Record search

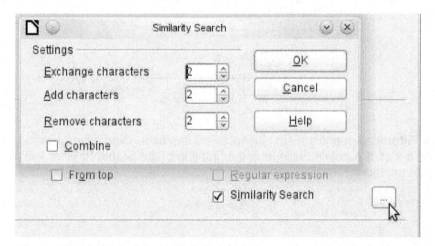

Figure 19: Limiting the similarity search

The similarity search function is useful when you need to exclude spelling mistakes. The higher the values that you set, the more records will be shown in the final list.

This search module is most suitable for people who know, from regular use, exactly how to achieve a given result. Most users are more likely to succeed in finding records by using a filter.

Chapter 4 of this handbook describes the use of forms for searching, and how the use of SQL and macros can accomplish a keyword search.

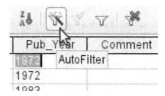

You can filter a table quickly by using the **AutoFilter**. Place the cursor in a field, and one click on the icon causes the filter to take over the content of this field. Only those records are shown for which the chosen field has the same content. The figure below shows filtering according to an entry in the **Pub_Year** column.

The filter is active, as shown by the filter icon with a green check mark. The filter symbol is shown pressed in. If the button is clicked again, the filter continues to exist, but all records are now shown. So, if you want, you can always return to the filtered state.

Clicking on the **Remove Filter/Sort** icon at the extreme right causes all existing filters and sorts to be removed. The filters become inactive and can no longer be recovered with their old values.

Tip	You can still enter records normally into a filtered table or one that has been restricted by a search. They remain visible in the table view until the table is updated by pressing the **Refresh** button.

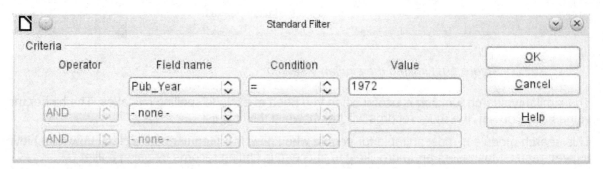

The **Standard Filter** icon opens a dialog inwhich you can filter using several simultaneous criteria, similar to doing a sort. If AutoFilter is in use, the first line of the Standard Filter will already show this existing filter criterion.

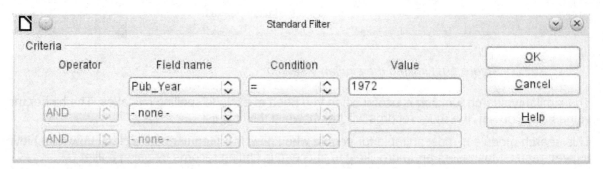

Figure 20: Multiple Data Filtering using the Standard Filter

The Standard Filter provides many of the functions of SQL data filtering. The following SQL commands are available.

GUI Condition	Description
=	Exact equality; corresponds to **like**, but without any additional placeholders
<>	Unequal
<	Less than
<=	Less than or equal
>	Greater than
>=	Greater than or equal
like	For text, written in quotation marks (' '); **"_"** for a variable character, **"%"** for an arbitrary number of variable characters
not like	Opposite of **like**, in SQL **NOT LIKE**
empty	No entry, not even a space character. In SQL this is expressed by the term **NULL**
Not empty	Opposite of empty, in SQL **NOT NULL**

Before one filter criterion can be combined with another, the following row must have at least one field name selected. In Figure 20, the word – *none* – is shown instead of a field name, so the combination is not active. The combination operators available are **AND** and **OR**.

The field name can be a new field name or a previously selected one.

Even for large data collections, the number of retrieved records can be reduced to a manageable set with skillful filtering using these three possible conditions.

In the case of filtering forms too, there are some further possibilities (described in the following chapter) which are not provided by the GUI.

Direct entry using SQL

Direct data entry using SQL is useful for entering, changing or removing multiple records with one command.

Entering new records

```
INSERT INTO "Table_name" [( "Field_name" [,...] )]
{ VALUES("Field value" [,...]) | <Select-Formula>};
```

If no "Field_name" is specified, all fields must be completed and in the right order (as laid down in the table). That includes the automatically incremented primary key field, where present. The values entered can also be the result of a query (<Select-Formula>). More exact information is given below.

```
INSERT INTO "Table_name" ("Field_name") VALUES ('Test');
CALL IDENTITY();
```

In the table, in the column "Field_name", the value 'Test' is inserted. The automatically incremented primary key field "ID" is not touched. The corresponding value for the "ID" needs to be created separately by using CALL IDENTITY(). This is important when you are using macros, so that the value of this key field can be used later on.

```
INSERT INTO "Table_name" ("Field_name") SELECT "Other_fieldname" FROM
"Name_of_other_table";
```

In the first table, as many new records are inserted into "Field_name", as are present in the column "Other_fieldname" in the second table. Naturally a Select-Formula can be used here to limit the number of entries.

Editing existing records

```
UPDATE "Table_name" SET "Field_name" = <Expression> [, ...] [WHERE
<Expression>];
```

When you are modifying many records at once, it is very important to check carefully the SQL command you are entering. Suppose that all students in a class are to be moved up one year:

```
UPDATE "Table_name" SET "Year" = "Year"+1
```

Nothing could be faster: All data records are altered with a single command. But of course you must now determine which students should *not* have been affected by this change. It would have been simpler to check a Yes/No field for the repetition of a year and then to move up only those students for which this field was not checked:

```
UPDATE "Table_name" SET "Year" = "Year"+1 WHERE "Repetition" = FALSE
```

These conditions only function when the field in question can only take the values **FALSE** and **TRUE**; it may not be **NULL**. It would be safer if the condition were formulated as **WHERE "Repetition" <> TRUE**.

Other calculation steps are also possible with Update. If, for example, wares costing more than $150.00 are to be included in a special offer and the price reduced by 10%, this can be carried out as follows:

```
UPDATE "Table_name" SET "Price" = "Price"*0,9 WHERE "Price" >= 150
```

Deleting existing records

```
DELETE FROM "Table_name" [WHERE <Expression>];
```

Without the conditional expression the command

```
DELETE FROM "Table_name"
```

deletes the entire content of the table.

For this reason it is preferable for the command to be more specific. For example, if the value of the primary key is given, only this precise record will be deleted.

```
DELETE FROM "Table_name" WHERE "ID" = 5;
```

If, in the case of a loan, the media record is to be deleted when the item is returned, this can be done using

```
DELETE FROM "Table_name" WHERE NOT "Return_date" IS NULL;
```

or alternatively with

```
DELETE FROM "Table_name" WHERE "Return_date" IS NOT NULL;
```

Problems with these data entry methods

Entry using a table alone takes no account of links to other tables. This is clear from an example of a media loan.

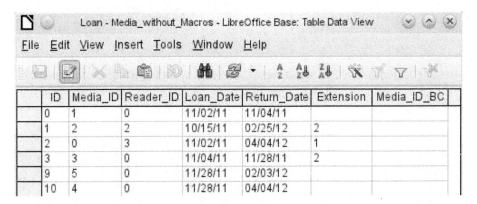

The **Loan** table consists of foreign keys for the item being lent (*Media_ID*) and the corresponding reader (*Reader_ID*) as well as a loan date (*Loan_Date*). In the table, therefore, we need to enter at the time of the loan two numeric values (Media number and Reader number) and a date. The primary key is automatically entered in the *ID* field. Whether the reader actually corresponds to the number is not apparent unless a second table for the readers is open at the same time. Whether the item was loaned out with the correct number is also not apparent. Here the loan must rely on the label on the item or on another open table.

All this is much easier to accomplish using forms. Here the users and the media can be looked up using list box controls. In forms, the names of user and item are visible and their numeric identifiers are hidden. In addition, a form can be so designed that a user can be selected first, then a loan date, and each set of media are assigned this one date by number. Elsewhere these numbers can be made visible with the exactly corresponding media descriptions.

Direct entry into tables is useful only for databases with simple tables. As soon as you have relationships between tables, a specially designed form is better. In forms, these relationships can be better handled by using sub-forms or list fields.

Chapter 4
Forms

Forms make data entry easier

Forms are used when direct entry into a table is inconvenient, to pick up errors in data entry promptly, or when too many tables make direct management of data impossible.

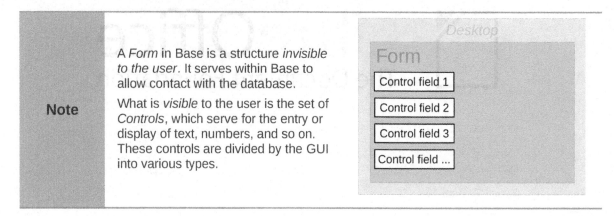

Note	A *Form* in Base is a structure *invisible to the user*. It serves within Base to allow contact with the database. What is *visible* to the user is the set of *Controls*, which serve for the entry or display of text, numbers, and so on. These controls are divided by the GUI into various types.

Creating forms

The simplest way to create a form is to use the Form Wizard. Use of the Wizard to create a form is described in Chapter 8, Getting Started with Base, in the *Getting Started with LibreOffice* guide. That chapter also explains how you can further modify the form after using the Wizard.

This handbook describes the creation of a form without using the Wizard. It also describes the properties of the various types of controls in a form.

A simple form

We start by using the task *Create Form in Design View* in the Forms area of the main Base window.

This calls up the Form Editor and the Form Shown in Design View window appears (Figure 21).

The Form Controls toolbar is docked on the left side. The Form Design toolbar (Figure 22) is docked at the bottom. If these toolbars do not appear automatically, use **View > Toolbars** to display them. Without these toolbars, it is not possible to create a form.

The blank area shows a grid of dots. This grid helps you to position the controls accurately, especially in relation to each other. The symbols at the right end of the Form Design toolbar show that the grid is visible and active.

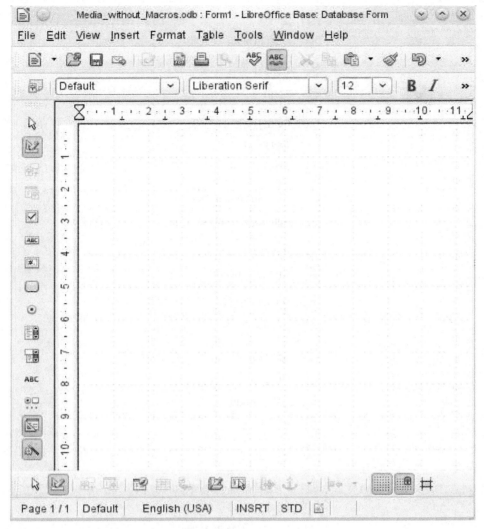

Figure 21: Form shown in Design View

Toolbars for form design

Now we will create a form on the empty page. This can be done in two ways:

- Invoke the Form Navigator to set up a form, or
- Design the form controls and set up the form by using the context menu.

Setting up a form with the Form Navigator

To display the Form Navigator, click the Form Navigator button (shown in Figure 22). A window appears (Figure 23); it shows only one folder, labeled **Forms**. This is the highest level of the area that we are editing. Several forms can be accommodated here.

Figure 22: Available buttons on the Form Design toolbar

Figure 23: Using the Form Navigator to create a new form

In the Form Navigator (Figure 23), right-click on **Forms** to open a context menu. Choose **New > Form** to create a new form. The other choices in the context menu (**Open in Design Mode** and **Automatic Control Focus**) correspond to buttons in Figure 22; we will discuss them later.

The form carries the default name **Form**. You can change this name immediately or later. It has no significance unless you need to access some part of the form using macros. The only thing you need to ensure is that two elements with the same name do not occur on the same level in the folder tree.

The context menu of the form (shown below) provides the way to create form properties.

Creating a form using a form field

The Form Controls toolbar (Figure 24) makes available some fields for your form. The first four elements are identical to those of the Form Design toolbar; they are followed by commonly used form control types (a control consists of a field plus a label).

Figure 24: Available buttons on the Form Controls toolbar

Figure 25: Available buttons on the More Controls toolbar

When you select a form control, you automatically create a form. For example, suppose you choose a text field: the cursor changes shape and a rectangular shape may be drawn on the white surface of the form. Then, on the stippled surface of the form, a text field appears.

Now you can create the form by right-clicking and using the **context menu** for the control (Figure 26).

Select the **Form** menu option (highlighted in the illustration) to set properties for the form you have just created. The form has the default name Form.

Figure 26: Context menu for form

Form properties

When the form properties are called up using the context menu in the Form Navigator or the context menu of a form control, a Form Properties window appears. It has three tabs: **General**, **Data** and **Events.**

General tab

Here you can change the Name of the form. In addition there are design possibilities that have no significance inside Base. They show only the more general possibilities for design using a form editor; when you create a Web form you will need to use them.

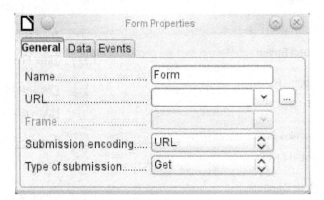

URL: Destination for the data.

Frame: Section of the destination website to be addressed where necessary.

Submission encoding: in addition to the normal character encoding for transmission to the URL, you can specify here text encoding and multipart coding (for example, for transfer of data).

Type of submission: GET (visible via the URL attached to the filename; you can see this often in the web if you use a search engine) or POST (not visible; suitable for large data volumes).

Data tab

For creating internal forms in Base, this is the most important tab. Here you can set the following initial properties for the form:

Content type: Choose between *Table*, *Query* and *SQL command*. While Table can always be used for data entry into a form, this is not always the case for Query (for more information, see Chapter 5, Queries, in this book) or direct entry of a SQL command. Here we are dealing with a query that is not visible in Base's query container but has in principle the same structure.

Content: According to whether Table or Query was chosen above, all *available tables and queries* are listed. If a SQL command is to be created, you can invoke the Query Editor by using the button with the three dots to the right of the Content field.

Analyze SQL command: If the analysis of SQL commands should not be permitted (because, for example, you are using code that the GUI cannot show correctly), you should choose **No** here. However this will prevent the form accessing the underlying data using a filter or a sort.

Filter: Here you can set a filter. To get help with this, click the button to the right of the field. See also Chapter 3, Tables, in this book.

Sort: Here you can set up a Sort for your data. To get help, click the button to the right of the field. See also Chapter 3, Tables.

Allow additions: Should the entry of new data be allowed? By default this is set to **Yes**.

Allow modifications: Should editing of the data be allowed? By default also **Yes**.

Allow deletions: The deletion of data is also allowed by default.

Add data only: If you choose this option, an empty form will always be displayed. There will be no access to existing data, which can neither be edited nor viewed.

Navigation bar: The appearance of the Navigation Bar at the bottom of the screen can be switched on or off. There is also a possibility, when you have a subform, always to show the Navigation Bar for the main form, so that activation of this toolbar affects the main form only. This setting for the Navigation Bar is not relevant to the internal navigation toolbar that can be added as a form control if required.

Cycle: The *Default* option for Base databases is that after entry into the last field in a form, the Tab key takes you to the first field of the next record – that is, a new record will be created. For databases, this has the same effect as *All records*. By contrast, if you choose *Active record*, the cursor will move only within the record; when it reaches the last field, it will jump back to the first field in that record. *Current page* refers particularly to HTML Forms. The cursor jumps from the end of a form to the next form on that page further down.

Events tab

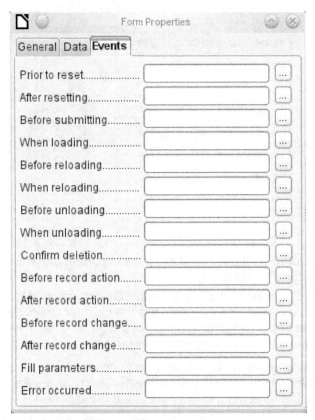

Events can trigger macros. A click on the button on the right (...) allows macros to be linked to the event.

Reset: The form is emptied of all new entries that have not yet been saved.

Before submitting: Before the form data are sent. This is only meaningful for Web forms.

When loading: Only when opening the form. Not when loading a new record into the form.

Reloading: This takes place when the content of the form is refreshed, for example by using a button on the Navigation Bar.

Unloading: This option seems not to function. It would be expected to refer to the closing of the form.

Record action: This includes, for example, storage using a button. In tests, this action regularly duplicates itself; macros run twice in succession.

Record change: The opening of a form counts as a record change. Whenever one record changes to another within the form, this action likewise occurs twice. Macros are therefore run twice in succession.

Fill parameters: This macro will be run if a parameter query is to be invoked in a subform, but for some reason the parameter is not correctly transmitted from the main form. If this event is not caught, a parameter query will follow the loading of the form.

Error occurred: This event could not be reconstructed.

Properties of controls

Once a form has been created, it can be filled with visible controls. Some controls allow the content of the database to be displayed, or data to be entered into the database. Other controls are used exclusively for navigation, for searching, and for carrying out commands (interaction). Some controls serve for additional graphical reworking of the form.

Data entry and Data display	
Control	**Use**
Text field	Text entry
Numeric field	Entering numbers
Date field	Entering dates
Time field	Entering times
Currency field	Numeric entry, preformated for currency
Formatted field	Display and entry with additional formatting, for example using measurement units
List box	Choosing between several different possibilities, also for transfer into the database of values other than those displayed
Combo box	Similar to a list field, but with only the displayed value transferred, or you can enter new values by hand
Check box	Yes/No Field
Options button	Radio button; allows you to choose from a small number of possibilities
Image control	Display of images from a database and entry of images into a database via a path selection
Pattern field	Entry into a preset mask; limits the entry possibilities to specific character combinations
Table control	Universal entry module, which can display a whole table. Integrated into this control are many of the above controls
Design	
Control	**Use**
Label field	Heading for the form, description of other controls
Group box	A frame around, for example, a set of option buttons
Interaction	
Control	**Use**
Button	Button with label
Image Button	Like a button, but with an additional graphic displayed on it
Navigation bar	Toolbar very similar to the one at the bottom edge of the screen
File selector	For selecting files, for example to upload in an HTML form—not further described
Spin box	Can only be used with a macro—not further described
Scrollbar	Can only be used with a macro—not further described

Default settings for many controls

As with forms, properties are grouped into three categories: General, Data and Events. General comprises everything that is visible to the user. The data category specifies the binding to a field in the database. The Events category controls actions, which can be bound to some macro. In a database without macros, this category plays no role.

General tab

Name..............................	Text Box 1	The name of a control must be unique within the form—used for access using macros.
Label Field......................		Does the field have a label? This groups field and label together.

Enabled...............	Yes	↕

Non-enabled fields cannot be used and are grayed out. Useful for control using macros. (Example: If Field 1 contains a value, Field 2 must not contain one; Field 2 is deactivated.)

Visible...............	Yes	↕

Usually **Yes**; invisible fields can be used as intermediate storage, for example in creating combination fields with macros. See Chapter 9, Macros.

Read-only...............	No	↕

Yes will exclude any modification of the value. This is useful, for example, for an automatically generated primary key.

Printable...............	Yes	↕

Sometimes it is useful to print a page from a form rather than a separate report. In this case, not all fields may be required to appear.

Tabstop...............	Yes	↕

Within a form, the *Tab* key is normally used for navigation. A field that is read-only does not need a tab stop; it can be skipped.

Tab order...............	0	↕	...

Does the field have a tab stop? Here the activation sequence within the form is specified.

Anchor...............	To Paragraph	↕

Anchoring of graphics within a text field.

PositionX...............	5,00cm	↕

Position of the top left corner relative to the left side of the form.

PositionY...............	0,33cm	↕

Position of the top left corner relative to the top of the form.

Width...............	3,83cm	↕

Width of the field.

Height...............	0,67cm	↕

Height of the field.

Font...............	(Default)		...

Font, font size, and font effects can be set here.

Alignment...............	Left	↕

Alignment. Here text entry is left-justified.

Vert. Alignment...............	Default	↕

Vertical alignment: Standard | Top | Middle | Bottom.

Background color............	Default	Background color of the text field.
Border.............................	Flat	Framing: No frame | 3D-Look | Flat.
Border color....................	☐ Light gray	If there is a frame, its color can be set here.
Hide selection.................	Yes	Highlighted text loses the highlight when the text field loses focus.
Additional information.....		Used for information to be read by macros. See Chapter 9, Macros.
Help text..........................		Appears as a tooltip when the mouse is hovered over the text field.
Help URL..........................		Points to a help file, useful mostly for HTML. Can be invoked using *F1* when the focus is on the field.

In addition, numeric, date fields, etc have the following properties.

Strict format....................	Yes	With testing enabled, only numbers and decimal points may be entered.
Mouse wheel scroll.........	Never	*Never* does not allow alterations using the mouse wheel; *When selected* allows such changes when the field is selected and the mouse is over the field; *Always* means whenever the mouse is over the field.
Spin Button......................	No	A spin symbol is incorporated into the right side of the field.
Repeat.............................	No	If a spin arrow is pressed down and held, this determines if the entry in the box should be incremented beyond the next value.
Delay...............................	50 ms	Determines the minimum delay after a mouse button press that triggers repetition.

Data tab

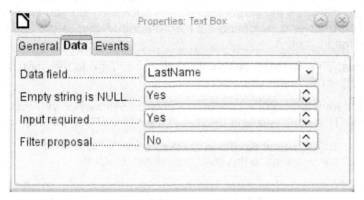

Data field: Here you create the binding with the table on which the form is based.

Empty string is NULL: Whether an empty string should be treated as (NULL) or the content simply deleted.

Entry required: This condition should match the one in the table. The GUI will prompt for entry if the user has not entered a value.

Filter proposal: When the data is to be filtered, the content of this field is temporarily stored as a suggestion. Caution – with large contents, this choice can use a lot of storage.

Events tab

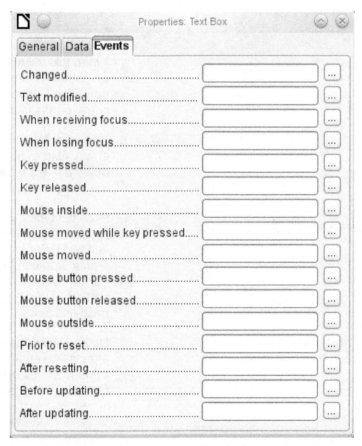

Changed: This event takes place when a control is modified and afterwards loses the focus.

Text modified: Refers to the content, which can in fact be text, numeric, or whatever. Occurs after each additional character is entered.

When receiving focus: The cursor enters the field. Under no circumstances must the macro create a message dialog on the screen; clicking in such a dialog causes the form field to lose the focus and then recover it, triggering the macro again. A loop is created which can only be broken by using the keyboard.

When losing focus: The cursor leaves the field. This can lead to the same kind of interplay when the handling of the event causes it to recur.

Key: Refers to the keyboard. For example, a key is pressed when you move through the form using the Tab key. This causes a field to receive the focus. Then the key is released.

Mouse: Self-explanatory; These events only takes place if the mouse is or was already within the field ("outside" corresponds to the javascript onMouseOut).

Reset: The form is emptied of all data. This happens, for example, when starting a new record. When a form is first loaded, the two events *Prior to reset* and *After resetting* occur in succession, before the form is available for input.

Updating: If the event is bound to a form control, update takes place when the focus is lost and jumps to another form control, after altering the content of the field. Changes in the form are accepted and displayed. When a form is closed, the two events *Before updating* and *After updating* occur in succession.

Text field

As well as the properties set out on page 70, text fields can have the following additional properties:

General tab

Max. text length................ `0`
> When this value is 0, entry is not permitted. Usually the length of the database field to which the text field corresponds is used here.

Default text........................ `[            ▼]`
> Should default text be put into an empty field? This text must be deleted if any other entry is to be made successfully.

Text type........................... `Single-line        ^⌄`
> Possible types: Single-line | Multi-line | Multi-line with formatting (the last two differ in tabbing behaviour and, in addition, a pattern field can not be bound to a database). The vertical alignment is not active for multi-line fields.

Text lines end with.......... `LF (Unix)          ⌄`
> Unix or Windows? This mainly affects line endings. Internally Windows lines end with two control characters (CR and LF).

Scrollbars........................ `None               ⌄`
> Only for multi-line fields: Horizontal | Vertical | Both.

Password character.......		Active only for single-line fields. Changes characters to see only points.

Data tab

Nothing of significance.

Events tab

Nothing of significance.

Numeric field

In addition to properties already described, the following properties exist:

General tab

Value min.........................	-1000000,00	Minimum value for the field. Should agree with the minimum value defined in the table.
Value max.........................	1000000,00	Maximum value.
Incr./decrement value......	1	Scrolling increment when using the mouse wheel or within a spin box.
Default value....................		Value displayed when a new record is being created.
Decimal accuracy...........	2	Number of decimal places, set to 0 for integers.
Thousands separator.....	No	Separator for thousands, usually a comma.

Data tab

There is no check on whether a field can be NULL. If there is no entry, the field will be NULL and not 0.

No filter proposal is offered.

Events tab

The "Changed" event is absent. Changes must be handled using the "Text modified" event (the word text is not to be taken literally here).

Date field

As well as the properties described on page 70, the following are to be noted.

General tab

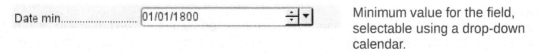

Date min.........................	01/01/1800	Minimum value for the field, selectable using a drop-down calendar.

| Date max | 12/31/2200 | | Maximum value. |

Short form as 10.02.12 or various forms using ' / ' instead of ' . ' or ' - ' in the American style.

| Date format | Standard (short) | | |

| Default date | | | Here you can enter a literal date but unfortunately not (yet) the current date (Today) at the time the form is opened. |

| Dropdown | No | | A month calender for selecting dates can be included. |

Data tab

There is no check on whether a field can be NULL. If there is no entry, the field will be NULL and not 0.

No filter proposal is offered.

Events tab

The "Changed" event is absent. Changes must be handled using the "Text modified" event (the word text is not to be taken literally here).

Time field

As well as the properties listed on page 70, the following features are available.

General tab

| Time min | 00:00:00 | | Minimum value for the field, by default set to 0. |

| Time max | 23:59:59 | | Maximum value, by default set to 1 second before 24:00. |

| Time format | 13:45 | | Short form without seconds, long form with seconds, and also 12-hour formats with AM and PM. |

| Default time | | | You can set a fixed time but unfortunately not (yet) the actual time of saving the form. |

Data tab

There is no check on whether a field can be NULL. If there is no entry, the field will be NULL and not 0.

No filter proposal is offered.

Events tab

The "Changed" event is absent. Changes must be handled using the "Text modified" event (the word text is not to be taken literally here).

Currency field

In addition to the properties already listed on page 70, the following features are available:

General tab

Min. value, Max. value, Increment, Default value, Decimal places, and Thousands separator. correspond to the general properties listed on page 75. In addition to these, there is only:

Currency symbol.............. | $ | The symbol is displayed but not stored in the table that underlies the form.

Prefix symbol.................. | No ◇ | Should the symbol be placed before or after the number?

Data tab

There is no check on whether a field can be NULL. If there is no entry, the field will be NULL and not 0.

No filter proposal is offered.

Events tab

The "Changed" event is absent. Changes must be handled using the "Text modified" event (the word text is not to be taken literally here).

Formatted field

In addition to the properties listed on page 70, the following features are offered:

General tab

Minimum and maximum values, and the default value, depend on the formatting. Behind the button for Formating is a flexible field that makes most currency and numeric fields unnecessary. Unlike a simple currency field, a pattern field can show negative sums in red.

Formatting........................ | | [...] The button to the right with the three dots provides a choice of numeric formats, as you usually do in Calc.

Among the numeric formats can be seen, alongside Date, Time, Currency or normal numeric format, possibilities for using fields with a measurement unit such as **kg** (see Figure 27). See also the general Help on numeric format codes.

Data tab

Nothing special to report.

Events tab

The "Changed" event is absent. Changes must be handled using the "Text modified" event (the word text is not to be taken literally here).

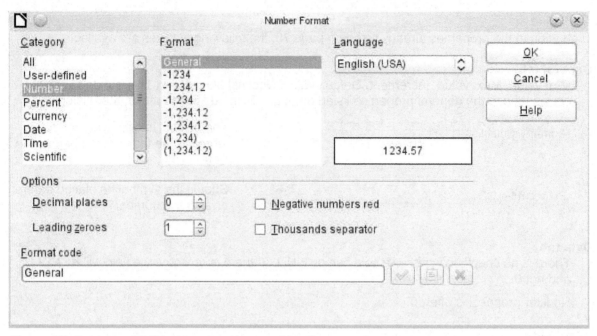

Figure 27: Formatted field with general numeric options

List box

When a list box is created, the List Box Wizard appears by default. This automatic appearance can be switched off if required using the Wizards On/Off button (shown in Figure 24).

Wizard

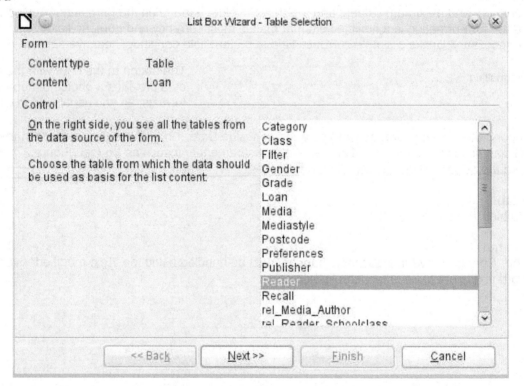

The form is already defined. It is bound to a *Table* named Loans. A list box shows the user different data from what is actually transmitted into the table. This data usually comes from another table in the database, and not from the table to which the form is bound.

The Loans table is supposed to show which Reader has borrowed which Media. However this table does not store the name of the reader but the corresponding primary key from the Reader table. It is therefore the Reader table that forms the basis for the list box.

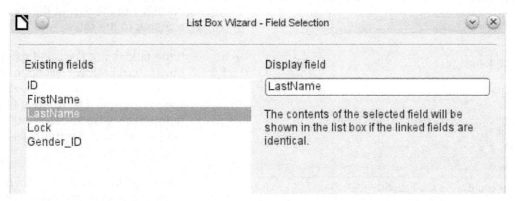

The *Surname* field from the Reader table should be visible in the list box. This serves as the Display field.

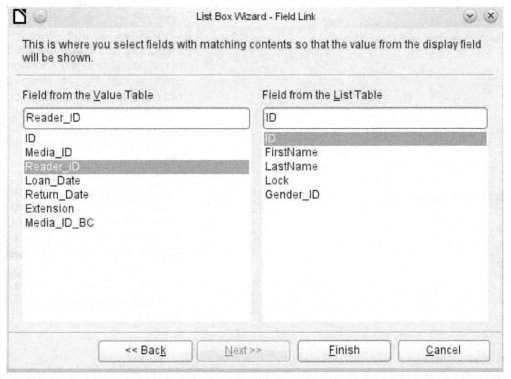

The *Reader_ID* field occurs in the Loan table which underlies the form. This table is described here as the *Value table*. The primary key ID from the Reader table must be bound to this field. The Reader table is described here as the *List table*.

The list box has now been created complete with data and default configuration and is fully functional.

In addition to the properties listed on page 70, the following features are available.

General tab

List entries....................... [▾]

The list entries have already been set using the Wizard. Here you could add further entries that are not from any table in the database. List entries here means the visible entries, not those that the form will transmit to the table.

Dropdown....................... [Yes   ▴▾]

If the field is not specified as drop-down, scroll arrows will appear on the right side of the list box when the form is loaded. The list field then automatically becomes a multi-line field, in which the actual value selected is highlighted.

Line count....................... [20   ▴▾]

If the field is drop-down, this property gives the maximum visible number of lines. If the content extends over more lines, a scrollbar appears when the list drops down.

Multiselection.................. [No   ▴▾]

Can more than one value be selected? In the above example, this is not possible since a foreign key is being stored. Usually this function is not used for databases, since each field should only contain one value. If necessary, macros can help in the interpretation of multiple entries in the list field.

Default selection............. [▾] [...]

As the deactivated button makes clear, a default selection makes little sense in the context of a binding with a database table, as created by the List Field Wizard. It could well be the case that the record corresponding to the default selection in the example table Readers is no longer present.

Data tab

In addition to the usual data properties *Data field* and *Input required*, there are significant properties which affect the binding between the displayed data and the data to be entered into the table that underlies the form.

Type of list contents: Valuelist | Table | Query | SQL | SQL [Native] | Tablefields

List contents Valuelist: If list entries have been created under **General**, the corresponding values to be stored are entered here. The list contents are loaded with individual items separated by **Shift – Enter**. The *List content* field then shows them as **"Value1";"Value2";"Value3"** … The *Bound Field* property is *inactive*.

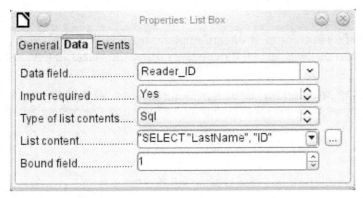

List contents Table: Here one of the database tables can be selected. However this is seldom possible as it requires the content of the table to be so structured that the first table field contains the values to be displayed in the list field, and one of the following fields contains the primary key which the table underlying the form uses as a foreign key. The position of this field within the table is specified in *Bound Field*, where the **Numbering begins with 0 for the first field of the database table**. But this 0 is reserved for the displayed value, in the above example the Surname, while the 1 refers to the ID field.

List contents Query: Here a query is first created separately and stored. The creation of such queries is described in Chapter 5, Queries. Using the query, it is possible to move the ID field from the first position in the underlying table to the second position, here represented by the bound field 1.

List contents SQL: The List Box Wizard fills this field. The query constructed by the Wizard looks like this:

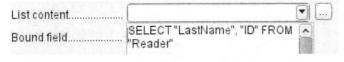

The query is the simplest possible. The Surname field occurs at position 0, the ID field at position 1. Both are read from the Reader table. As the bound field is Field 1, this SQL formula works. Here should be added **ORDER BY "LastName" ASC**. So you haven't to scroll to long through the list to find somebody. An additional problem might be, that *LastName* could be the same for more than one reader. So *FirstName* must be added in the view of the list box. When there are readers with the same *LastName* and the same *FirstName*, the primary key *ID* must also be shown. See Chapter 5, Queries, for information on how this works.

List contents SQL [Native]: The SQL formula is entered directly, not using the Wizard. Base does not evaluate the query. This is suitable when the query contains functions that might perhaps not be understood by the Base GUI. In this case the query is not checked for errors. More about **direct SQL Mode** can be found in Chapter 5, Queries.

List contents tablefields: Here *Field names* from a table are listed, not their content. For the Reader table, the List contents would be "ID", "Given name", "Surname", "Lock", "Gender_ID".

Events tab

In addition to the standard events, the following events are available:

Execute action: If a value is chosen by the keyboard or the mouse, the list box executes this action.

Item status changed: This could be the change of the displayed content of a list box through the use of the drop-down button. It could also be a click on the drop-down button of the field.

Error occurred: Unfortunately, this event cannot be reconstructed for list boxes.

Combo box

As soon as a combo box is created, a Wizard appears by default, just as with a list box. This automatic behavior can be switched off if necessary using the Wizards On/Off button (see Figure 24).

Combo boxes write the selected text directly into the table underlying the form. Therefore the following example shows both the table linked to the form and the one selected for the control as the Reader table.

Wizard

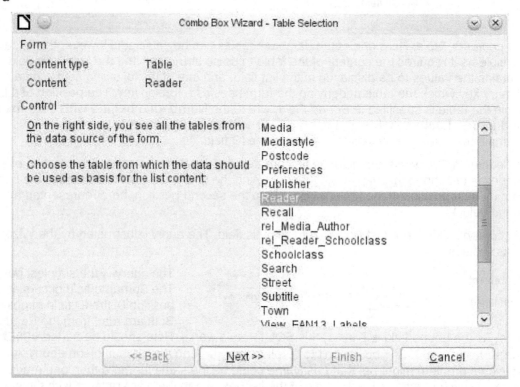

Again the form is predefined, this time with the Reader table. As the data to be displayed in the combo box is also to be stored in this table, the source selected for the data for the list is likewise the Reader table.

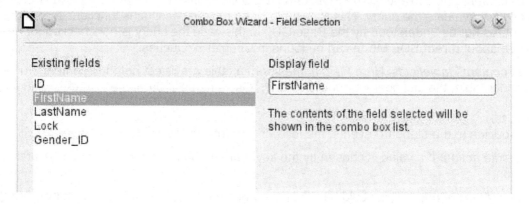

In the Reader table the FirstName field occurs. This should be displayed in the combo box.

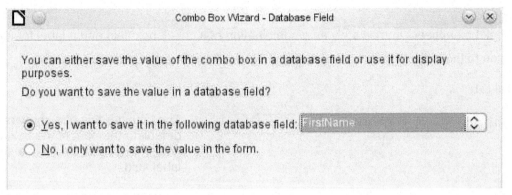

In a database, there seems to be little point in not storing the value of a combo box within a field. We want to read given names from the Reader table, and also to make them available for new readers, so that new records do not need to be created for a given name that already exists in the database. The combo box shows the first name, and text input is not necessary.

If a new value does need to be entered, this can be done easily in a combo box, as the box shows exactly what is going into the underlying table for the form.

In addition to the properties shown on page 70 and described for list boxes, the following features are available.

General tab

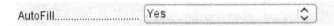

AutoFill.............................. Yes ⌄   During entry of new values, a list of matching values (if any) is displayed for possible selection.

Data tab

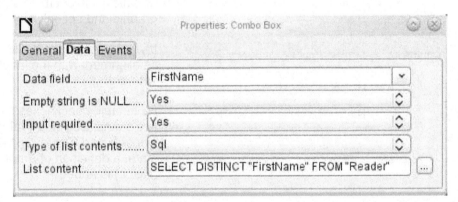

The data fields conform to the existing default settings and the settings for a list box. The SQL command however shows a special feature:

```
SELECT DISTINCT "FirstName" FROM "Reader"
```

Adding the **DISTINCT** keyword ensures that duplicate given names are shown only once. However, creation using the Wizard once more makes it impossible for the content to be sorted.

Events tab

The events correspond to those for a list box.

Check box

The check box appears immediately as a combination of a check box field and a label for the box.

In addition to the properties described on page 70, the following features are available.

General tab

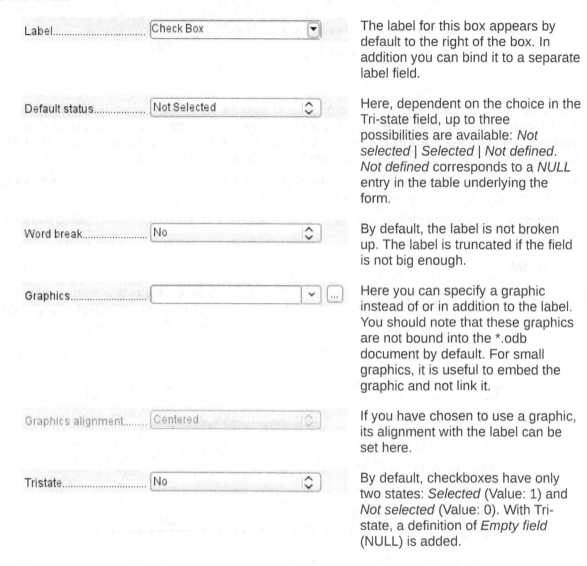

Label................................ Check Box ▾

The label for this box appears by default to the right of the box. In addition you can bind it to a separate label field.

Default status................. Not Selected ↕

Here, dependent on the choice in the Tri-state field, up to three possibilities are available: *Not selected* | *Selected* | *Not defined*. *Not defined* corresponds to a *NULL* entry in the table underlying the form.

Word break....................... No ↕

By default, the label is not broken up. The label is truncated if the field is not big enough.

Graphics........................... ▾ ...

Here you can specify a graphic instead of or in addition to the label. You should note that these graphics are not bound into the *.odb document by default. For small graphics, it is useful to embed the graphic and not link it.

Graphics alignment........ Centered ↕

If you have chosen to use a graphic, its alignment with the label can be set here.

Tristate............................ No ↕

By default, checkboxes have only two states: *Selected* (Value: 1) and *Not selected* (Value: 0). With Tri-state, a definition of *Empty field* (NULL) is added.

Data tab

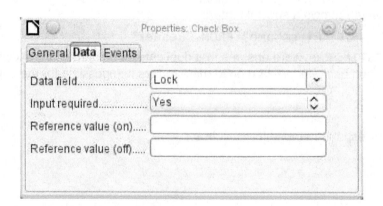

The check box can be given a reference value. However only the values of 1 (for On) or 0 (for Off) can be transferred to the underlying data field (check boxes act as fields for the choice of Yes and No).

Events tab

The fields "Changed", "Text modified". "Before updating" and "After updating" are all absent.

Additional fields for a check box are "Execute action" (see List box) und "Item status changed" (corresponds to "Changed").

Option button

The option button is similar to the check box described above, except for its general properties and its external (round) form.

When several option buttons in the form are linked to the same table field, only one of the options can be selected.

General tab

Group name...................... [   ]

The option button is designed to be used in groups. One of several options can then be selected. That is why a Group name appears here, under which the options can be addressed.

Data tab

See under Check box. Here, however, reference values that are entered are actually transferred to the data field.

Events tab

See under Check box.

Image control

A image control handles the entry and display of graphical material in the database. The underlying data field must be a binary field.

Entry into a image control takes place either by a double-click with the mouse to open a file selection dialog, or a right-click to choose whether an existing graphic is to be deleted or replaced.

A graphical control by default has no Tab stop.

In addition to the properties described on page 70, the following features are available.

General tab

Graphics.......................... [⌄] [...]

The graphic selected here is only shown inside the control, while the form is being edited. It has no significance for later input.

Scale.......................... Keep Ratio |↕|

No: The image will not be fitted to the field. If it is too big, the field will show a window into the image. The image is not distorted.
Keep ratio: The image is fitted to the control but not distorted (aspect ratio preserved).
Autom. Size: The image is fitted to the control and may be shown in a distorted form.

Data tab

Nothing further to report.

Events tab

The events "Changed", "Text modified", "Before updating" and "After updating" are missing..

Pattern field

An input mask is used to control input into the field. Characters are pre-specified for particular positions, determining the properties of entered characters. The preset characters are stored along with the entered ones.

In addition to the properties described on page 70, the following features are available.

General tab

Edit mask....................... [   ]   This determines what characters can be entered.

Literal mask.................... [   ]   This is what the form user sees.

The following content is taken from LibreOffice Help:

The length of the edit mask determines how many characters may be entered. If the user's entry does not match the mask, the entry is rejected on leaving the control. The following characters are available for defining the edit mask.

Character	Meaning
L	A text constant. This position cannot be edited. The actual character is displayed at the corresponding position in the literal mask.
a	Represents any of the letters a-z/A-Z. Capital letters are not converted into lower case.
A	Represents any of the letters A-Z. If lower-case letters are entered, they will automatically be converted to upper case.
c	Represents any of the characters a-z/A-Z plus the digits 0-9. Capital letters are not converted into lower case.
C	Represents any of the letters A-Z plus the digits 0-9. If lower-case letters are entered, they will automatically be converted to upper case.
N	Only the digits 0-9 can be entered.
x	All printable characters are allowed.
X	All printable characters are allowed. If lower-case letters are entered, they will automatically be converted to upper case.

So, for example, you can define the literal mask as "__/__/2012" and the edit mask as "NNLNNLLLLL", to allow the user to enter four characters only for a date.

Data tab

Nothing further to report.

Events tab

The "Changed" event is absent.

Table control

This is the most comprehensive control. It provides a table, which can then be provided with controls for individual columns. This not only allows the actual data to be viewed during input, but also the previously entered data, without the need to use the Navigation bar to scroll through the records.

Not every field that is possible in a form can be selected for a table control field. Push buttons, image buttons and option buttons are not available.

The Table Control Wizard assembles in a window the fields that will appear afterwards in the table.

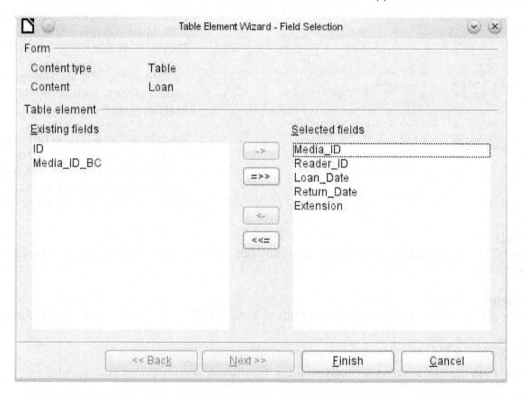

In the control the Loans table is available for editing. In addition to the ID (primary key) field and the Media_ID_BC field (entry of media using a bar-code scanner), all fields are to be used in the control.

The previously created table control must now be further developed, to allow entry into the Loans table. For fields such as *Reader_ID* or *Media_ID*, it would be more useful to be able to choose the reader or the media directly, rather than a number representing the reader or media. For this purpose, controls such as list boxes can be placed within the table control. This is declared later. The formatting of the *Extension* field with two decimal places was certainly not intended.

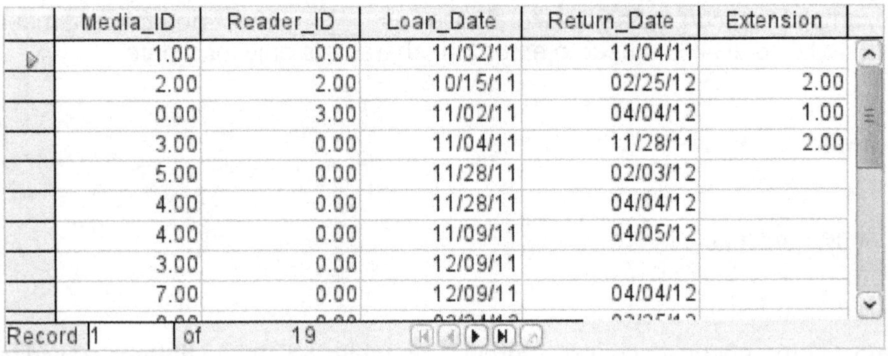

	Media_ID	Reader_ID	Loan_Date	Return_Date	Extension	
▷	1.00	0.00	11/02/11	11/04/11		⌃
	2.00	2.00	10/15/11	02/25/12	2.00	
	0.00	3.00	11/02/11	04/04/12	1.00	
	3.00	0.00	11/04/11	11/28/11	2.00	
	5.00	0.00	11/28/11	02/03/12		
	4.00	0.00	11/28/11	04/04/12		
	4.00	0.00	11/09/11	04/05/12		
	3.00	0.00	12/09/11			
	7.00	0.00	12/09/11	04/04/12		⌄

Record 1   of   19   [◀][◀][▶][▶][⟲]

Figure 28: Output of the Table Control Wizard

In addition to the properties listed on page 70, the following features are available.

General tab

Row height............. [⌄]   Height of individual lines. With no value here, the height is automatically adjusted to the font size. Multi-line text fields are then shown as single lines to be scrolled.

Navigation bar.......... [Yes   ⌄]   As with tables, the lower edge of the control shows the record number and navigation aids.

Record marker............ [Yes   ⌄]   By default there is a record marker on the left edge of the control. It indicates the current record. You can use the record marker to access the delete function for the whole record.

Data tab

Since this is a field that contains no data itself but manages other fields, there are no data properties.

Events tab

The "Changed" and "Text modified" events are missing. The "Error occurred" event is added.

Label field

In addition to the properties described on page 70, the following features are available.

General tab

Word break............. [No   ⌄]   By default a label is not wrapped. If it is too long for the field, it is truncated. Caution: word wrapping does not recognize spaces, so if the field is too small, a break can occur within a word.

Data tab

None.

Events tab

The label field reacts only to events that are connected with the mouse, a key or the focus.

Group box

A group box graphically groups several controls and provides them with a collective label.

If a group box is created with Wizards active, the Wizard proceeds from the assumption that several option buttons will occur together within this frame.

This form is based on the Reader table. We are dealing with the choice of gender. The entries are the labels of the option buttons.

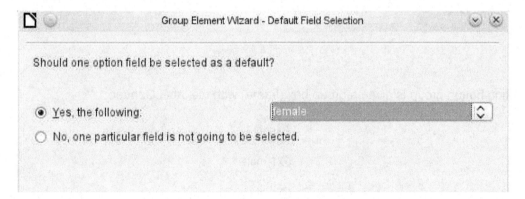

Here the default option is "female". If there is to be no default field, the default entry in the underlying table is *NULL*.

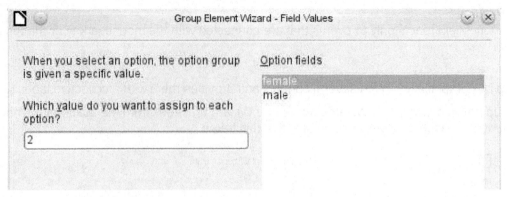

The Wizard gives the option buttons separate values by default, here 1 for female and 2 for male. These values correspond to the examples of primary key fields in the Gender table.

The value selected by clicking an option button is transferred to the *Gender_ID* field of the form's underlying table Readers. In this way the Readers table is provided with the corresponding foreign key from the Gender table by using the option button.

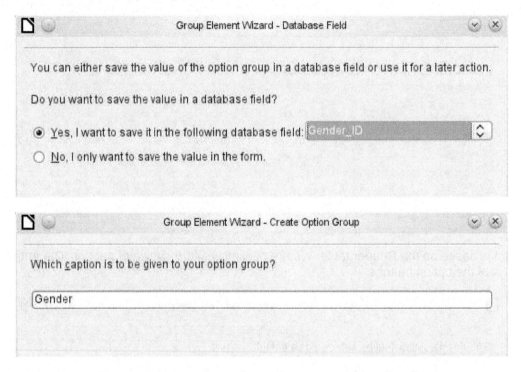

The option button group is given a group box (frame) with the label Gender.

If female is selected in the active form, male is deselected. This is a characteristic of option buttons that are bound to the same field in the underlying table. In the example shown above, the option buttons replace a two-element list box.

In addition to the properties described on page 70, the following features are available.

General tab

The label can be changed from its default value. At present the frame properties (Line thickness, line color) cannot be changed but you can change the font formatting.

Data tab

None, since this control serves only for visual grouping of fields.

Events rab

The group box reacts to events involving the mouse, a key, or the focus.

Push button

In addition to the properties described on page 70, the following features are available.

General tab

Label.....................	Push Button ▼	Label on the button.
Take Focus on Click........	Yes ◇	The button receives the focus when it is clicked.
Toggle.............................	No ◇	If Yes, the button can be shown pressed in. The button state is shown as for a switch. When you press it a second time, it shows an unpressed button.
Default status..............	Not Selected ◇	Active, when Toggle is set to *Yes*. *Selected* corresponds to the pressed-in button.
Word break......................	No ◇	Word wrapping if the button is too narrow.
Action.............................	None ◇	A variety of actions similar to those for the navigation bar are available.
URL.................................	∨ ...	HTML: File to be called up with this button.
Frame.............................	∨	Only for HTML forms: The target-frame (frame arrangement for different HTML pages) in which the file should be opened.
Default button.................	No ◇	The default button is framed when this is set to *Yes*. When there are several alternative buttons on a form, the one most often used should have this characteristic. It is activated by pressing the Enter key, when no other action needs to depend on this key. Only one button on the form can be the default button.

Graphics............................ [▾] [...]	Should a graphic appear on the button?
Graphics alignment......... [Centered ◇]	Only active when a graphic has been selected. Specifies the alignment of the graphic to the text.

Data tab

None. A button only carries out actions.

Events tab

"Approve action", "Execute action" and "Item status changed".

Image button

In addition to the properties already described on page 70, the following features are available.

General tab

Similar to a normal button. However this button has no text and the button itself is not visible. You see only a frame around the graphic.

By default, an image button has no tab stop.

Caution: at the time of writing, hardly any actions work with this button. It is practically only usable with macros.

Data tab

None; this control only carries out actions.

Events tab

"Approve action" and all events involving the mouse, a key, or the focus.

Navigation bar

Figure 29: Navigation bar control

The standard Form Navigation bar is inserted into forms at the lower edge of the screen. The insertion of this toolbar can cause a brief rightward shift of the form as it builds up on the screen. This can be distracting in cases where the navigation bar is switched off again for some parts of the visible form, for example when there are subforms or more than one form in the visible form.

By contrast, a navigation bar control that is part of the form, separate from the corresponding items, makes it clear through which items you navigate with the toolbar. The form for Loans, for example, needs to search first through the readers and then show the media loaded to the reader. The navigation bar control is positioned near the reader, so the user notices that the navigation bar is used for the reader and not for the media loaned to the reader.

The standard Form Navigation bar makes available the buttons shown in Figure 30. The navigation bar control shows the same buttons except those for Find Record, Form-Based Filters and Data source as Table.

Figure 30: Navigation buttons

In addition to the properties listed on page 70, the following features are available for the Navigator Bar control.

General tab

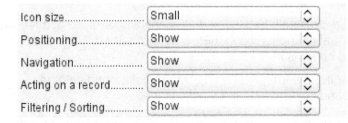

The icon size is adjustable. In addition you can choose which groups are displayed. These are shown in Figure 29 from left to right using a vertical line as a group separator: Positioning, Navigation, Acting on a record, and groups of commands for Filtering and Sorting.

Data tab

None, as this control only carries out actions.

Events tab

All events that involve the Mouse, a key, or the focus.

Independent of this form control, the **insertable navigation bar** naturally continues to exist with the same items as the above figure.

This insertable navigation bar provides additionally the *general record search*, the *form-based filter* and the display of the form's underlying *data source in table view* above the form.

If you are working not just with a form but with subforms and ancillary forms, you must be careful that this insertable navigation bar does not disappear as you switch forms. That creates a disturbing effect on the screen.

Multiple selection

If you use the Select icon (Figure 24) to select a large region or several elements of a form, the following modifications may be carried out (see Figure 31).

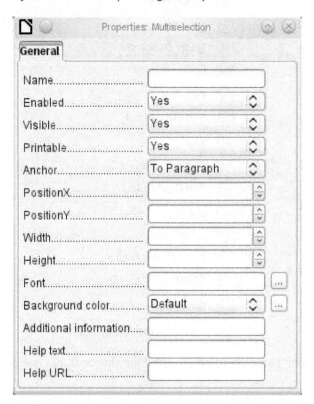

Figure 31: General properties of form fields in a multiple selection

You should not alter the name. That would cause all the selected elements suddenly to acquire the same name. It would make finding individual elements using the Form Navigator difficult, and management of the form by using named controls in macros impossible.

Multiple selection is more useful for changing the font, the height or the background color of controls. Note that changing the background color affects the labels as well.

If you want to alter only the labels, hold down the *Control* key and click these controls directly or in the Navigator, or right-click on a field to call up the control properties. Now the choice of properties that you can change is greater as you are dealing only with similar fields. You can change anything here that is available in a label field.

The possibilities of multiple selection depend therefore on the choice of fields. You can simultaneously change controls of the same kind that have all the properties that exist for a single instance.

A simple form completed

A simple form has form controls for writing or reading records from a single table or query. Its construction is shown by the following example.

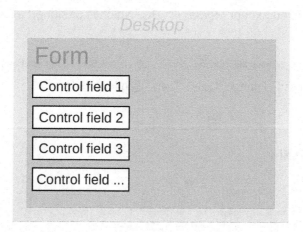

The example of a simple form for library loans is shown here using several variants. The quick way to use the Form Wizard is described in Chapter 8, Getting Started with Base, in the *Getting Started with LibreOffice* guide. Here we describe the creation in Design View.

The heading for the form was created using a label field. The font was changed. The label field is anchored to a paragraph in the top left corner of the document. Using the context menu of the label field, a form was created that was linked to the Loans table (see "Form properties" on page 66). The page has also been given a uniformly colored background.

Adding groups of fields

A quick variant for direct entry of fields with labels is to use the *Add Field* function.

This function, available on the Formula Design toolbar (see Figure 22), allows all fields of the underlying table to be selected.

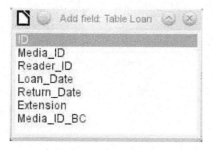

Double-click on the fields to insert them into the form as a group with labels (unfortunately all on the same spot). The group needs to be separated out so that the form eventually looks like the following illustration. For a better view, all unnecessary toolbars have been removed from the window, which has also been compressed so that not all elements of the Navigation bar are visible.

All fields have been selected except *Media_ID_BC*, which is designed to be used only with a barcode scanner.

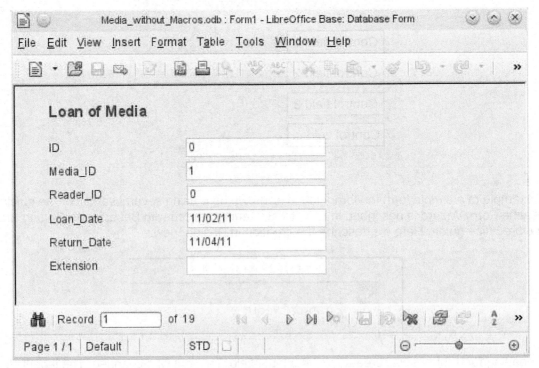

Figure 32: Simple form made by using Add Field

For each table field, an appropriate form control has been automatically selected. Numbers are in numeric fields and are declared as integers without decimal places. Date fields are represented correctly as date controls. All fields have been given the same width. If a graphical control had been included, it would have been given a square field.

Adjusting field proportions

We can now do some creative things, including adjusting the length of the fields and making the dates into drop-down fields. More important still is for the *Media_ID* and the *Reader_ID* fields to be made more user-friendly, unless every library user has a library ID card and every medium is supplied with an ID on accession. That will not be assumed in what follows.

To adjust individual fields, we must edit the group. This can be done with a right-click on the group and then following the context menu (Figure 33). For future work, it will be clearer if we use the Form Navigator.

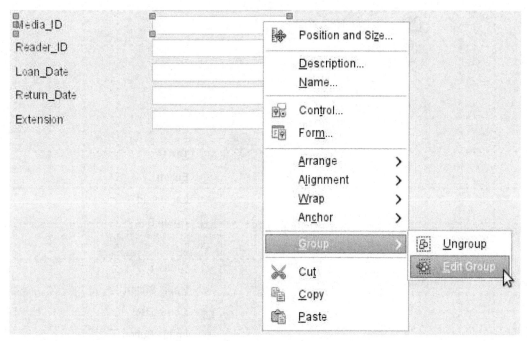

Figure 33: Form controls: editing the group

The Form Navigator displays all the elements of the form with their labels. For controls, the names are taken directly from the names of the fields in the underlying table. The names of the labels have the suffix *Label*.

A click on *Media_ID* selects this field (Figure 34). Right-click to replace the selected field with a different type of field, using the context menu (Figure 35).

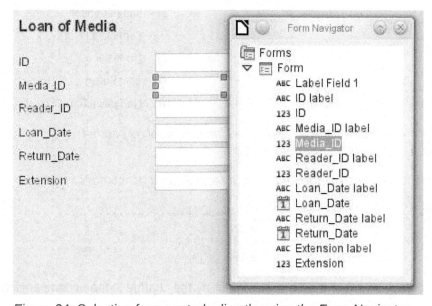

Figure 34: Selecting form controls directly using the Form Navigator

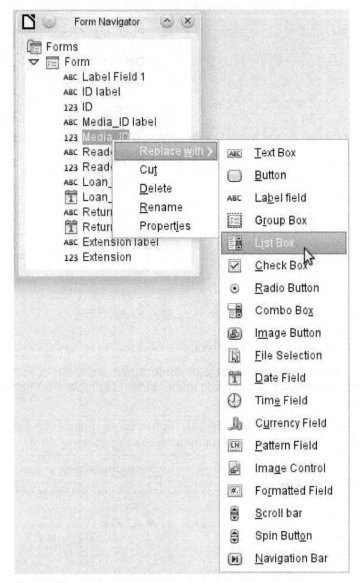

*Figure 35: Replacing one kind of control by another
using the Form Navigator*

This replacement is carried out for the *Media_ID* and *Reader_ID* controls.

The change is made visible in the Form Navigator by the change in the accompanying icon.

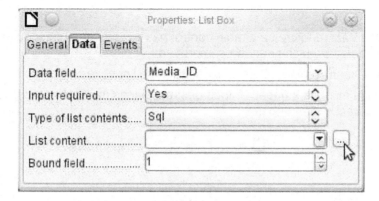

The SQL query for the list field can now be created through the graphical user interface by clicking on the button at the right. This is carried out automatically when a list box is created directly, but not when it is formed by conversion from another type of control. For the SQL command, see Chapter 5, Queries.

Since the list boxes are to be made drop-down, the following defects can be corrected at the same time:

- The labels for the list boxes should be *Media* instead of *Media_ID* and *Reader* instead of *Reader_ID*.

- The *ID* control should be declared as read-only.

- Any fields which are not absolutely necessary for issuing loans for a new medium do not need a tab stop. Without it, the form can be traversed much faster. If necessary, the tab stop can also be adjusted using the activation sequence (see page 70). Only the *Media*, *Reader* and *Loan date* fields must be accessible in all cases using the *Tab* key.

- If the form is intended for carrying out loans, it is unnecessary and also confusing for returned media to be displayed. Media with a return date should be filtered out. In addition, the display order could be sorted by Reader, so that media on loan to the same person are displayed successively. See the note on "Form properties" on page 66. However there is a problem here in that readers can be sorted only by ID, not alphabetically, because the table underlying the form only contains the ID.

Adding single fields

The addition of single fields is a bit more complicated. The fields must be selected, dragged onto the form surface, and the appropriate field from the underlying table specified. In addition, the type of field must be correctly chosen; for example, numeric fields have two decimal places by default.

Only when creating list boxes does the Wizard come into play, making it easier for a novice to carry out the steps for creating correct fields—up to a point. Beyond that point, the Wizard ceases to meet requirements because:

- The entries are not automatically sorted.

- Combining several fields in the list box content is not possible.

Here again we need to make retrospective improvements, so that the required SQL code can be created quite quickly using the built-in query editor.

When adding single controls, the field and its label must be explicitly associated (see "Default settings for many controls" on page 70). In practice it could be better if you do not associate fields with the labels. So you must not choose **Edit Group** before changing the properties of a field.

Table control

The use of the Table Wizard to create a table control has already been described on page 87. It has however some defects which need to be improved:

- The *Media_ID* and *Reader_ID* fields must become list boxes.
- Numeric fields must be stripped of their decimal places, since the Wizard always specifies two decimal places for numbers.

Changing fields within the table control is not possible using the same method as described for other controls. In the Navigator, the description of fields ends with the table control. The Navigator knows nothing about the controls that lie within the table control, referring to fields in the underlying table. This equally applies later, when attempts are made to access the fields using macros. They cannot be accessed by name.

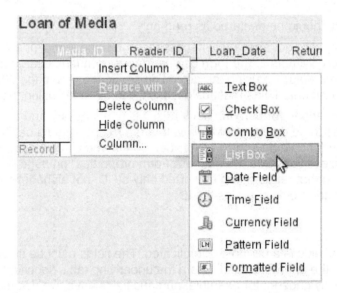

The controls within the table control are called columns. Using the context menu, it is now possible to replace one type of field by another. However the whole range of types is not available. There are no push buttons, option boxes, or graphical controls.

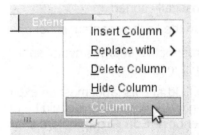

The properties of the fields are hidden in the context menu behind the concept of columns. Here, for example, the numeric field *Extension* can be changed so that no decimal places are shown.

Also the default minimum value of –1,000,000.00 hardly makes sense for a loan extension. The number should always remain small and positive.

As soon as the properties of a column are called up, you can select another column without shutting the properties dialog. In this way you can work on all the fields, one after another, without having to save in between.

End by saving the entire form, and finally the database itself.

The properties of the fields built into a table control are not so comprehensive as for those outside. The font, for example, can be set only for the entire table control. In addition, you do not have the option of skipping individual columns by removing their tab stops.

Tip	You can move through a form using either the mouse or the *Tab* key. If you tab into a table control, the cursor will move one field to the right for each additional tab; at the end of the line, it will move back to the first field of the next record in the table control. To exit the table control, use *Ctrl+Tab*.

The order of the columns can be changed by dragging the column header:

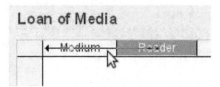

If this is done in form design view, it is permanent. A temporary change in order can be carried out during data entry by using the same method.

If only certain fields should be visible during use, you can use several different table controls in the form, as the *Tab* is captured by default by each table control.

The form shown in Figure 36 is for the loan of media. Only the fields immediately necessary are shown in the upper table control. The lower one shows all the fields, so that it is apparent which person and medium the return is for.

Loan of Media

Reader	Medium	Loan_Date
Lederstrumpf, Bert	Das sogennante Böse	11/02/11
Gerd, Lisa	Eine kurze Geschichte der Zeit	10/15/11
Mirinda, Monika	Der kleine Hobbit	11/02/11
Lederstrumpf, Bert	Traditionelle und kritische Theori	11/04/11
Lederstrumpf, Bert	I hear you knocking	11/28/11
Lederstrumpf, Bert	Die neue deutsche Rechtschreib	11/28/11
Lederstrumpf, Bert	Die neue deutsche Rechtschreib	11/09/11

Record 1 of 19

Reader	Medium	Loan_Date	Extension	Return_Date
Leders	Das sogenn	11/02/11		11/04/11
Gerd, Lisa	Eine kurze G	10/15/11	2	02/25/12
Mirinda, Mor	Der kleine H	11/02/11	1	04/04/12
Lederstrum	Traditionelle	11/04/11	2	11/28/11
Lederstrum	I hear you kn	11/28/11		02/03/12
Lederstrum	Die neue de	11/28/11		04/04/12
Lederstrum	Die neue de	11/09/11		04/05/12

Record 1 of 19

Figure 36: A form with multiple table controls

This figure shows an aesthetic failing that needs urgent attention. In the upper table control, the same medium sometimes occurs more than once. This happens because the table also shows media that have been returned earlier. Therefore the data needs to be filtered to show only the loans. Records with a return date should not appear.

This filtering is possible either by a query or directly using the form properties. If it is done using the form properties, the filter can be temporarily switched off during input. Filtering using a query is described in Chapter 5, Queries. Here we describe how to do it using form properties.

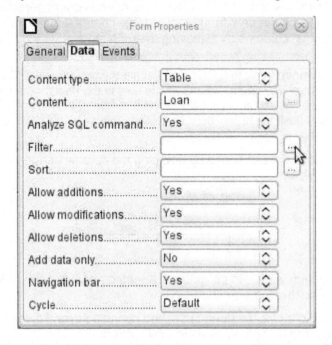

The filtering is carried out using the button with the three dots, which opens the dialog shown below. You can also enter the filter directly into the *Filter* text field if you know the SQL coding.

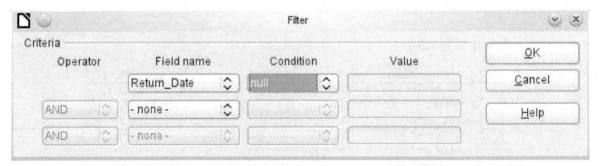

Using the GUI, you can now select the field named *Return_Date*. It will show only the records for which the field is empty, where "empty" stands for the SQL designation NULL.

The cleaned-up form (shown in Figure 37) now looks rather simpler.

Of course there is still room for improvement, but compared with the earlier form, this version has a clear advantage in that all the media are visible at a glance.

The processing of data using table controls is similar to using an actual table. A right-click on the record header of an existing record causes it to be deleted, and an entry can be canceled or saved in the case of new records.

When you leave a line, the record is automatically saved.

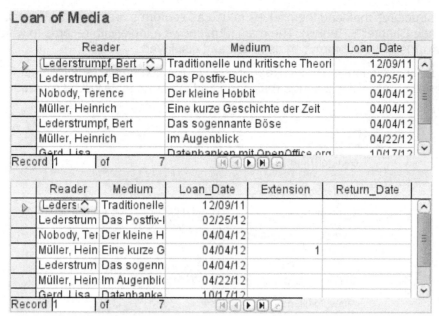

Loan of Media

	Reader	Medium	Loan_Date	
▷	Lederstrumpf, Bert ◇	Traditionelle und kritische Theori	12/09/11	⌃
	Lederstrumpf, Bert	Das Postfix-Buch	02/25/12	
	Nobody, Terence	Der kleine Hobbit	04/04/12	≡
	Müller, Heinrich	Eine kurze Geschichte der Zeit	04/04/12	
	Lederstrumpf, Bert	Das sogennante Böse	04/04/12	
	Müller, Heinrich	Im Augenblick	04/22/12	
	Gerd Lisa	Datenbanken mit OpenOffice org	10/17/12	⌄

Record 1   of   7   ⊣ ◁ ▶ ⊩ ⟲

	Reader	Medium	Loan_Date	Extension	Return_Date	
▷	Leders ◇	Traditionelle	12/09/11			⌃
	Lederstrum	Das Postfix-I	02/25/12			
	Nobody, Ter	Der kleine H	04/04/12			≡
	Müller, Hein	Eine kurze G	04/04/12	1		
	Lederstrum	Das sogenn	04/04/12			
	Müller, Hein	Im Augenbli	04/22/12			
	Gerd Lisa	Datenbanke	10/17/12			⌄

Record 1   of   7   ⊣ ◁ ▶ ⊩ ⟲

Figure 37: Amended form

We can still improve the Loan of Media form in a number of ways.

- It would be nice if selecting a reader in one part of the form caused the media on loan to this reader to be displayed in another.

- In the table shown above, you can see a lot of records that are not necessary because these media are already on loan. The table was created to allow loans to be made, so it would be better if only an empty page appeared, which could then be filled with the new loan.

Such solutions are available using further forms that are hierarchically arranged and make possible separate views of the data.

Main forms and subforms

A subform lies within a form like a form control. Like a form control, it is bound to data from the main form. However its data source can be another table or a query (or a SQL command). The important thing for a subform is that its data source is somehow linked to the data source of the main form.

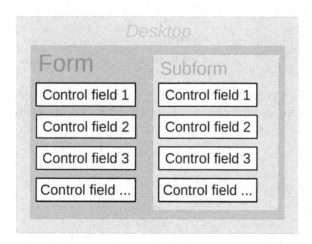

Typical table structures that lend themselves to use as subforms are tables with a one-to-many relationship (see Chapter 3, Tables). The main form shows a table with records to which many dependent records in the subform can be linked and displayed.

First we will use the relationship of the Reader table to the Loan table (see Chapter 3, Tables). The Reader table will form the basis for the main form and the Loan table will be reproduced in the sub-form.

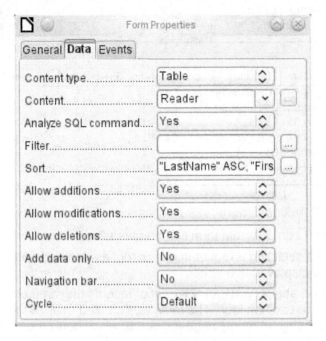

Here the main form is linked to the Reader table. To speed up the search for readers, the table is sorted alphabetically. We will do without a navigation bar, since the content of the subform would come between the main form and the navigation bar. Instead we will use the built-in form control (Figure 29).

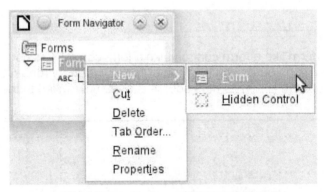

Right-click on the main form in the Form Navigator to use the context menu to create a new form. Once again this form has the default name of Form, but it is now an element in the subfolder of the main form.

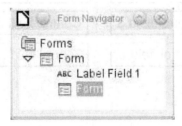

The properties of the subform must now be set up to give it the right data source, in order to reproduce the data for the correct reader.

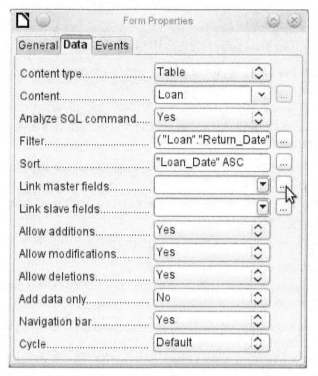

The Loans table is chosen for the subform. For the filter we specify that the Return date field should be empty ("**Return_Date" IS NULL**). This prevents any media that have already been returned from appearing. The records should be sorted by loan date. The ascending sort shows the medium on loan for the longest period at the top.

Link master fields and *Link slave fields* are used to create a linkage to the main form, in which the subform lies. The button with three dots shows once again that a helpful dialog is available for creating these.

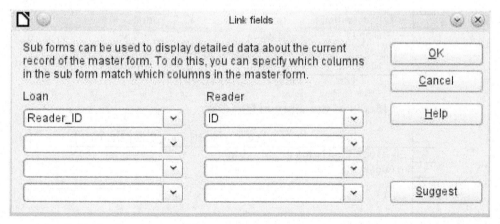

Under *Loans*, the fields in the Loans table are shown, under *Readers* those of the Reader table. The *Reader_ID* from *Loans* should be set as equivalent to the *ID* from the *Reader* table.

Although this linkage has already been created in the database using **Tools > Relationships** (see Chapter 3, Tables), the function that lies behind the Suggest button in this dialog does not reference this and would suggest that the first foreign key in the Loan table, namely *Media_ID*, should be linked with *ID* from the Reader table. The Form Creation Wizard solves this better by reading the relation from the relationship of the database.

The chosen link between the table for the subform and the table for the main form is now specified in terms of fields from the tables.

To create a table control for the main form, we must now select the main form in the Form Navigator. Then, if the Table Control Wizard is enabled, it will show the fields available in the main form. We deal with the subform in a similar way.

Once the table controls have been set up, we need to carry out the modifications already discussed when creating the simpler form:

- Replacing the numeric field *Media_ID* in the subform with a list box.
- Renaming the *Media_ID* field *Media*.
- Modifying the numeric fields to a format without decimal places.
- Limiting the minimum and maximum values.
- Renaming other fields, to save space or to add non-ASCII characters which should not be used in field names in database tables.

Sort and filter functions are supplemented for the main form by adding a navigation bar. The other fields on the navigation bar are not needed, as they are mostly available from the table control (record display, record navigation) or else carried out by movement through the table control (data storage).

The final form might look like the figure below.

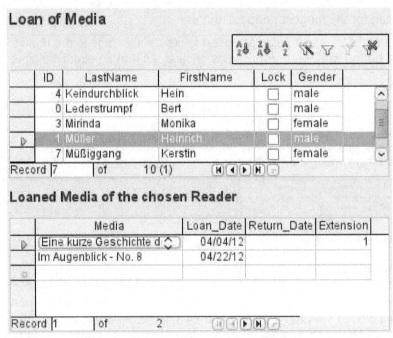

Figure 38: Form consisting of a main form (above) and a subform (below).

If a reader is now selected in the main form, the subform will show the media on loan to that reader. When an item is returned, it continues to appear on the form until the form itself is refreshed. This occurs automatically when another record is loaded into the main form. If the original reader is selected again, returned media are no longer displayed.

This delayed updating is actually desirable in this case, as it allows one to inspect the media currently lying on the library counter and see at once whether these have been registered.

This form structure is significantly easier to use than the previous one with only a single form. However there are still details that can be improved:

- Media and loan dates might be changed when the media is to be loaned out for longer. Changing the media date might make it impossible to trace which item is still available in the library and which is on loan. Changing the loan date could lead to errors. Recall notices could not be verified.

- If a reader record is not selected by clicking on the record header at the left, only the little green arrow on the header shows which record is currently active. It is quite possible that the active record will be scrolled right out of the table control window.

- Instead of the text "*Loaned Media of the chosen Reader*", it would be better to have the reader's name.

- It is possible to loan out the same medium twice without it having been returned.

- It is possible to delete the record for an item on loan quite easily.

- Data can be changed or deleted in the main form. This can be useful for small libraries with little public traffic. However when things become hectic at the loans counter, editing of user data should not take place at the same time as issuing loans. It would be better if new users could be registered but existing user data left untouched. For libraries, this applies equally to deletions or complete name changes.

First let us improve the selection of readers. This should protect us from changes to the loan records. A simple solution would be not to allow any modification except the entry of new records. This still requires a search function when a reader wishes to borrow an item. It would be better to use a list box to find the reader and carry out the issue and return operations in separate table controls.

For the main form we need a table, into which the list box can write a value linked to this table. The table requires an integer field and a primary key. It will always contain only one record, so the primary key field ID can safely be declared as Tiny Integer. The following table named Filter should therefore be created.

Table name: Filter	
Field name	**Field type**
ID	Tiny Integer, Primary key
Integer	Integer

The table is given a primary key with the value 0. This record will be repeatedly read and rewritten by the main form.

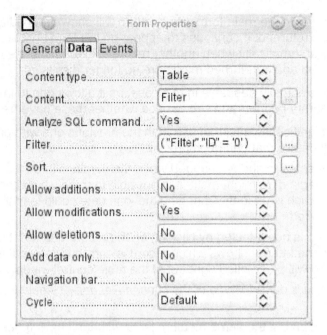

The main form is based on the Filter table. It will just read the value from the table which is associated with the primary key (*ID*) of 0. No data will be added; the current record will just be repeatedly rewritten. As only edits of a single record are allowed, a navigation bar would be superfluous.

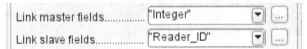

This main form is linked to the subform in such a way that the value of the Integer field in the Filter table is the same as the value of the *Reader_ID* field in the Loan Table. The subform's properties are unchanged from the version shown above.

Before we create a list box in the main form, we must switch off the wizards. The list box Wizard only allows you to create a box that shows the content of a single field; it would be impossible to have surname and given name and an additional number in the display area of a list box. As in the simpler form, we now enter for the list box contents *Surname, Given name – ID Nr*. The list box transmits the ID to the underlying table.

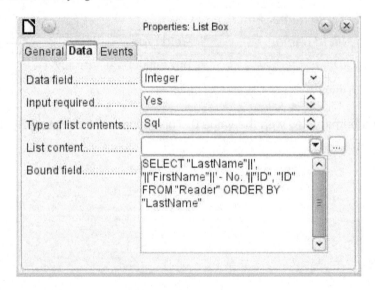

Next to the list box, a button is created. This button is actually part of the subform. It takes over two functions: saving the record in the main form and updating the table in the subform. It is good enough to entrust the update to the button in the subform. The save process for the modified main form is then carried out automatically.

The button can simply be labeled *OK*. The action assigned to it in the general properties of the button is *Refresh Form*.

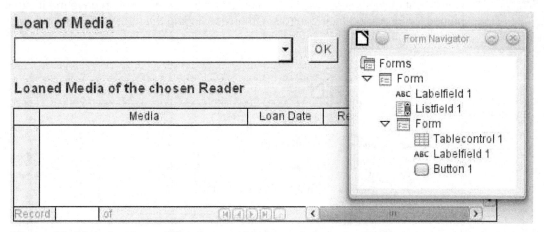

Figure 39: Main form as a filter for a subform

The main form consists only of the heading and the list box; the subform contains another heading, the table control from the previous version and the button.

The form now functions better in that:

- No reader can now be edited, altered or deleted, and
- Readers can be found more quickly by typing into the control than by using a filter.

For a greater degree of functionality (returns without alteration of previous data) a second subform must be created, linked to the same Loans table. To ensure the functionality of the list box in Figure 39, both subforms must be placed one level further down, as subforms of a subform. Data is updated hierarchically from the main form down through the subforms. The button in the previously described form must now be placed in the first subform and not in the two subforms that come under it.

Here the Form Navigator is used to show the different levels. In the main form we have the text field for the form title and the list box for finding the reader. The list box appears at the bottom of the form, as it is declared after the subform. Unfortunately this display sequence cannot be altered. The subform has only one button, for updating its contents and at the same time saving the main

---

form. One level further down are the two additional subforms. These are given different names when created so that no confusion arises in any level of the tree.

Note	Basically the names of forms and controls are without significance. However if these names are to be accessed by macros, they must be distinguishable. You cannot distinguish identical names at the same level. Naturally it makes sense, when creating larger form structures to have meaningful names for forms and their controls. Otherwise finding the right field could quickly become problematic.

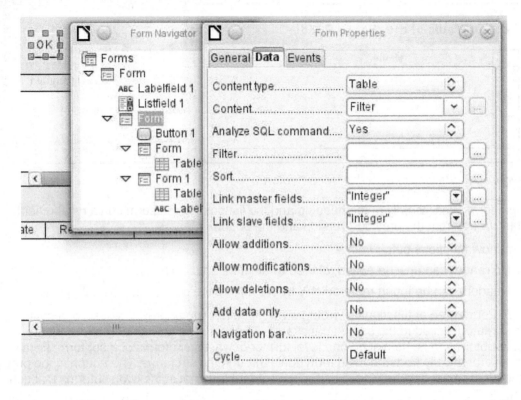

The main form and the subform use the same table. In the subform, no data are entered. That is why all the fields for this form are set to *No*. The main form and the subform are linked through the field, whose value is to be transmitted to the sub-subforms: the Integer field in the Filter table.

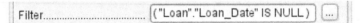

In the first sub-subform, no existing data are displayed; it is used only for creating new data. For this, the suggested filter is adequate. Only records matching the *Reader_ID* and with an empty loan date field ("*Loan_Date" IS NULL*) will be displayed. In practice, this means an empty table control. As the table control is not continuously updated, newly loaned media will remain within it until the *OK* update button is used either to select a new name or to transfer the data into the second sub-subform.

The second sub-subform requires more settings. This form too contains data from the "Loans" table. Here the data is filtered for an empty return date. ("*Return_Date" IS NULL*). The data are sorted as in the previous form, so that the media on loan for the longest time are immediately visible.

The following points are also important. Old records can be changed, but no new records can be added. Deletion is also impossible. This is the first necessary step to prevent loan records from being simply deleted later on. But it would still be possible to change the medium and the loan date. Therefore the properties of the columns will require adjustment. Eventually the medium and the loan date should be displayed but protected from modification.

The table control is simply duplicated after the creation of the form. This is done by selecting it, copying, deselecting, and then pasting it in from the clipboard. The copy will be at the same position as the original, and will therefore need to be dragged away. After that, both table controls can be edited separately. The table control for the media return can be left practically the same. Only the write access for the *Media* and *Loan date* columns need to be changed.

While for the Loan date it is only necessary to choose *Read only*, this is not sufficient for list boxes. This setting does not prevent the list box from being used to make changes. However if *Enabled* is set to *No*, a choice cannot be made there. A list box contained within the table control is then displayed as a read-only text field.

In the above table control, all fields that have nothing to do with the loan are removed. Only the medium as a selection field and the loan date *Loan_Date* remain.

If finally the query for the list box in the upper table control is selected, only those media are displayed which can actually be loaned out. More about this is in Chapter 5, Queries.

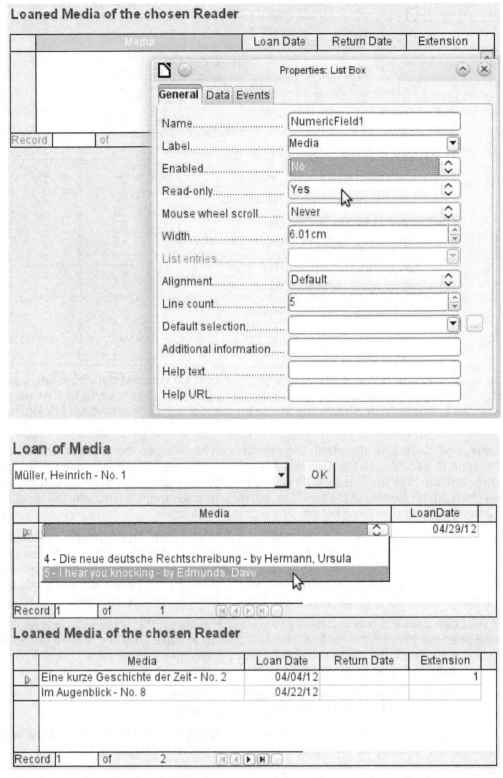

Figure 40: The selection field in the upper subform shows only media that are not on loan.

The media loan form is already significantly more useful. When a reader arrives at the loan counter, his or her name is searched. The media to be loaned can be selected using the list box and the loan date entered. The *Tab* key then takes you to the next record.

A final improvement is also desirable: at present the loan date must be selected each time. Imagine a day in the library with perhaps 200 loan transactions, perhaps just one person, who has to loan out about 10 media each time. That would require the same entry for the date field over and over again. There must be a way to simplify this.

Our main form is linked to the Filter table. The main form works only with the record that has as its primary key the "ID" 0. But additional fields can be built into the Filter table. At present there is no field that can store a date, but we can easily create a new field with the field name Date and the field type *Date*. In the Filter table we now have stored not only the *Reader_ID* ("Filter"."Integer") but also the *Loan_Date* ("Filter"."Date").

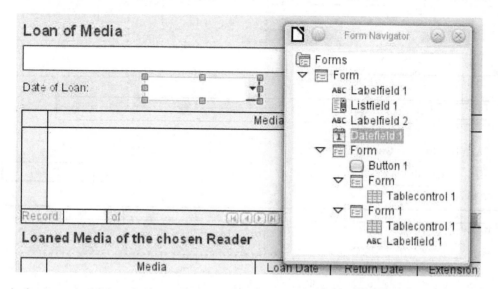

In the main form, an additional date field appears, along with a label referring to its content. The value from the date field is stored in the Filter table and transferred by the linkages from subform to sub-subform.

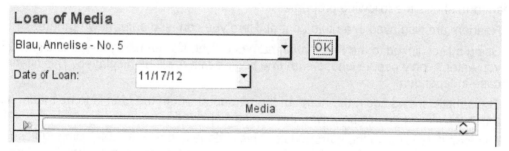

The linkage between the two forms now refers to two fields. The *Integer* field is bound to the *Reader_ID* field of the sub-subform. The *Date* field is bound to the *Loan_Date* field. This ensures that the *Loan_Date* is automatically transferred from the Filter table to the Loans table when the loan is made.

Loan of Media

Blau, Annelise - No. 5   OK

Date of Loan: 11/17/12

Media

Figure 41: The date of the loan is entered only once. When the Reader changes, it must be reentered.

The date field is now removed from the table control, so that the latter contains only one search field. This would be the ideal requirement for speeding up even more the work of the library. For in fact each medium will have a printed accession number, so why does that have to be searched?

You can just enter the number directly. Or, better still, it could be scanned in with a barcode reader. Then media can be loaned as rapidly as the borrower can stow them in his bag.

This is illustrated in the example database. The above example should suffice for understanding the initial form design but, as the example database, Media_without_Macros.odb, develops the form further, the extra refinements are briefly presented below.

Loan

	First Name	Last Name	ID		Filter (Last Name)	
	Annelise	Blau	5			OK
	Greta	Garbo	6			
	Lisa	Gerd	2			
	Hein	Keindurchblick	4			
	Bert	Lederstrumpf	0			
	Monika	Miranda	3			

Record 3 of 10 (1)

Record 3 of 10

Loan for Reader Gerd, Lisa

Loan Date: 11/17/12 [ ] Refresh

current Loan

	Medium	Loan Date	
	1 - Das sogennante Böse - by Lorenz, Konrad	11/17/12	

Record 1 of 1

Return

	Medium	Loan Date	Return Date	Extension	Loan Days	Balance Time
	6 - Datenbanken mit OpenOffice.org 3 - by ?	11/07/12			10 Days	4 Days

Record 1 of 1

The Loan form shows the following properties:

- Readers are displayed in a table control. Here you can also enter new readers.
- Using a filter, linked to the Filter table, names can be filtered using their initial letter. So, if you enter A, only people whose surname begins with A will be displayed. This filtering is case-independent.
- The subtitle shows again the name of the person to whom the loan is to be made. If a lock has been placed on this borrower, this is also displayed.
- The loan date is set to the current date. This is done in the filter table using SQL such that, when no date is entered, the default value to be stored is the current date.
- Loanable media are selected using a list box. When the Update button is pressed, the loan is transferred to the table control below.
- The table control in the middle serves only to display the actual date of loan for the media. Here it is also possible to correct an error retrospectively by deleting the line.

- In the lower table control, as in the above example, alteration of media and loan dates is not possible. Nor is it possible to delete records.

- Apart from the entry of the return date or, if appropriate, an extension of the loan, this table also displays the number of days for which the medium can be loaned and how many days remain of the current loan period.

- If this remaining time becomes negative, the medium must be returned immediately. The issue is then locked. It becomes possible again only when the medium is returned. After the return, the Update button need only be pressed once.

This form, made by using queries, is significantly more complex in its structure than the previously shown version. You can learn more about the essentials of this in Chapter 5, Queries.

One view – many forms

While the example for the Loans form only involves entries into one table (the Loans table) and additionally allows entry into the simpler form for new readers, the entry procedure for media is significantly more extensive. In its final form, the media table is surrounded by a total of eight additional tables (see Chapter 3, Tables).

The Subtitle and rel_Media_author tables are linked to subforms of the Media form through a n:1 relationship. By contrast, tables with a 1:n relationship to the Media table should be represented by forms that lie above the Media table. As there are several such tables, their values are entered into the main form using list boxes.

The table of a main form stands to the table of a subform in a 1:n relationship, or in some exceptional cases 1:1. Therefore, after long use of the database, the main form usually manages a table which has significantly fewer records in it than the table belonging to the subform.

Multiple main forms cannot include the same subform. Therefore it is not possible to create a form arrangement for many simultaneous 1:n relationships in which the subform has the same content. When there is a 1:n relationship for the table belonging to a form, you can use a list box. Here there are only a few terms available from another table, those whose foreign keys can be entered into the main form's table in this way.

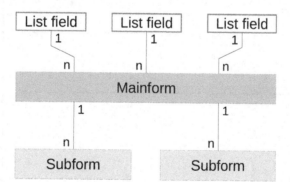

Using list boxes, the main form based on the Media table can be assigned values from the Category, Town or Publisher tables. Subforms are used to link the rel_Media_Author and Subtitle tables with the main form and through it with the Media table.

The subform for the rel_Media_Author table again consists of two list boxes so that the foreign keys from the Authors and Author_Add_ID (additions might be for example editor, photographer, and so on) do not have to be entered directly as numbers.

For the media entry form, the list boxes usually have to be filled up gradually during the entry process. For this purpose, further forms are built in alongside the main form. They exist independently of the main form.

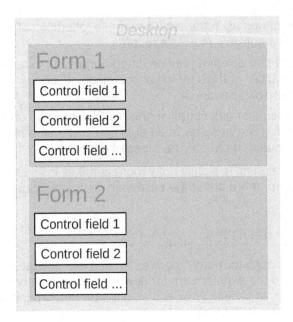

The overall form for entering media looks like this:

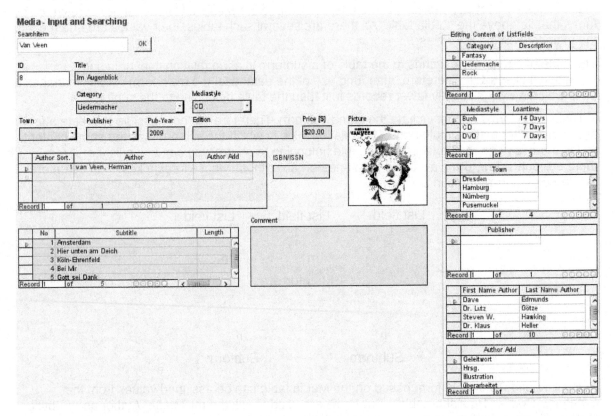

On the left side is the main form with a view to searching and entry of new media. On the right side of the form is a group box with the label *Edit list box contents*, providing a separate area intended for filling up the list boxes in the main form. If the database has not existed for long, it will often be necessary to make entries into these fields. However, the more entries that are available for the list boxes of the main form, the less often will access to the table controls in the group box be necessary.

The following table controls are all subordinated as individual side forms to the main form, the entry form.

Editing Content of Listfields

	Category	Description	
▷	Fantasy		
	Liedermache		
	Rock		
◌			

Record 1   of   3   ⏮ ◀ ▶ ⏭

	Mediastyle	Loantime	
▷	Buch	14 Days	
	CD	7 Days	
	DVD	7 Days	
◌			

Record 1   of   3   ⏮ ◀ ▶ ⏭

	Town	
▷	Dresden	
	Hamburg	
	Nürnberg	
	Pusemuckel	

Record 1   of   4   ⏮ ◀ ▶ ⏭

	Publisher	
▷		

Record 1   of   1   ⏮ ◀ ▶ ⏭

	First Name Author	Last Name Author	
▷	Dave	Edmunds	
	Dr. Lutz	Götze	
	Steven W.	Hawking	
	Dr. Klaus	Heller	

Record 1   of   10   ⏮ ◀ ▶ ⏭

	Author Add	
▷	Geleitwort	
	Hrsg.	
	Illustration	
	überarbeitet	

Record 1   of   4   ⏮ ◀ ▶ ⏭

Here in each case the complete data for a table are entered. In the early stages, it is often necessary to have recourse to these side forms, since not many authors are yet stored in the corresponding table.

When a new record is stored in one of the table controls, it is necessary to find the corresponding list box in the main form and use the Update control (see Navigation bar) to read in the new values.

The Form Navigator shows a correspondingly large list of forms.

The forms have been individually named to aid recognition. Only the main form still has the name of *MainForm* given to it by the Wizard. Altogether there are eight parallel forms. The *Filter* form hosts a search function while the *MainForm* form is the main input interface. All the other forms relate to one or other of the table controls shown above.

Without the table controls, the main form looks somewhat simpler.

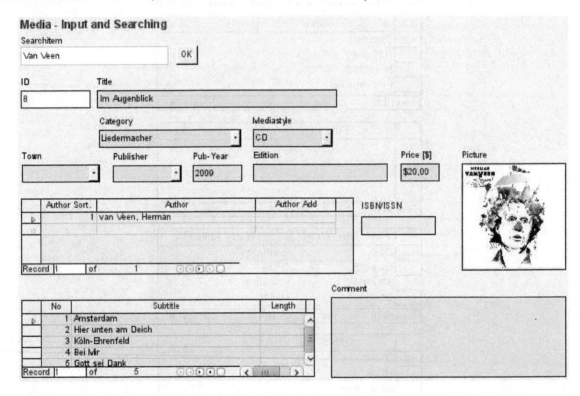

The field for the search term lies in the *Filter* form, the two *table controls* (for the author and the subtitle) lie in the *subform* of the Media Entry main form.

In the Form Navigator, this form looks much more complex, as all the controls and labels appear there. In the previous form, most of the fields were actually columns within the table controls and were thus invisible to the Form Navigator.

Unfortunately the sequence within the Form Navigator cannot easily be changed. So, for example, it would seem more sensible to place the subforms *Subtitle* and *Author* as branches of *MainForm* right at the beginning. But within the Form Navigator, individual controls and subforms are simply shown in the order in which they were created.

Chapter 5
Queries

General information on queries

Queries to a database are the most powerful tool that we have to use databases in a practical way. They can bring together data from different tables, calculate results where necessary, and quickly filter a specific record from a mass of data. The large Internet databases that people use every day exist mainly to deliver a quick and practical result for the user from a huge amount of information by thoughtful selection of keywords – including the search-related advertisements that encourage people to make purchases.

Entering queries

Queries can be entered both in the GUI and directly as SQL code. In both cases a window opens, where you can create a query and also correct it if necessary.

Creating queries using the Query Design dialog

The creation of queries using the Wizard is briefly described in Chapter 8 of the *Getting Started* guide, Getting Started with Base. Here we shall explain the direct creation of queries in Design View.

In the main database window, click the Queries icon in the Databases section, then in the Tasks section, click *Create Query in Design View*. Two dialogs appear. One provides the basis for a design-view creation of the query; the other serves to add tables, views, or queries to the current query.

As our simple form refers to the Loan table, we will first explain the creation of a query using this table.

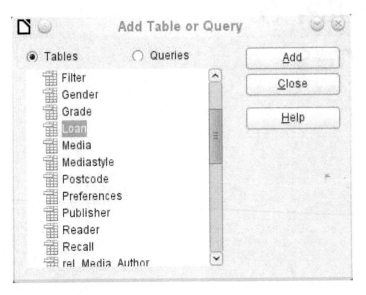

From the tables available, select the Loan table. This window allows multiple tables (and also views and queries) to be combined. To select a table, click its name and then click the **Add** button. Or, double-click the table's name. Either method adds the table to the graphical area of the Query Design dialog.

When all necessary tables have been selected, click the **Close** button. Additional tables and queries can be added later if required. However no query can be created without at least one table, so a selection must be made at the beginning.

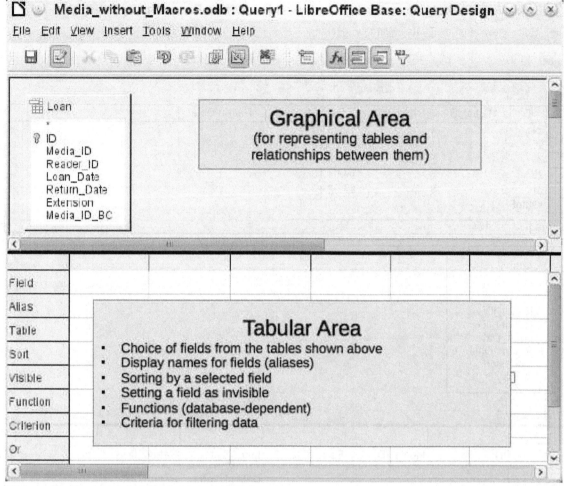

Figure 42: Areas of the Query Design dialog

Figure 42 shows the basic divisions of the Query Design dialog: the graphical area displays the tables that are to be linked to the query. Their relationships to each other in relation to the query may also be shown. The table area is for the selection of fields for display, or for setting conditions related to these fields.

Click on the field in the first column in the table area to reveal a down arrow. Click this arrow to open the drop-down list of available fields. The format is **Table_name.Field_name** – which is why all field names here begin with the word *Loan*.

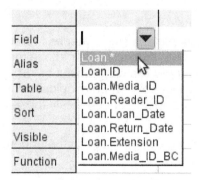

The selected field designation **Loan.*** has a special meaning. Here one click allows you to add all fields from the underlying table to the query. When you use this field designation with the *wildcard* * for all fields, the query becomes indistinguishable from the table.

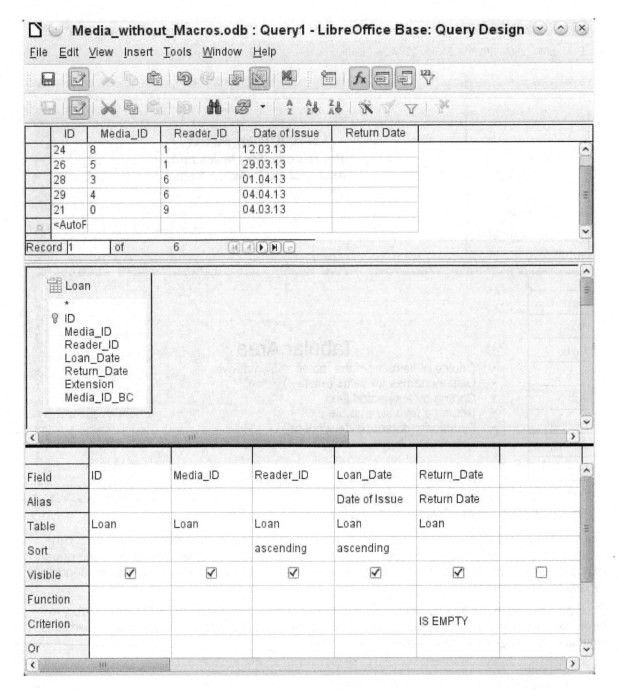

The first five fields of the Loan table are selected. Queries in Design Mode can always be run as tests. This causes a tabular view of the data to appear above the graphical view of the Loan table with its list of fields. A test run of a query is always useful before saving it, to clarify for the user whether the query actually achieves its goal. Often a logical error prevents a query from retrieving any data at all. In other cases it can happen that precisely those records are displayed that you wished to exclude.

In principle a query that produces an error message in the underlying database cannot be saved until the error is corrected.

	ID	Media_ID
▷	22	2
	24	8
	26	5
	28	3
	29	4
	21	0
○	<AutoF	

	Media_ID	Rea
▷	2	1
	8	1
	5	1
	3	6
	4	6
	0	9

Figure 43: An editable query   *Figure 44: A non-editable query*

In the above test, special attention should be paid to the first column of the query result. The active record marker (green arrow) always appears on the left side of the table, here pointing to the first record as the active record. While the first field of the first record in Figure 43 is highlighted, the corresponding field in Figure 44 shows only a dashed border. The highlight indicates that this field can be modified. The records, in other words, are editable. The dashed border indicates that this field cannot be modified. Figure 43 also contains an extra line for the entry of a new record, with the ID field already marked as *<AutoField>*. This also shows that new entries are possible.

Tip	A basic rule is that no new entries are possible if the primary key in the queried table is not included in the query.

Field	ID	Media_ID	Reader_ID	Loan_Date	Return_Date
Alias				Date of Issue	Return Date

The Loan_Date and Return_Date fields are given aliases. This does not cause them to be renamed but only to appear under these names for the user of the query.

	ID	Media_ID	Reader_ID	Date of Issue	Return Date
▷	22	2	1	04.03.13	

The table view above shows how the aliases replace the actual field names.

Return_Date
Return Date
Loan
✓
IS EMPTY

The Return_Date field is given not just an alias but also a search criterion, which will cause only those records to be displayed for which the Return_Date field is empty. (Enter *IS EMPTY* in the Criterion row of the Return_Date field.) This exclusion criterion will cause only those records to be displayed that relate to media that have not yet been returned from loan.

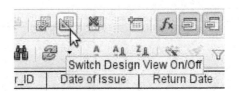

To learn the SQL language better, it is worth switching from time to time between Design Mode and SQL Mode.

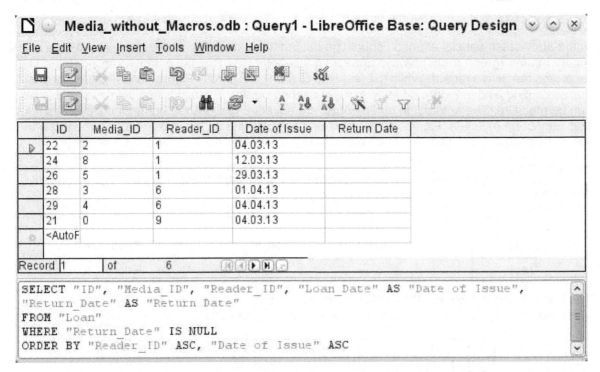

```
SELECT "ID", "Media_ID", "Reader_ID", "Loan_Date" AS "Date of Issue",
"Return_Date" AS "Return Date"
FROM "Loan"
WHERE "Return_Date" IS NULL
ORDER BY "Reader_ID" ASC, "Date of Issue" ASC
```

Here the SQL formula created by our previous choices is revealed. To make it easier to read, some line breaks have been included. Unfortunately the editor does not store these line breaks, so when the query is called up again, it will appear as a single continuous line breaking at the window edge.

SELECT begins the selection criteria. *AS* specifies the field aliases to be used. *FROM* shows the table which is to be used as the source of the query. *WHERE* gives the conditions for the query, namely that the Return_date field is to be empty (*IS NULL*). *ORDER BY* defines the sort criteria, namely ascending order (ASC – ascending) for the two fields Reader_ID and Loan date. This sort specification illustrates how the alias for the Loan_Date field can be used within the query itself.

Tip	When working in Design View Mode, use *IS EMPTY* to require a field be empty. When working in SQL Mode, use *IS NULL* which is what SQL (Structured Query Language) requires.
	When you want to sort by descending order using SQL, use *DESC* instead of *ASC*.

So far the Media_ID and Reader_ID fields are only visible as numeric fields. The readers' names are unclear. To show these in a query, the Reader table must be included. For this purpose we return to Design Mode. Then a new table can be added to the Design view.

Here further tables or queries can subsequently be added and made visible in the graphical user interface. If links between the tables were declared at the time of their creation (see Chapter 3, Tables), then these tables are shown with the corresponding direct links.

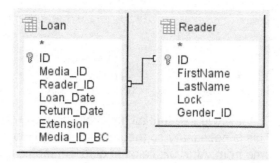

If a link is absent, it can be created at this point by dragging the mouse from "Loan"."Reader_ID" to "Reader"."ID".

Now fields from the Reader table can be entered into the tabular area. The fields are initially added to the end of the query.

Reader_ID	Loan_Date	Return_Date	FirstName	LastName
	Date of Issue	Return Date		
Loan	Loan	Loan	Reader	Reader

The position of the fields can be corrected in the tabular area of the editor using the mouse. So for example, the First_name field has been dragged into position directly before the Loan_date field.

ID	Media_ID	Reader_ID	FirstName	LastName	Date of Issue	Return Date
22	2	1	Heinrich	Müller	04.03.13	
24	8	1	Heinrich	Müller	12.03.13	
26	5	1	Heinrich	Müller	29.03.13	
28	3	6	Greta	Garbo	01.04.13	
29	4	6	Greta	Garbo	04.04.13	
21	0	9	Terence	Nobody	04.03.13	

Record 1 of 6

Now the names are visible. The Reader_ID has become superfluous. Also sorting by Surname and First_name makes more sense than sorting by Reader_ID.

This query is no longer suitable for use as a query that allows new entries into the resulting table, since it lacks the primary key for the added Reader table. Only if this primary key is built in, does the query become editable again. In fact it then becomes completely editable so that the readers' names can also be altered. For this reason, making query results editable is a facility that should be used with extreme caution, if necessary under the control of a form.

| Caution | Having a query that you can edit can create problems. Editing data in the query also edits data in the underlying table and the records contained in the table. The data may not have the same meaning. For example, change the name of the reader, and you have also changed what books the reader has borrowed and returned.

If you have to edit data, do so in a form so you can see the effects of editing data. |

Even when a query can be further edited, it is not so easy to use as a form with list boxes, which show the readers' names but contain the Reader_ID from the table. List boxes cannot be added to a query; they are only usable in forms.

```
SELECT "Loan"."ID", "Loan"."Media_ID", "Loan"."Reader_ID",
"Reader"."FirstName", "Reader"."LastName", "Loan"."Loan_Date" AS "Date of
Issue", "Loan"."Return_Date" AS "Return Date"
FROM "Loan", "Reader"
WHERE "Loan"."Reader_ID" = "Reader"."ID" AND "Loan"."Return_Date" IS NULL
ORDER BY "Loan"."Reader_ID" ASC, "Date of Issue" ASC
```

If we now switch back to SQL View, we see that all fields are now shown in double quotes: **"Table _name"."Field_name"**. This is necessary so that the database knows from which table the previously selected fields come from. After all, fields in different tables can easily have the same field names. In the above table structure this is particularly true of the ID field.

Note	The following query works without putting table names in front of the field names:
	
	`    SELECT "ID", "Number", "Price" FROM "Stock", "Dispatch"`
	`    WHERE "Dispatch"."stockID" = "Stock"."ID"`
	
	Here the ID is taken from the table which comes first in the FROM definition. The table definition in the WHERE Formula is also superfluous, because stockID only occurs once (in the Dispatch table) and ID was clearly taken from the Stock table (from the position of the table in the query).

If a field in the query has an alias, it can be referred to – for example in sorting – by this alias without a table name being given. Sorting is carried out in the graphical user interface according to the sequence of fields in the tabular view. If instead you want to sort first by "Loan date" and then by "Loan"."Reader_ID", that can be done if:

- The sequence of fields in the table area of the graphical user interface is changed (drag and drop "Loan date" to the left of "Loan"."Reader_ID", or
- An additional field is added, set to be invisible, just for sorting (however, the editor will register this only temporarily if no alias was defined for it) [add another "Loan date" field just before "Loan"."Reader_ID" or add another "Loan"."Reader_ID" field just after "Loan date"], or
- The text for the ORDER BY command in the SQL editor is altered correspondingly (ORDER BY "Loan date", "Loan"."Reader_ID").

Specifying the sort order *may not be completely error-free*, depending on the LibreOffice version. From version 3.5.3, sorting from the SQL view is correctly registered and displayed in the graphical user interface, including the fields that are used in the query but are not visible in the query output. (These fields do not have a check in the Visible row.)

Tip	A query may require a field that is not part of the query output. In the graphic in the next section, Return_Date is an example. This query is searching for records that do **not** contain a return date. This field provides a criterion for the query but no useful visible data.

Using functions in a query

The use of functions allows a query to provide more than just a filtered view of the data in one or more tables. The following query calculates how many media have been loaned out, depending on the Reader_ID.

Field	ID	Reader_ID	Return_Date
Alias	Count		
Table	Loan	Loan	Loan
Sort			
Visible	☑	☑	☐
Function	Count	Group	
Criterion			IS EMPTY

For the ID of the Loan table, the *Count* function is selected. In principle it makes no difference which field of a table is chosen for this. The only condition is: *The field must not be empty in any of the records*. For this reason, the primary key field, which is never empty, is the most suitable choice. All fields with a content other than NULL are counted.

For the Reader_ID, which gives access to reader information, the *Grouping* function is chosen. In this way, the records with the same Reader_ID are grouped together. The result shows the number of records for each Reader_ID.

As a search criterion, the Return_Date is set to "IS EMPTY", as in the previous example. (Below, the SQL for this is *WHERE "Return_Date" IS NULL*.)

	Count	Reader_ID
▷	1	9
	3	1
	2	6

Record 1   of   3 |◄| ◄ | ► | ►|

```
SELECT COUNT( "ID" ) AS "Count", "Reader_ID"
FROM "Loan"
WHERE "Return_Date" IS NULL
GROUP BY "Reader_ID"
```

The result of the query shows that Reader_ID '0' has a total of 3 media on loan. If the *Count* function had been assigned to the Return_Date instead of the ID, every Reader_ID would have '0' media on loan, since Return_date is predefined as NULL.

The corresponding Formula in SQL code is shown above.

Altogether the graphical user interface provides the following functions, which correspond to functions in the underlying HSQLDB.

For an explanation of the functions, see "Query enhancement using SQL Mode" on page 134.

Group
(no function)
Average
Count
Maximum
Minimum
Sum
Every
Any
Some
STDDEV_POP
STDDEV_SAMP
VAR_SAMP
VAR_POP
Collect
Fusion
Intersection
Group

If one field in a query is associated with a function, all the remaining fields mentioned in the query must also be associated with functions if they are to be displayed. If this is not ensured, you get the following error message:

A somewhat free translation would be: The following expression contains no aggregate function or grouping.

Tip	When using Design View Mode, a field is only visible if the *Visible* row contains a check mark for the field. When using SQL Mode, a field is only visible when it follows the keyword, SELECT.

Note	When a field is **not** associated with a function, the number of rows in the query output is determined by the search conditions. When a field is associated with a function, the number of rows in the query output is determined by whether there is any grouping or not. If there is no grouping, there is only one row in the query output. If there is grouping, the number of rows matches the number of distinct values that the grouping field has. So, all of the visible fields must either be associated with a function or **not be associated with a function** to prevent this conflict in the query output.
	After this, the complete query is listed in the error message, but unfortunately without the offending field being named specifically. In this case the field Return_Date has been added as a displayed field. This field has no function associated with it and is not included in the grouping statement either.
	The information provided by using the More button is not very illuminating for the normal database user. It just displays the SQL error code.

To correct the error, remove the check mark in the Visible row for the Return_Date field. Its search condition (Criterion) is applied when the query is run, but it is not visible in the query output.

Using the GUI, basic calculations and additional functions can be used.

Field	ID	Media_ID	Reader_ID	Date	Count("Recall"."Date") * 2	Return_Date
Alias				RecallCount	RecallAmount	
Table	Loan	Loan	Loan	Recall		Loan
Sort						
Visible	☑	☑	☑	☑	☑	☐
Function	Group	Group	Group	Count		
Criterion						IS EMPTY

Suppose that a library does not issue recall notices when an item is due for return, but issues overdue notices in cases where the loan period has expired and the item has not been returned. This is common practice in school and public libraries that issue loans only for short, fixed periods. In this case the issue of an overdue notice automatically means that a fine must be paid. How do we calculate these fines?

In the query shown above, the Loan and Recalls tables are queried jointly. From the count of the data entries in the table Recalls, the total number of recall notices is determined. The fine for overdue media is set in the query to 2.00 €. Instead of a field name, the field designation is given as **Count(Recalls.Date)*2**. The graphical user interface adds the quotation marks and converts the term "count" into the appropriate SQL command.

Caution ⚠	**Only for people who use a comma for their decimal separator:**
	If you wish to enter numbers with decimal places using the graphical user interface, you must ensure that a decimal point rather than a comma is used to separate the decimal places within the final SQL statement. Commas are used as field separators, so new query fields are created for the decimal part.
	An entry with a comma in the SQL view always leads to a further field containing the numerical value of the decimal part.

	ID	Media_ID	Reader_ID	RecallCount	RecallAmount	
▷	24	8	1	1	2	
	22	2	1	1	2	

Record 1   of   2   ⊮ ◂ ▸ ⊯

```
SELECT "Loan"."ID", "Loan"."Media_ID", "Loan"."Reader_ID",
COUNT( "Recall"."Date" ) AS "RecallCount",
COUNT( "Recall"."Date" ) * 2 AS "RecallAmount"
FROM "Recall", "Loan"
WHERE "Recall"."Loan_ID" = "Loan"."ID"
AND "Loan"."Return_Date" IS NULL
GROUP BY "Loan"."ID", "Loan"."Media_ID", "Loan"."Reader_ID"
```

The query now yields for each medium still on loan the fines that have accrued, based on the recall notices issued and the additional multiplication field. The following query structure will also be useful for calculating the fines due from individual users.

Field	Reader_ID	Date	Count("Recall"."Date") * 2	Return_Date
Alias		RecallCount	RecallAmount	
Table	Loan	Recall		Loan
Sort				
Visible	☑	☑	☑	☐
Function	Group	Count		
Criterion				IS EMPTY

The "Loan"."ID" and "Loan"."Media_ID" fields have been removed. They were used in the previous query to create by grouping a separate record for each medium. Now we will be grouping only by the reader. The result of the query looks like this:

	Reader_ID	RecallCount	RecallAmount
▷	1	2	4

Record 1 of 1

Instead of listing the media for Reader_ID = 0 separately, all the "Recalls"."Date" fields have been counted and the total of 8.00€ entered as the fine due.

Relationship definition in the query

When data is searched for in tables or forms, the search is usually limited to one table or one form. Even the path from a main form to a subform is not navigable by the built-in search function. For such purposes, the data to be searched for are better collected by using a query.

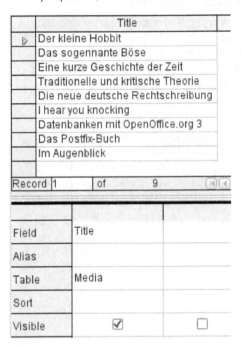

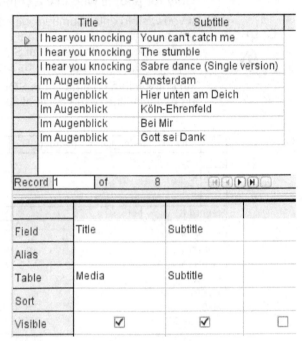

The simple query for the Title field from the Media table shows the test entries for this table, 9 records in all. But if you enter Subtitle into the query table, the record content of the Media table is reduced to only 2 Titles. Only for these two Titles are there also Subtitles in the table. For all the other Titles, no subtitles exist. This corresponds to the join condition that only those records for which the Media_ID field in the Subtitle table is equal to the ID field in the Media table should be shown. All other records are excluded.

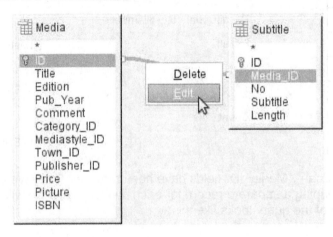

The join conditions must be opened for editing to display all the desired records. We refer here **not** to joins between tables in *Relationship design* **but** to joins within *queries*.

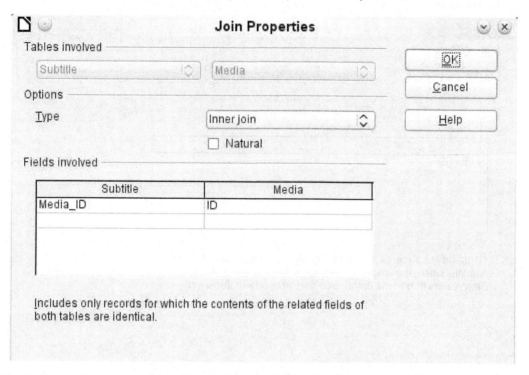

By default, relationships are set as *Inner Joins*. The window provides information on the way this type of join works in practice.

The two previously selected tables are listed as Tables Involved. They are not selectable here. The relevant fields from the two tables are read from the table definitions. If there is no relationship specified in the table definition, one can be created at this point for the query. However, if you have planned your database in an orderly manner using HSQLDB, there should be no need to alter these fields.

The most important setting is the *Join* option. Here relationships can be so chosen that all records from the Subtitle table are selected, but only those records from Media which have a subtitle entered in the Subtitle table.

Or you can choose the opposite: that in any case all records from the table Media are displayed, regardless of whether they have a subtitle.

The *Natural* option specifies that the linked fields in the tables are treated as equal. You can also avoid having to use this setting by defining your relationships properly at the very start of planning your database.

For the type *Right join*, the description shows that all records from the Media table will be displayed (Subtitle RIGHT JOIN Media). As there is no Subtitle that lacks a title in Media but there are certainly Titles in Media that lack a Subtitle, this is the right choice.

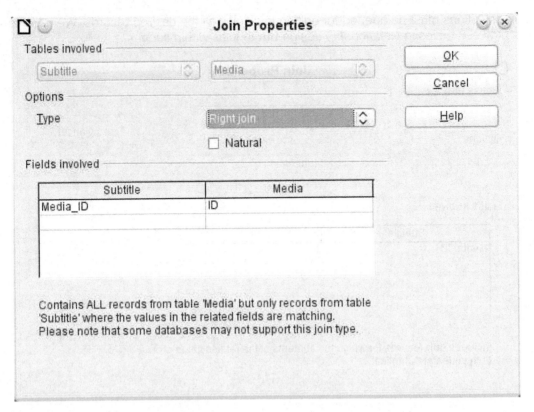

After confirming the *right join* the query results look as we wanted them. Title and Subtitle are displayed together in one query. Naturally Titles appear more than once as with the previous relationship. However as long as hits are not being counted, this query can be used further as a basis for a search function. See the code fragments in this chapter, in Chapter 9 (Macros), and in Chapter 8 (Database Tasks).

	Title	Subtitle	
▷	Der kleine Hobbit		
	Das sogennante Böse		
	Eine kurze Geschichte der Zeit		
	Traditionelle und kritische Theorie		
	Die neue deutsche Rechtschreibung		
	I hear you knocking	Youn can't catch me	
	I hear you knocking	The stumble	
	I hear you knocking	Sabre dance (Single version)	
	Datenbanken mit OpenOffice.org 3		
	Das Postfix-Buch		
	Im Augenblick	Amsterdam	
	Im Augenblick	Hier unten am Deich	
	Im Augenblick	Köln-Ehrenfeld	
	Im Augenblick	Bei Mir	
	Im Augenblick	Gott sei Dank	

Record 1 of 15

Query enhancement using SQL Mode

If during graphical entry you use **View > Switch Design View On/Off** to switch design view off, you see the SQL command for what previously appeared in Design View. This is the best way for beginners to learn the Standard Query Language for Databases. Sometimes it is also the only way to enter a query into the database when the GUI cannot translate your requirements into the necessary SQL commands.

```
SELECT * FROM "Table_name"
```

This will show everything that is in the Table_name table. The "*" represents all the fields of the table.

```
SELECT * FROM "Table_name" WHERE "Field_name" = 'Karl'
```

Here there is a significant restriction. Only those records are displayed for which the field Field_name contains the term 'Karl' – the exact term, not for example 'Karl Egon'.

Sometimes queries in Base cannot be carried out using the GUI, as particular commands may not be recognized. In such cases it is necessary to switch Design View off and use **Edit > Run SQL command directly** for direct access to the database. This method has the disadvantage that you can only work with the query in SQL Mode.

Direct use of SQL commands is also accessible using the graphical user interface, as the above figure shows. Click the icon highlighted (*Run SQL command directly*) to turn the Design View Off/On icon off. Now when you click the *Run* icon, the query runs the SQL commands directly.

Here is an example of the extensive possibilities available for posing questions to the database and specifying the type of result required:

```
SELECT [{LIMIT <offset> <limit> | TOP <limit>}][ALL | DISTINCT]
{ <Select-Formulation> | "Table_name".* | * } [, ...]
[INTO [CACHED | TEMP  | TEXT] "new_Table"]
FROM "Table_list"
[WHERE SQL-Expression]
[GROUP BY SQL-Expression [, ...]]
[HAVING SQL-Expression]
[{ UNION [ALL | DISTINCT] | {MINUS [DISTINCT] | EXCEPT [DISTINCT] } |
INTERSECT [DISTINCT] } Query statement]
[ORDER BY Order-Expression [, ...]]
[LIMIT <limit> [OFFSET <offset>]];
```

[{LIMIT <offset> <limit> | TOP <limit>}]:

This limits the number of records to be displayed. **LIMIT 10 20** starts at the 11th record and shows the following 20 records. **TOP 10** always shows the first 10 records. This is the same as **LIMIT 0 10**. **LIMIT 10 0** omits the first 10 records and displays all records starting from the 11th.

You can do the same thing by using the last SELECT condition in the formula **[LIMIT <limit> [OFFSET <offset>]]**. **LIMIT 10** shows only 10 records. Adding **OFFSET 20** causes the display to begin at the 21st record. Before you use this final form of display limitation, you need to include a sorting condition (ORDER BY ...).

Limiting the display of query results is only possible using direct SQL commands. By doing this, you determine how the query data is sorted and hence what data will be shown.

[ALL | DISTINCT]

SELECT ALL is the default. All records are displayed that fulfill the search conditions. Example: **SELECT ALL "Name" FROM "Table_name"** yields all names; if "Peter" occurs three times and "Egon" four times in the table, these names are displayed three and four times respectively. **SELECT DISTINCT "Name" FROM "Table_name"** suppresses query results that have the same content. In this case, 'Peter' and 'Egon' occur only once. **DISTINCT** refers to the whole of the record that is accessed by the query. So if, for example, the surname is asked for as well, records for 'Peter Müller' and 'Peter Maier' will count as distinct. Even if you specify the **DISTINCT** condition, both will be displayed.

\<Select-Formulation>
```
{ Expression | COUNT(*) |
{ COUNT | MIN | MAX | SUM | AVG | SOME | EVERY | VAR_POP | VAR_SAMP |
STDDEV_POP | STDDEV_SAMP }
([ALL | DISTINCT]] Expression) } [[AS] "display_name"]
```
Field names, calculations, record totals are all possible entries. In addition different functions are available for the field shown. Except for **COUNT(*)** (which counts all the records) none of these functions access **NULL** fields.

```
COUNT | MIN | MAX | SUM | AVG | SOME | EVERY | VAR_POP | VAR_SAMP |
STDDEV_POP | STDDEV_SAMP
```

COUNT("Name") counts all entries for the field Name.
MIN("Name") shows the first name alphabetically. The result of this function is always formatted just as it occurs in the field. Text is shown as text, integers as integers, decimals as decimals and so on.
MAX("Name") shows the last name alphabetically.
SUM("Number") can add only the values in numerical fields. The function fails for date fields.
AVG("Number") shows the average of the contents of a column. This function too is limited to numerical fields.
SOME("Field_Name"), **EVERY("Field_Name")**: Fields used with these functions must have the Yes/No [BOOLEAN] field type (contains only 0 or 1). Furthermore, they produce a summary of the field content to which they are applied.

SOME returns *TRUE* (or *1*) if at least one entry for the field is *1*, and it returns *FALSE* (or *0*) only if all the entries are *0*. **EVERY** returns *1* only if every entry for the field is *1*, and returns *FALSE* if at least one entry is *0*.

Tip	The Boolean field type is Yes/No[BOOLEAN]. However, this field contains only 0 or 1. In query search conditions, use either *TRUE*, *1*, *FALSE* or *0*. For the *Yes* condition, you can use either *TRUE* or *1*. For the *No* condition, use either *FALSE* or *0*. If you try to use either "Yes" or "No" instead, you get an error message. Then you will have to correct your error.

Example:

```
SELECT "Class", EVERY("Swimmer") FROM "Table1" GROUP BY "Class";
```

Class contains the names of the swimming class. *Swimmer* is a Boolean field describing whether a student can swim or not (1 or 0). *Students* contains the names of the students. *Table1* contains these fields: its primary key, Class, Swimmer, and Students. Only Class and Swimmer are needed for this query.

Because the query is grouped by the entries of the field Class, EVERY will return a value for the field, Swimmer, for each class. When every person in a swimming class can swim, EVERY returns TRUE. Otherwise EVERY returns FALSE because at least one student of the class can not swim. Since the output for the Swimmer field is a checkbox, A check mark indicates TRUE, and no check mark indicates FALSE.

VAR_POP | VAR_SAMP | STDDEV_POP | STDDEV_SAMP are statistical functions and affect only integer and decimal fields.
All these functions return 0, if the values within the group are all equal.

The statistical functions do not allow the **DISTINCT** limitation to be used. Basically they calculate over all values covered by the query, whereas **DISTINCT** excludes records with the same values from the display.

[AS] "display_name": The fields can be given a different designation (alias) within the query.

"Table_name".* | * [, ...]

Each field to be displayed is given with its field names, separated by commas. If fields from several tables are entered into the query, a combination of the field name with the table name is necessary: **"Table_name"."Field_name"**.

Instead of a detailed list of all the fields of a table, its total content can be displayed. For this you use the symbol "*". It is then unnecessary to use the table name, if the results will only apply to the one table. However, if the query includes all of the fields of one table and at least one field from a second table, use:
"Table_name 1".*, "Table_name 2"."Field_name".

[INTO [CACHED | TEMP | TEXT] "new_table"]

The result of this query is to be written directly into a new table which is named here. The field properties for the new table are defined from the field definitions contained in the query. Writing into a new table does not work from SQL Mode as this handles only displayable results. Instead you must use **Tools > SQL**. The resultant table is initially not editable as it lacks a primary key.

FROM <Table_list>

```
"Table_name 1" [{CROSS | INNER | LEFT OUTER | RIGHT OUTER} JOIN
"Table_name 2" ON Expression] [, ...]
```

The tables which are to be jointly searched are usually in a list separated by commas. The relationship of the tables to one another is then additionally defined by the keyword **WHERE**.

If the tables are bound through a **JOIN** rather than a comma, their relationship is defined by the term beginning with **ON** which occurs directly after the second table.

A simple **JOIN** has the effect that only those records are displayed for which the conditions in both the tables apply.

Example:

SELECT "Table1"."Name", "Table2"."Class" FROM "Table1", "Table2" WHERE "Table1"."ClassID" = "Table2"."ID"

is equivalent to:

```
SELECT "Table1"."Name", "Table2"."Class" FROM "Table1" JOIN "Table2"
ON "Table1"."ClassID" = "Table2"."ID"
```

Here the names and the corresponding classes are displayed. If a name has no class listed for it, that name is not included in the display. If a class has no names, it is also not displayed. The addition of **INNER** does not alter this.

```
SELECT "Table1"."Name", "Table2"."Class" FROM "Table1" LEFT JOIN
"Table2" ON "Table1"."ClassID" = "Table2"."ID"
```

If **LEFT** is added, all "Names" from "Table1" are displayed even if they have no "Class". If, on the contrary, **RIGHT** is added, all Classes are displayed even if they have no names in them. Addition of **OUTER** need not be shown here. (Right Outer Join is the same thing as Right Join; Left Outer Join is the same thing as Left Join.)

```
SELECT "Table1"."Player1", "Table2"."Player2" FROM "Table1" AS
"Table1" CROSS JOIN "Table2" AS "Table1" WHERE "Table1"."Player1" <>
"Table2"."Player2"
```

A **CROSS JOIN** requires the table to be supplied with an alias, but the addition of the term **ON** is not always necessary. All records from the first table are paired with all records from the second table. Thus the above query yields all possible pairings of records from the first table with those of the second table except for pairings between records for the same player. In the case of a **CROSS JOIN**, the condition must not include a link between the tables specified in the **ON** term. Instead, **WHERE** conditions can be entered. If the conditions are formulated exactly as in the case of a simple JOIN, you get the same result:

```
SELECT "Table1"."Name", "Table2"."Class" FROM "Table1" JOIN "Table2"
ON "Table1"."ClassID" = "Table2"."ID"
```

gives the same result as

```
SELECT "Table1"."Name", "Table2"."Class" FROM "Table1" AS "Table1"
CROSS JOIN "Table2" AS "Table2" WHERE "Table1"."ClassID" =
"Table2"."ID"
```

[WHERE SQL-Expression]

The standard introduction for conditions to request a more accurate filtering of the data. Here too the relationships between tables are usually defined if they are not linked together with JOIN.

[GROUP BY SQL-Expression [, ...]]

Use this when you want to divide the query data into groups before applying the functions to each one of the groups separately. The division is based upon the values of the field or fields contained in the GROUP BY term.

Example:

```
SELECT "Name", SUM("Input"-"Output") AS "Balance" FROM "Table1" GROUP
BY "Name";
```

Records with the same name are summed. In the query result, the sum of **Input – Output** is given for each person. This field is to be called **Balance**. Each row of the query result contains a value from the "Name" table and the calculated balance for that specific value.

Tip	When fields are processed using a particular function (for example **COUNT, SUM** ...), all fields that are not processed with a function but should be displayed are grouped together using **GROUP BY**.

[HAVING SQL-Expression]

The **HAVING** formula closely resembles the **WHERE** formula. The difference is that the WHERE formula applies to the values of selected fields in the query. The HAVING formula applies to selected calculated values. Specifically, the WHERE formula can not use an aggregate function as part of a search condition; the HAVING formula does.

The HAVING formula serves two purposes as shown in the two examples below. In the first one, the search condition requires that the minimum run-time be less than 40 minutes. In the second example, the search condition requires that an individual's balance must be positive.

The query results for the first one lists the names of people whose run-time has been less than 40 minutes at least one time and the minimum run-time. People whose run-times have all be greater than 40 minutes are not listed.

The query results for the second one lists the names of people who have a total greater output than input and their balance. People whose balance is 0 or less are not listed.

Examples:

```
SELECT "Name", "Runtime" FROM "Table1" GROUP BY "Name", "Runtime"
HAVING MIN("Runtime") < '00:40:00';
SELECT "Name", SUM("Input"-"Output") AS "Balance" FROM "Table1" GROUP
BY "Name" HAVING SUM("Input"-"Output") > 0;
```

[SQL Expression]

SQL expressions are combined according to the following scheme:

```
[NOT] condition [{ OR | AND } condition]
```

Example:

```
SELECT * FROM "Table_name" WHERE NOT "Return_date" IS NULL AND
"ReaderID" = 2;
```

The records read from the table are those for which a "Return_date" has been entered and the "ReaderID" is 2. In practice this means that all media loaned to a specific person and returned can be retrieved. The conditions are only linked with **AND**. The **NOT** refers only to the first condition.

```
SELECT * FROM "Table_name" WHERE NOT ("Return_date" IS NULL AND
"ReaderID" = 2);
```

Parentheses around the condition, with **NOT** outside them shows only those records that do not fulfill the condition in parentheses completely. This would cover all records, except for those for "ReaderID" number 2, which have not yet been returned.

[SQL Expression]: conditions

```
{ value [|| value]
```

A value can be single or several values joined by two vertical lines **||**. Naturally this applies to field contents as well.

```
SELECT "Surname" || ', ' || "First_name" AS "Name" FROM "Table_name"
```

The content of the fields "Surname" and "First_name" are displayed together in a field called "Name". Note that a comma and a space are inserted between "Surname" and "First_name".

```
| value { = | < | <= | > | >= | <> | != } value
```

These signs correspond to the well-known mathematical operators:
{ Equal to | Less than | Less than or equal to | Greater than | Greater than or equal to | Not equal to | Not equal to }

```
| value IS [NOT] NULL
```

The corresponding field has no content, because nothing has been written to it. This cannot be determined unambiguously in the GUI, since a visually empty text field does not mean that the field is completely without content. However the default set-up in Base is that empty fields in the database are set to **NULL**.

```
| EXISTS(Query_result)
```

Example:

```
SELECT "Name" FROM "Table1" WHERE EXISTS (SELECT "First_name" FROM
"Table2" WHERE "Table2"."First_name" = "Table1"."Name")
```

The names from Table1 are displayed for which first names are given in Table2.

```
| Value BETWEEN Value AND Value
```

BETWEEN value1 AND value2 yields all values from value1 up to and including value2. If the values are letters, an alphabetic sort is used in which lower-case letters have the same value as the corresponding upper-case ones.

```
SELECT "Name" FROM "Table_name" WHERE "Name" BETWEEN 'A' AND 'E';
```

This query yields all names beginning with A, B, C or D (and also with the corresponding lower-case letters). As E is set as the upper limit, names beginning with E are not included. The letter E itself occurs just *before* the names that begin with E.

```
| value [NOT] IN ( {value [, ...] | Query result } )
```

This requires either a list of values or a query. The condition is fulfilled if the value is included in the value list or the query result.

```
| value [NOT] LIKE value [ESCAPE] value }
```

The **LIKE** operator is one that is needed in many simple search functions. The value is entered using the following pattern:

'%' stands for any number of characters (including 0),

'_' replaces exactly one character.

To search for '%' or '_' itself, the characters must immediately follow another character defined as **ESCAPE**.

```
SELECT "Name" FROM "Table_name" WHERE "Name" LIKE '\_%' ESCAPE '\'
```

This query displays all names that begin with an underscore. '\' is defined here as the **ESCAPE** character.

[SQL Expression]: values

```
[+ | -] { Expression [{ + | - | * | / | || } Expression]
```

The values may have a preceding sign. Addition, subtraction, multiplication, division and concatenation of expressions are allowed. An example of concatenation:

```
SELECT "Surname"||', '||"First_name" FROM "Table"
```

In this way records are displayed by the query with a field containing "Surname, First_name". The concatenation operator can be qualified by the following expressions.

```
| ( Condition )
```

See the previous section for this.

```
| Function ( [Parameter] [,...] )
```

See the section on Functions in the appendix.

The following queries are also referred to as sub-queries (subselects).

```
| Query result which yields exactly one answer
```

As a record can only have one value in each field, only a query which yields precisely one value can be displayed in full.

```
| {ANY|ALL} (Queryresult which yields exactly one answer from a whole column)
```

Often there is a condition that compares an expression with a whole group of values.

Combined with **ANY** this signifies that the expression must occur at least once in the group. This can also be specified using the **IN** condition. = **ANY** yields the same result as **IN**.

Combined with **ALL** it signifies that all values of the group must correspond to the one expression.

[SQL Expression]: Expression

```
{ 'Text' | Integer | Floating-point number
| ["Table".]"Field" | TRUE | FALSE | NULL }
```

Basically values serve as arguments for various expressions, dependent on the source format. To search for the content of text fields, place the content in quotes. Integers are written without quotes, as are floating-point numbers.

Fields stand for the values that occur in those fields in the table. Usually fields are compared either with each other or with specific values. In SQL, field names should be placed in double quotes, as they may not be correctly recognized otherwise. Usually SQL assumes that text without double quotes is without special characters, that is a single word without spaces and in upper case. If several tables are contained in the query, the table name must be given in addition to the field name, separated from the latter by a period.

TRUE and **FALSE** usually derive from Yes/No fields.

NULL means no content. It is not the same thing as 0 but rather corresponds to "empty".

UNION [ALL | DISTINCT] Query_result

This links queries so that the content of the second query is written under the first. For this to work, all fields in both queries must match in type. This linkage of several queries functions only in direct SQL command mode.

```
SELECT "First_name" FROM "Table1" UNION DISTINCT SELECT "First_name"
FROM "Table2";
```

This query yields all first names from table1 and Table2; the additional term **DISTINCT** means that no duplicate first names will be displayed. **DISTINCT** is the default in this context. By default the first names are sorted alphabetically in ascending order. **ALL** causes all first names in Table1 to be displayed, followed by the first name in Table2. In this case the default is to sort by primary key.

MINUS [DISTINCT] | EXCEPT [DISTINCT] Query_result

```
SELECT "First_name" FROM "Table1" EXCEPT SELECT "First_name" FROM
"Table2";
```

Shows all first names from table1 except for the first names contained in Table 2. **MINUS** and **EXCEPT** lead to the same result. Sorting is alphabetic.

INTERSECT [DISTINCT] Query_result

```
SELECT "First_name" FROM "Table1" INTERSECT SELECT "First_name" FROM
"Table2";
```

This displays the first names that occur in both tables. Sorting is again alphabetic. At present this only works in direct SQL command mode.

[ORDER BY Ordering-Expression [, ...]]

The expression can be a field name, a column number (beginning with 1 from the left), an alias (formulated with AS for example) or a composite value expression (see [SQL Expression]: values). The sort order is usually ascending (**ASC**). If you want a descending sort you must specify **DESC** explicitly.

```
SELECT "First_name", "Surname" AS "Name" FROM "Table1" ORDER BY "Surname";
```

is identical to

```
SELECT "First_name", "Surname" AS "Name" FROM "Table1" ORDER BY 2;
```

is identical to

```
SELECT "First_name", "Surname" AS "Name" FROM "Table1" ORDER BY "Name";
```

Using an alias in a query

Queries can reproduce fields with changed names.

```
SELECT "First_name", "Surname" AS "Name" FROM "Table1"
```

The field *Surname* is called *Name* in the display.

If a query involves two tables, each field name must be preceded by the name of the table:

```
SELECT "Table1"."First_name", "Table1"."Surname" AS "Name",
"Table2"."Class" FROM "Table1", "Table2" WHERE "Table1"."Class_ID" =
"Table2"."ID"
```

The table name can also be given an alias, but this will not be reproduced in table view. If such an alias is set, all the table names in the query must be altered accordingly:

```
SELECT "a"."First_name", "a"."Surname" AS "Name", "b"."Class" FROM
"Table1" AS "a", "Table2" AS "b" WHERE "a"."Class_ID" = "b"."ID"
```

The assignment of an alias for a table can be carried out more briefly without using the term AS:

```
SELECT "a"."First_name", "a"."Surname" AS "Name", "b"."Class" FROM
"Table1" "a", "Table2" "b" WHERE "a"."Class_ID" = "b"."ID"
```

This however makes the code less readable. Because of this, the abbreviated form should be used only in exceptional circumstances.

Queries for the creation of list box fields

List box fields show a value that does not correspond to the content of the underlying table. They are used to display the value assigned by a user to a foreign key rather than the key itself. The value that is finally saved in the form must not occur in the first position of the list box field.

```
SELECT "First_name", "ID" FROM "Table1";
```

This query would show all first names and the primary key "ID" values that the form's underlying table provides. Of course it is not yet optimal. The first names appear unsorted and, in the case of identical first names, it is impossible to determine which person is intended.

```
SELECT "First_name"||' '||"Surname", "ID" FROM "Table1" ORDER BY
"First_name"||' '||"Surname";
```

Now the first name and the surname both appear, separated by a space. The names become distinguishable and are also sorted. But the sort follows the usual logic of starting with the first letter of the string, so it sorts by first name and only then by surname. A different sort order to that in which the fields are displayed would only be confusing.

```
SELECT "Surname"||', '||"First_name", "ID" FROM "Table1" ORDER BY
"Surname"||', '||"First_name";
```

This now leads to a sorting that corresponds better to normal custom. Family members appear together, one under another; however different families with the same surname would be interleaved. To distinguish them, we would need to group them differently within the table.

There is one final problem: if two people have the same surname *and* first name, they will still not be distinguishable. One solution might be to use a name suffix. But imagine how it would look if a salutation read Mr "Müller II"!

```
SELECT "Surname"||', '||"First_name"||' - ID:'||"ID", "ID" FROM
"Table1" ORDER BY "Surname"||', '||"First_name"||"ID";
```

Here all records are distinguishable. What is actually displayed is "Surname, First name – ID:ID value".

In the loan form, there is a list box which only shows the media that have not yet been loaned out. It is created using the following SQL formula:

```
SELECT "Title" || ' - Nr. ' || "ID", "ID" FROM "Media" WHERE "ID" NOT
IN (SELECT "Media_ID" FROM "Loan" WHERE "Return_Date" IS NULL) ORDER
BY "Title" || ' - Nr. ' || "ID" ASC
```

Queries as a basis for additional information in forms

If you wish a form to display additional Information that would otherwise not be visible, there are various query possibilities. The simplest is to retrieve this information with independent queries and insert the results into the form. The disadvantage of this method is that changes in the records may affect the query result, but unfortunately these changes are not automatically displayed.

Here is an example from the sphere of stock control for a simple checkout.

The checkout table contains totals and foreign keys for stock items, and a receipt number. The shopper has very little information if there is no additional query result printed on the receipt. After all, the items are identified only by reading in a barcode. Without a query, the form shows only:

Total	Barcode
3	17
2	24

What is hidden behind the numbers cannot be made visible by using a list box, as the foreign key is input directly using the barcode. In the same way, it is impossible to use a list box next to the item to show at least the unit price.

Here a query can help.

```
SELECT "Checkout"."Receipt_ID", "Checkout"."Total", "Stock"."Item",
"Stock"."Unit_Price", "Checkout"."Total"*"Stock"."Unit_price" AS
"Total_Price" FROM "Checkout", "Item" WHERE "Stock"."ID" =
"Checkout"."Item_ID";
```

Now at least after the information has been entered, we know how much needs to be paid for 3 * Item'17'. In addition only the information relevant to the corresponding Receipt_ID needs to be filtered through the form. What is still lacking is what the customer needs to pay overall.

```
SELECT "Checkout"."Receipt_ID",
SUM("Checkout"."Total"*"Stock"."Unit_price") AS "Sum" FROM "Checkout",
"Stock" WHERE "Stock"."ID" = "Checkout"."Item_ID" GROUP BY
"Checkout"."Receipt_ID";
```

Design the form to show one record of the query at a time. Since the query is grouped by Receipt_ID, the form shows information about one customer at a time.

Data entry possibilities within queries

To make entries into a query, the primary key for the table underlying the query must be present. This also applies to a query that links several tables together.

In the loaning of media, it makes no sense to display for a reader items that have already been returned some time ago.

```
SELECT "ID", "Reader_ID", "Media_ID", "Loan_date" FROM "Loan" WHERE
"Return_Date" IS NULL;
```

In this way a form can show within a table control field everything that a particular reader has borrowed over time. Here too the query must filter using the appropriate form structure (reader in the main form, query in the sub-form), so that only media that are actually on loan are displayed. The query is suitable for data entry since the primary key is included in the query.

The query ceases to be editable, if it consists of more than one table and the tables are accessed via an alias. It makes no difference in that case whether or not the primary key is present in the query.

```
SELECT "Media"."ID", "Media"."Title", "Category"."Category",
"Category"."ID" AS "Kat_ID" FROM "Media", "Category" WHERE
"Media"."Category_ID" = "Category"."ID";
```

This query is editable as both primary keys are included and can be accessed in the tables without using an alias.

```
SELECT "m"."ID", "m"."Title", "Category"."Category", "Category"."ID"
AS "Kat_ID" FROM "Media" AS "m", "Category" WHERE "m"."Category_ID" =
"Category"."ID";
```

In this query the "Media" table is accessed using an alias. The query cannot be edited.

In the above example, this problem is easily avoided. If, however, a correlated subquery (see page 145) is used, you need to use a table alias. A query is only editable in that case if it contains only one table in the main query.

Use of parameters in queries

If you often use the same basic query but with different values each time, queries with parameters can be used. In principle queries with parameters function just like queries for a subform:

```
SELECT "ID", "ReaderID", "Media_ID", "Loan_date" FROM "Loans" WHERE
"Return_Date" IS NULL AND "Reader_ID"=2;
```

This query shows only the media on loan to the reader with the number 2.

```
SELECT "ID", "Reader_ID", "Media_ID", "Loan_date" FROM "Loans" WHERE
"Return_Date" IS NULL AND "Reader_ID" = :Readernumber;
```

Now when you run the query, an entry field appears. It prompts you to enter a reader number. Whatever value you enter here, the media currently on loan to that reader will be displayed.

When using forms, the parameter can be passed from the main form to a subform. However it sometimes happens that queries using parameters in subforms are not updated, if data is changed or newly entered.

Often it would be nice to alter the contents of list boxes using settings in the main form. So for example, we could prevent library media from being loaned to individuals who are currently banned from borrowing media. Unfortunately controlling list box settings in this personalized way by using parameters is not possible.

Subqueries

Subqueries built into fields can always only return one record. The field can also return only one value.

```
SELECT "ID", "Income", "Expenditure", ( SELECT SUM( "Income" ) -
SUM( "Expenditure" ) FROM "Checkout") AS "Balance" FROM "Checkout";
```

This query allows data entry (primary key included). The subquery yields precisely one value, namely the total balance. This allows the balance at the till to be read after each entry. This is still not comparable with the supermarket checkout form described in "Queries as a basis for additional information in forms". Naturally it lacks the individual calculations of Total * Unit_price, but also the presence of the receipt number. Only the total sum is given. At least the receipt number can be included by using a query parameter:

```
SELECT "ID", "Income", "Expenditure", ( SELECT SUM( "Income" ) -
SUM( "Expenditure" ) FROM "Checkout" WHERE "Receipt_ID" =
:Receipt_Number) AS "Balance" FROM "Checkout" WHERE "Receipt_ID" =
:Receipt_Number;
```

In a query with parameters, the parameter must be the same in both query statements if it is to be recognized as a parameter.

For subforms such parameters can be included. The subform then receives, instead of a field name, the corresponding parameter name. This link can only be entered in the properties of the subform, and not when using the Wizard.

Note	Subforms based on queries are not automatically updated on the basis of their parameters. It is more appropriate to pass on the parameter directly from the main form.

Correlated subqueries

Using a still more refined query, an editable query allows one to even carry the running balance for the till:

```
SELECT "ID", "Income", "Expenditure", ( SELECT SUM( "Income" ) -
SUM( "Expenditure" ) FROM "Checkout" WHERE "ID" <= "a"."ID" ) AS
"Balance" FROM "Checkout" AS "a" ORDER BY "ID" ASC
```

The Checkout table is the same as Table "a". "a" however yields only the relationship to the current values in this record. In this way the current value of ID from the outer query can be evaluated within the subquery. Thus, depending on the ID, the previous balance at the corresponding time is determined, if you start from the fact that the ID, which is an autovalue, increments by itself.

Queries as source tables for queries

A query is required to set a lock against all readers who have received a third overdue notice for a medium.

```
SELECT "Loan"."Reader_ID", '3rd Overdue - the reader is blacklisted'
AS "Lock"
FROM (SELECT COUNT( "Date" ) AS "Total_Count", "Loan_ID"  FROM
"Recalls" GROUP BY "Loan_ID") AS "a", "Loan"
WHERE "a"."Loan_ID" = "Loan"."ID" AND "a"."Total_Count" > 2
```

First let us examine the **inner query**, to which the outer query relates. In this query the number of date entries, grouped by the foreign key Loan_ID is determined. This must not be made dependent on the Reader_ID, as that would cause not only three overdue notices for a single medium but also three media with one overdue notice each to be counted. The inner query is given an alias so that it can be linked to the Reader_ID from the outer query.

The **outer query** relates in this case only to the conditional formula from the inner query. It shows only a Reader_ID and the text for the Lock field when the "Loan"."ID" *and* "a"."Loan_ID" are *equal* and "a"."Total_Count" > 2 .

In principle all fields in the inner query are available to the outer one. So for example the sum "a"."Total_Count" can be merged into the outer query to give the actual fines total.

However it can happen, in the Query Design dialog, that the Design View Mode no longer works after such a construction. If you try to open the query for editing again you get the following warning:

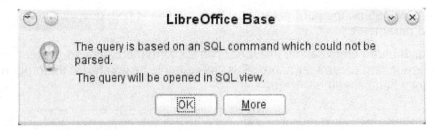

If you then open the query for editing in SQL view and try to switch from there into the Design View, you get the error message:

The Design View Mode cannot find the field contained in the inner query "Loan_ID", which governs the relationship between the inner and outer queries.

When the query is run in SQL Mode, the corresponding content from the subquery is reproduced without error. Therefore you do *not* have to use direct SQL mode in this case.

The **outer query** used the results of the **inner query** to produce the final results. These are a list of the "Loan_ID" values that should be locked and why. If you want to further limit the final results, use the sort and filter functions of the graphical user interface.

Summarizing data with queries

When data is searched for over a whole database, the use of simple form functions often leads to problems. A form refers after all to only one table, and the search function moves only through the underlying records for this form.

Getting at all the data is simpler when you use queries, which can provide a picture of all the records. The section on "Relationship definition in the query" suggests such a query construction. This is constructed for the example database as follows:

```
SELECT "Media"."Title", "Subtitle"."Subtitle", "Author"."Author"
FROM "Media"
LEFT JOIN "Subtitle" ON "Media"."ID" = "Subtitle"."Media_ID"
LEFT JOIN "rel_Media_Author" ON "Media"."ID" =
"rel_Media_Author"."Media_ID"
LEFT JOIN "Author" ON "rel_Media_Author"."Author_ID" = "Author"."ID"
```

Here all "Titles", "Subtitles" and "Authors" are shown together.

The Media table contains a total of 9 Titles. For two of these titles, there are a total of 8 Subtitles. Without a **LEFT JOIN**, both tables displayed together yield only 8 records. For each Subtitle, the corresponding Title is searched for, and that is the end of the query. Titles *without* Subtitle are not shown.

Now to show all Media including those *without* a Subtitle: Media is on the left side of the assignment, Subtitle on the right side. A **LEFT JOIN** will show every Title from Media, but only a Subtitle for those that have a Title. Media becomes the decisive table for determining which records are to be displayed. This was already planned when the table was constructed (see

Chapter 3, Tables). As Subtitles exist for two of the nine Titles, the query now displays $9 + 8 - 2 = 15$ records.

Note	The normal linking of tables, after all tables have been counted, follows the keyword WHERE.
	
	If there is a **LEFT JOIN** or a **RIGHT JOIN**, the assignment is defined directly after the two table names using **ON**. The sequence is therefore always
	`Table1 LEFT JOIN Table2 ON Table1.Field1 = Table2.Field1`
	`LEFT JOIN Table3 ON Table2.Field1 = Table3.Field1 ...`

Two titles of the Media table do not yet have an author entry or a Subtitle. At the same time one Title has a total of three Authors. If the Author Table is linked without a **LEFT JOIN,** the two Media *without* an Author will not be shown. But as one medium has three authors instead of one, the total number of records displayed will still be 15.

Only by using **LEFT JOIN** will the query be instructed to use the Media table to determine which records to show. Now the records without Subtitle or Author appear again, giving a total of 17 records.

Using appropriate Joins usually increases the amount of data displayed. But this enlarged data set can easily be scanned, since authors and subtitles are displayed in addition to the titles. In the example database, all of the media-dependent tables can be accessed.

More rapid access to queries using table views

Views in SQL are quicker than queries, especially for external databases, as they are anchored directly into the database and the server returns only the results. By contrast queries are first sent to the server and processed there.

If a new query relates to another query, the SQL view in Base makes the other query look like a table. If you create a View from it, you can see that you are actually working with a subquery (Select used within another Select). Because of this, a Query 2 that relates to another Query 1 cannot be run by using **Edit > Run SQL command directly**, since only the graphical user interface and not the database itself knows about Query 1.

The database gives you no direct access to queries. This also applies to access using macros. Views, on the other hand, can be accessed from both macros and tables. However, no records can be edited in a view. (They must be edited in a table or form.)

Tip	A query created using **Create Query in SQL View** has the disadvantage that it cannot be sorted or filtered using the GUI. There are therefore limits to its use. A *View* on the other hand can be managed in Base just like a normal table – with the exception that no change in the data is possible. Here therefore even in direct SQL-commands all possibilities for sorting and filtering are available.

Views are a solution for many queries, if you want to get any results at all. If for example a Subselect is to be used on the results of a query, create a **View** that gives you these results. Then use the subselect on the View. Corresponding examples are to be found in Chapter 8, Database Tasks.

Creating a View from a query is rather easy and straight forward.
1) Click the **Table** object in the Database section.
2) Click **Create View**.
3) Close the Add Table dialog.

4) Click the Design View On/OFF icon. (This is the SQL Mode for a View.)
5) Getting the SQL for the View:
   a) Edit the query in SQL View.
   b) Use *Control+A* to highlight the query's SQL.
   c) Use *Control+C* to copy the SQL.
6) In the SQL Mode of the View use *Control+V* to paste the SQL.
7) Close, Save, and Name the View.

The Document Foundation

Chapter 6
Reports

Creating reports using the Report Builder

Reports are used to present data in a way that makes it readily understood by people without knowledge of the database. Reports can:

- Present data in easy-to-read tables
- Create charts for displaying data
- Make it possible to use data for printing labels
- Produce form letters such as bills, recall notices, or notifications to people joining or leaving an association

To create a report requires careful preparatory work on the underlying database. Unlike a form, a report cannot include subreports and thus incorporate additional data sources. Neither can a report present different data elements than those that are available in the underlying data source, as a form can do using list boxes.

Reports are best prepared using queries. In this way all variables can be determined. In particular, if sorting within the report is required, always use a query that makes provision for sorting. This means that queries in direct SQL mode should be avoided under these conditions. If you must use a query of this type in your database, you can carry out the sort by first creating a view from the query. Such a view can always be sorted and filtered using the graphical user interface (GUI) of Base.

Caution	When using the Report Builder, you should frequently save your work during editing. In addition to saving within the Report Builder itself after each significant step, you should also save the whole database.
	Depending on the version of LibreOffice that you are using, the Report Builder can sometimes crash during editing.
	The functionality of completed reports is not affected even if they were created under another version, in which the problem does not occur.

The user interface of the Report Builder

To start the Report Builder from within Base, use **Reports > Create Report in Design View**.

The initial window of the Report Builder (Figure 45) shows three parts. On the left is the current division of the report into Page header, Detail, and Page footer; in the middle are the corresponding areas where the content will be entered; and, to the right, the properties of these regions are shown.

At the same time the Add fields dialog is displayed. This dialog corresponds to the one in form creation. It creates fields with their corresponding field labels.

Without content from the database, a report has no proper function. For this reason, the dialog opens at the Data tab. Here you can set the content of the report; in the example it is the *View_Report_Recall* table. As long as **Analyze SQL command** is set to *Yes*, the report can be subjected to sorting, grouping, and filtering. A view has been chosen for the basis of this report, so no filter will be applied; it has already been included in the query underlying the view.

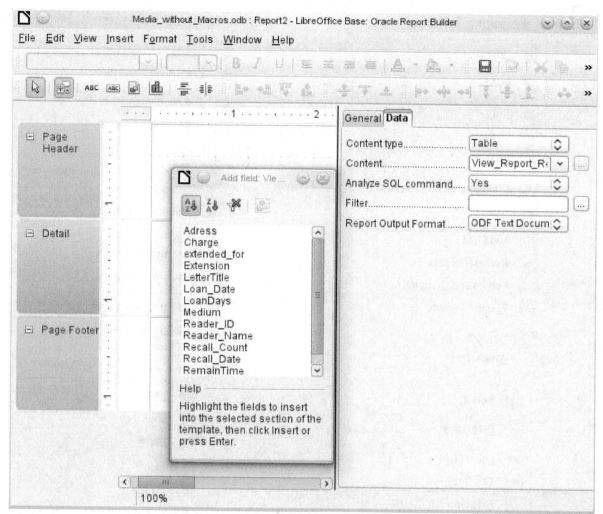

Figure 45: Initial window of Report Builder

Two output formats for reports are available for selection: *ODF Text document* (a Writer document) or *ODF Spreadsheet* (a Calc document). If you just want a tabular view of your data, the Calc document should definitely be chosen for your report. It is significantly faster to create and is also easier to format subsequently, as there are fewer options to consider and columns can easily be dragged to the required width afterward.

By default, the Report Builder looks for its data source in the first table in the database. This ensures that at least a test of the functions is possible. A data source has to be chosen before the report can be provided with fields.

The Report Builder provides a lot of additional buttons, so the table on the next page shows the buttons with their descriptions. The buttons for aligning elements are not further described in this chapter. They are useful for quick adjustment of fields in a single area of the Report Builder, but in principle everything can be done by direct editing of field properties.

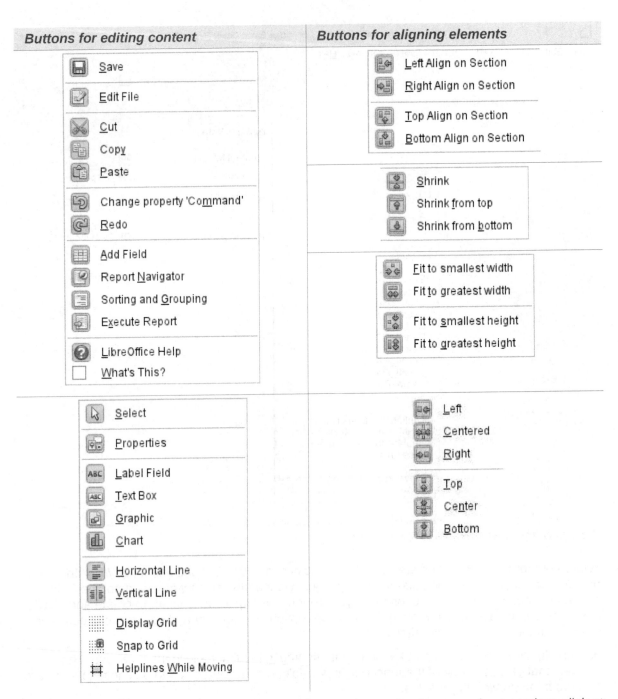

Buttons for editing content	Buttons for aligning elements
Save	Left Align on Section
Edit File	Right Align on Section
Cut	Top Align on Section
Copy	Bottom Align on Section
Paste	Shrink
Change property 'Command'	Shrink from top
Redo	Shrink from bottom
Add Field	Fit to smallest width
Report Navigator	Fit to greatest width
Sorting and Grouping	Fit to smallest height
Execute Report	Fit to greatest height
LibreOffice Help	
What's This?	
Select	Left
Properties	Centered
Label Field	Right
Text Box	Top
Graphic	Center
Chart	Bottom
Horizontal Line	
Vertical Line	
Display Grid	
Snap to Grid	
Helplines While Moving	

Just as with forms, it is helpful to use the appropriate navigator. So, for example, a careless click at the start of the Report Builder can make it difficult to find the properties of the data for the report. Such data may only be reachable through the report navigator. Left-click on *Report* and the properties of the report are once more accessible.

Initially the navigator shows, in addition to the visible sections of the document (Page header, Groups, Detail, and Page footer), the possibility of including functions. Groups can be used, for example, to assign all media being recalled to the person who has borrowed them, to avoid multiple recall notices. Detail areas show the records belonging to a group. Functions are used for calculations such as sums.

To obtain useful output in the above example, the content of the view must be reproduced with suitable grouping. Each reader should be linked to the recall notices for all of their loaned and overdue media.

View > Sorting and Grouping or the corresponding button starts the grouping function.

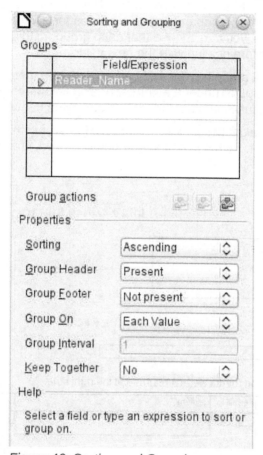

Figure 46: Sorting and Grouping

Here grouping and sorting are by the *Reader_Name* field. Additional fields could also be included in the table above. For example, if you also want to group and sort by the *Loan_Date* field, choose this as the second line.

Directly under the table, several grouping actions are available for selection. You can move a group up or down the list or completely remove it. As only one group is necessary for the planned report, Figure 46 shows only the *Delete* symbol at the extreme right of the group actions as available.

The *Sorting* property is self-explanatory.

When the entry was created, the left side of the Report Builder immediately showed a new division. Next to the field description *Reader_Name* you can now see *Header*. This section is for the group header in the report. The header might contain the name of the person who will receive the recall notice. In this case there is no group footer. Such a footer could contain the fine due, or the place and current date and a space for the signature of the person sending the notice.

By default there is a new group for each value. So if the *Reader_Name* changes, a new group is started. Alternatively you can group by initial letter. In the case of a recall notice, however, this would put all readers with the same initial together in one group. Schmidt, Schulze, and Schulte would receive a common recall notice, which would be quite pointless in this example.

When grouping by initial letter, you can additionally specify how many letters later the next group should begin. One can imagine for example a grouping for a small telephone directory. According to the size of the contact list, one might imagine a grouping on every second initial letter. So A and B would form the first group, then C and D, and so on.

A group can be set either to be kept together with the first details section, or, as far as possible, as a complete group. By default, this option is set to *No* . For recall notices, you would probably want the group to be arranged so that a separate page is printed for each person who is to receive a recall letter. In another menu, you can choose that each group (in this case, each reader name) be followed by a page break before dealing with the next value.

If you have chosen to have a group header and perhaps a group footer, these elements will appear as sections in the report navigator under the corresponding fieldname *Reader_Name*. Here too you have the possibility of using functions, which will then be limited to this group.

To add fields, use the *Add field* function, as with forms. However in this case, the label and the field contents are not tied together. Both can be independently moved, changed in size and dragged to different sections.

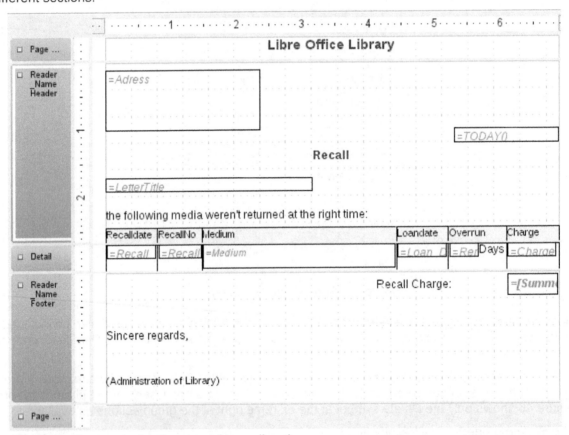

Figure 47: Report design for example recall notice

Figure 47 shows the report design for the recall notice. In the page header is the heading Libre Office Library, inserted as a label field. Here you could also have a letterhead with a logo, since the incorporation of graphics is possible. The fact that this level is called *Page header* does not imply that there is no space above it. That depends on the page settings; if an upper margin has been set, it lies above the page header.

Reader_Name header is the header for the grouped and sorted data. In the fields that are to contain data, the names of the corresponding data fields are shown in light gray. So, for example, the view underlying the report has a field named Address, containing the complete address of the recipient with street and town. To put this into a single field requires line breaks in the query. You can use **CHAR(13)** to create them.

Example:

```
SELECT "FirstName"||' '||"LastName"||CHAR(13)||"Street"||' '||"No"||
CHAR13||"Postcode"||' '||"Town" FROM "FirstName"
```

The *=TODAY()* field represents a built-in function, which inserts the current date into this position.

In *Reader_Name header*, in addition to the salutation, we see the column headings for the following table view. These elements should appear only once, even if several media are listed.

In the background of these column headers is a gray rectangle, which also serves as a frame for the data.

The details area is repeated as often as there are separate records with the same *Reader_Name* data. Here are listed all media that have not been returned on time. There is another rectangle in the background to frame the contents. This rectangle is filled with white rather than gray.

Note	In principle LibreOffice provides for the possibility of adding horizontal and vertical lines. These are displayed in design mode. At present they do not appear when the report is complete.
	These lines have the further disadvantage that they are interpreted only as hairlines. They can be reproduced better if rectangles are used. Set the background of the rectangle to black and the size to, for example, 17cm wide and 0.03cm high. This will create a horizontal line with a thickness of 0.03cm and a length of 17cm.

The *Reader_Name footer* closes the letter with a greeting formula and an area for the signature. The footer is so defined that an additional page break will occur after this area. Also, contrary to the default setup, it is specified that this area should be kept together in all cases. After all, it would look rather odd if many recall notices had the signature on a separate page.

Keep together refers here to the page break. If you want the content of a record to be kept together independently of the break, this is only possible at present if the record is not read in as Details but is used as the basis for a grouping. You can choose *Keep together = Yes*, but it does not work; the Details area becomes separated. You have to put the content of Details in a separate group to keep it together.

A built-in function is used for calculating the total fines.

Below is what an actual recall notice would look like. The details area contains 5 media that the reader has taken out on loan. The group footer contains the total fine due.

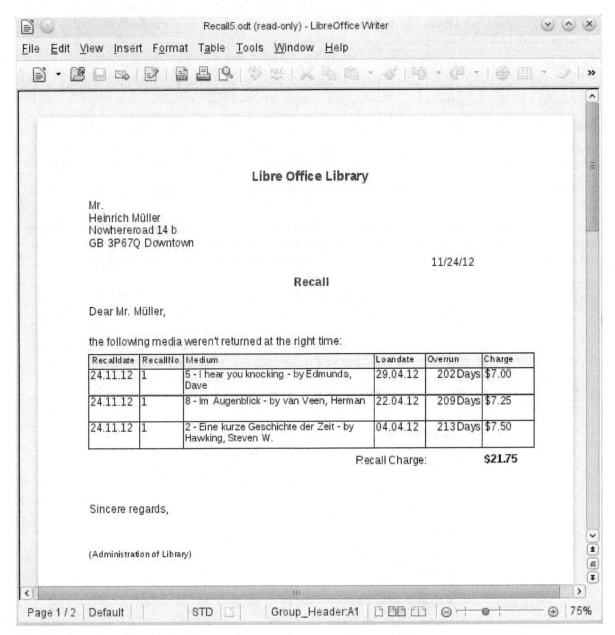

Note	Reports for single records can also extend over more than one page. The size of the report is quite separate from the page size. However, stretching the details area over more than one page can lead to faulty breaks. Here the Report Builder still has problems in calculating the spacing correctly. If both grouping areas and graphical elements are included, this may result in unpredictable sizes for certain areas.
	So far individual elements can be moved to positions outside the size of a single page only with the mouse and cursor keys. The properties of the elements always provide the same maximum distance from the upper corner of any area that lies on the first page.

General properties of fields

There are only three types of field for the presentation of data. In addition to text fields (which, contrary to their name, can also contain numbers and formatting), there is also a field type that can contain images from the database. The chart field displays a summary of data.

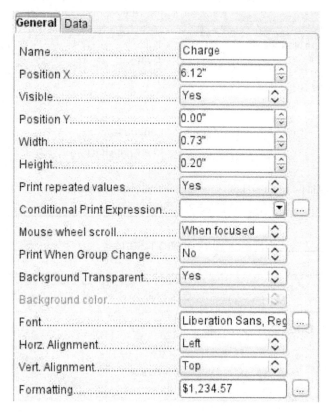

As with forms, fields are given names. By default, the name is that of the underlying database field.

A field can be set to be invisible. This may seem a bit pointless in the case of fields but is useful for group headers and footers, which may be required to carry out other functions of the grouping without containing anything that needs to be displayed.

If *Print repeated values* is deactivated, display of the field is inhibited when a field with the same content is loaded directly before. This functions correctly only for data fields that contain text. Numeric fields or date fields ignore the deactivation instruction, Label fields are completely faded out when deactivated, even if they occur only once.

In the Report Builder the display of certain content can be inhibited by using *Conditional Print Expression* or the value of the field can be used as a base for formatting text and background. More on conditional expressions is given in "Conditional print" on page 169.

The setting for the mouse wheel has no effect because report fields are not editable. It seems to be a leftover from the form definition dialog.

The *Print When Group Change* function could not be reproduced in reports either.

If the background is not defined as transparent, a background color can be defined for each field.

The other entries deal with the internal content of the field in question. This covers the font (for font color, font weight, and so on, see Figure 48), the alignment of the text within the field, and formatting with the corresponding Character dialog (see Figure 49).

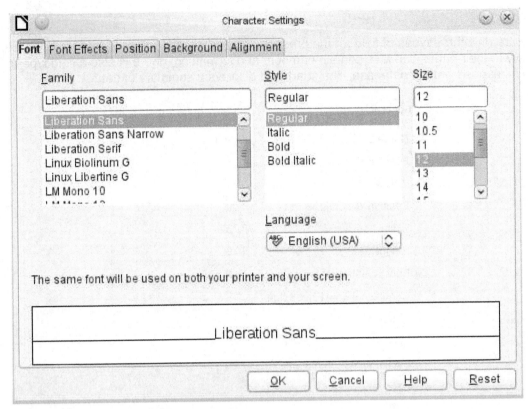

Figure 48: Fonts: Character Settings

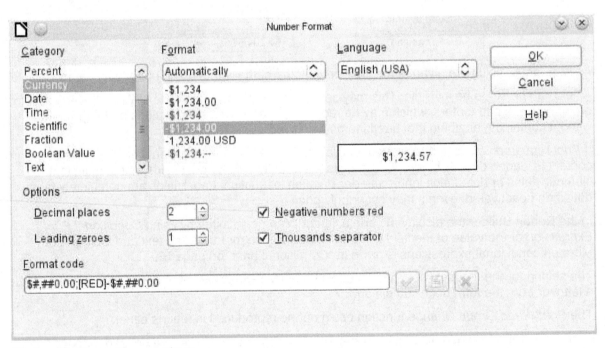

Figure 49: Formatting numbers

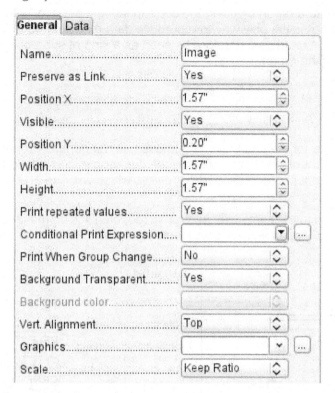

A graphical control can contain graphics from both inside and outside the database. Unfortunately it is not possible at present to store a graphic such as a logo permanently in Base. Therefore it is essential that the graphic is available in the search path, even when you are presented with the choice of embedding rather than linking images and the first field *Set up as link* can be set (literally closed) to a corresponding planned functionality. This is one of several functions that are planned for Base and are in the GUI but have not actually been implemented yet—so the buttons and checkboxes have no effect.

Alternatively, of course, a graphic can be stored in the database itself and so becomes available internally. But in that case, it must be accessible through one of the fields in the query underlying the report.

To take up an *external graphic,* use the selection button beside the *Graphic* field to load it. To load a graphical database field, specify the field under the *Data* tab.

The vertical alignment setting does not seem to have any effect during the design stage. When you call up the report, however, the graphic appears in the correct position.

When scaling, you can select *No*, *Keep aspect ratio*, or *Autom. Size*. This corresponds to the settings for a form:

- *No*: The image is not fitted to the control. If it is too large, a cropped version is shown. The original image is not affected by this.
- *Keep aspect ratio*: The image is fitted to the control but not distorted.
- *Automatic size*: The image is fitted to the control and in some cases may be distorted.

Incorporating charts into the report

You can insert charts into a report by using the corresponding control or with **Insert > Report controls > Chart**. A chart is the only way to reproduce data that is not found in the data source specified for the report. A chart can therefore be seen as a kind of subreport, but also as a free-standing component of the report.

You must draw the place for the chart using the mouse. In the general properties, in addition to the familiar fields, you can choose a *Chart type* (see the corresponding types in Calc). In addition, you can set a maximum number of records for the preview, which will give an impression of how the chart will finally look.

Charts can be formatted in the same way as in Calc (double-click on the chart). For further information, see the description in the *LibreOffice Calc Guide*.

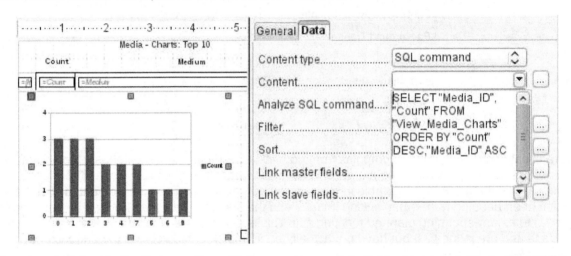

The chart is linked in the Data section with the necessary data fields. Here, in a Media Top 10 list example, the chart shows the frequency with which particular media are borrowed. The Query Editor is used to create a suitable SQL command, as you would do for a listbox in a form. The first column in the query will be used to provide the labels for the vertical bars in the chart, while the second column yields the total number of loan transactions, shown in the height of the bars.

In the example above, the chart shows very little at first, since only limited test loans were carried out before the SQL command was issued.

The chart on the next page, from the membership database of a society (German: Mitgliederstatistik), has been prepared from a query that needs to be entered in direct SQL mode, as the graphical user interface does not understand it. For this reason *No* (German: Nein) has been chosen for *Analyze SQL command*, a choice that excludes any filtering and sorting with the internal tools of the Report Builder. These fields are therefore grayed out. In the data properties of the chart, **Query** (German: Abfrage) has been entered.

Fields are linked together in the same way as for a main form with a subform. In the report itself, the age distributions of male and female members are listed in tabular form. They are grouped by gender. Each group is given its own chart. So that the chart only contains data for the correct gender, the *Gender* field (German: Geschlecht) in the report is linked to the *Gender* in the chart.

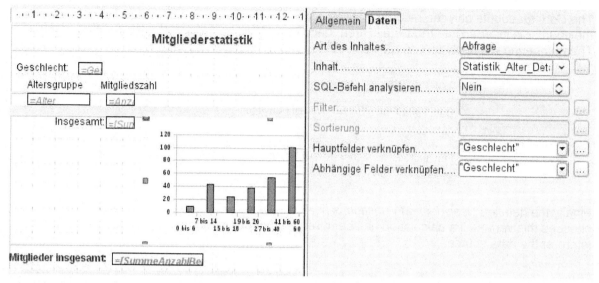

Figure 50: Linked fields for a chart, same as in forms. This example is not translated, because the report is nt part of the example database.

| Note | The creation of charts works at present only in Versions 3.3.x and 3.4.x. From Version 3.5, LibreOffice can no longer open these reports. They can still be produced, however. |
| | LibreOffice is not the only program to have problems with charts. In Version 3.3 of OpenOffice.org, the display does not work either. OpenOffice.org does open the reports, but with the charts missing. |

Data properties of fields

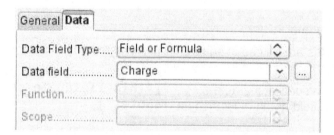

In the properties dialog, the Data tab shows by default only the database field from which the data for this report field will be read. However, in addition to the field types *Field* and *Formula*, the types *Function*, *Counter*, and *User-defined function* are available.

You can select in advance the *Sum, Minimum,* and *Maximum* functions. They will apply either to the current group or to the whole report. These functions can lead to problems if a field is empty (NULL). In such fields, if they have been formatted as numbers, "NaN" appears; that is, there is no numerical value present. For empty fields, no calculation is carried out and the result is always 0.

Such fields can be reformatted to display a value of 0 by using the following formula in the Data area of the view.

```
IF([numericfield];[numericfield];0)
```

This function calculates with the actual value of a field that has no value. It would seem simpler to formulate the underlying query for the report so that 0 is given instead of NULL for numeric fields.

The *Counter* counts only the records that will occur either in the group or in the report as a whole. If the counter is inserted into the Details area, each record will be provided with a running number. The numbering will apply only to records in the group or in the whole report.

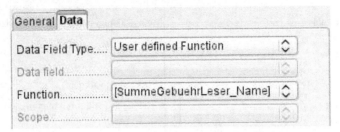

Finally the detailed *User-defined Function* is available. It may happen that the Report Builder itself chooses this variant, if a calculation has been requested, but for some reason it cannot correctly interpret the data source.

Functions in the Report Builder

The Report Builder provides a variety of functions, both for displaying data and for setting conditions. If these are not sufficient, user-defined functions can be created using simple calculation steps, which are particularly useful in group footers and summaries.

Entering formulas

The Report Builder is based on the Pentaho Report Builder. A small part of its documentation is at http://wiki.pentaho.com/display/Reporting/9.+Report+Designer+Formula+Expressions.

A further source is the Specifications for the OpenFormula Standard: http://www.oasis-open.org/committees/download.php/16826/openformula-spec-20060221.html

Basic principles:

Formulas start with an equals sign.	`=`
References to data fields are placed in square brackets.	`[Field name]`
If the data fields contain special characters (including spaces), the field name must also be enclosed in quotes.	`["This fieldname should be in quotes"]`
Text entry must always be in double quotes.	`"Text entry"`
The following operators are allowed.	+, -, * (Multiplication), / (Division), % (divide the preceding number by 100), ^ (Raise to the power of the following number), & (concatenate text),
The following relationships are possible.	= , <> , < , <= , > , >=
Round brackets are allowed.	( )
Default error message.	**NA** (Not available)
Error message for an empty field that was defined as a number.	**NaN** (Perhaps "not a number"?)

All formula input applies only to the current record. Relationships with previous or following records are therefore not possible.

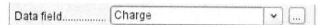

Next to the date field is a button with three dots whenever a formula can be entered. This button starts the Function Wizard.

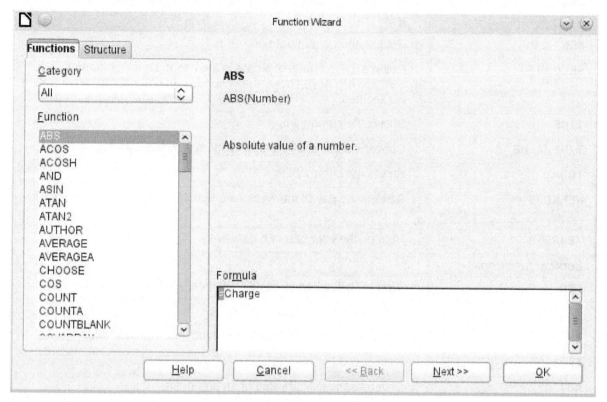

However there are far fewer functions than in Calc. Many functions do have Calc equivalents. There the Wizard calculates the result of the function directly.

The Function Wizard does not always work perfectly. For instance, text entries are not taken up with double quotes. However, only entries with double quotes are processed when starting the function.

The following functions are available:

Function	Description
Date and Time Functions	
DATE	Produces a valid date from numeric values for the year, the month and the day.
DATEDIF *(DAY | MONTH | YEAR)*	Returns the total years, months or days between two date values.
DATEVALUE	Converts an American date entry in text form (quoted) into a date value. The American variant that is produced can then be reformatted.
DAY	Returns the day of the month for a given date. DAY([Date field])

DAYS	Returns the number of days between two dates.
HOUR	Returns the hours of a given time in 24-hour format. HOUR([DateTimeField]) calculates the hours in the field.
MINUTE	Returns the minutes of a date in the internal numeric format MINUTE([Timefield]) calculates the minutes part of the time.
MONTH	Returns the month for an entered date as a number. MONTH([Datefield])
NOW	Returns the current date and time.
SECOND	Returns the seconds of a date in the internal numeric format SECOND(NOW()) shows the seconds part of the time the command is executed.
TIME	Shows the current time.
TIMEVALUE	Converts a text entry for a time into a time value for calculations.
TODAY	Shows the current date.
WEEKDAY	Returns the day of the week as a number. Day number 1 is Sunday.
YEAR	Returns the year part of a date entry.

Logical functions	
AND	Yields TRUE when all its arguments are TRUE.
FALSE	Defines the logical value as FALSE.
IF	If a condition is TRUE, then this value, else another value.
IFNA	(since LO 3.5)
NOT	Reverses the logical value of an argument.
OR	Yields TRUE when one of its conditions is TRUE.
TRUE	Defines the logical value as TRUE.
XOR	Yields TRUE when only one of the linked values is TRUE.

Rounding functions	
INT	Rounds down to the previous integer.

Mathematical functions	
ABS	Returns the absolute (non-negative) value of a number.
ACOS	Calculates the arccosine of a number. - arguments between -1 and 1. (since LO 3.5)
ACOSH	Calculates the areacosine (inverse hyperbolic cosine) – argument >= 1. (since LO 3.5)
ASIN	Calculates the arcsine of a number – argument between -1 and 1. (since LO 3.5)

ATAN	Calculates the arctangent of a number. (since LO 3.5)
ATAN2	Calculates the arctangent of an x-coordinate and a y-coordinate. (since LO 3.5)
AVERAGE	Gives the average of the entered values. (occurs twice in the LO 3.3.4 Formula Wizard)
AVERAGEA	Gives the average of the entered values. Text is treated as zero. (since LO 3.5)
COS	Argument is the angle in radians whose cosine is to be calculated. (since LO 3.5)
EVEN	Rounds a positive number up or a negative number down to the next even integer.
EXP	Calculates the exponential function (Base 'e'). (since LO 3.5)
LN	Calculates the natural logarithm of a number. (since LO 3.5)
LOG10	Calculates the logarithm of a number (Base '10'). (since LO 3.5)
MAX	Returns the maximum of a series of numbers.
MAXA	Returns the maximum value in a row. Any text is set to zero.
MIN	Returns the smallest of a series of values.
MINA	Returns the minimum value in a row. Any text is set to zero.
MOD	Returns the remainder for a division when you enter the dividend and divisor.
ODD	Rounds a positive number up or a negative number down to the next odd integer.
PI	Gives the value of the number 'π'. (since LO 3.5)
POWER	Raises the base to the power of the exponent. (Since LO 3.5)
SIN	Calculates the sine of a number. (since LO 3.5)
SQRT	Calculates the square root of a number. (since LO 3.5)
SUM	Sums a list of numeric values
SUMA	Sums a list of numeric values. Text and Yes/No fields are allowed. Unfortunately this function (still) ends with an error message. (since LO 3.5)
VAR	Calculates the variance, starting from a sample. (since LO 3.5)

Text functions	
EXACT	Shows if two text strings are exactly equal.
FIND	Gives the offset of a text string within another string.
LEFT	The specified number of characters of a text string are reproduced starting from the left.
LEN	Gives the number of characters in a text string.
LOWER	Converts text to lower case.
MESSAGE	Formats the value into the given output format. (since LO 3.5)
MID	The specified number of characters of a text string are reproduced starting from a specified character position.
REPLACE	Replaces a substring by a different substring. The starting position and the length of the substring to be replaced must be given.
REPT	Repeats text a specified number of times.
RIGHT	The specified number of characters of a text string are reproduced starting from the right.
SUBSTITUTE	Replaces specific parts of a given text string by new text. Additionally you can specify which of several occurrences of the target string are to be replaced.
T	Returns the text, or an empty text string if the value is not text (for example a number).
TEXT	Conversion of numbers or times into text.
TRIM	Removes leading spaces and terminal spaces, and reduces multiple spaces to a single space.
UNICHAR	Converts a Unicode decimal number into a Unicode character. For example, 196 becomes 'Ä' ('Ä' has the hexadecimal value 00C4, which is 196 in decimals without leading zeros).
UNICODE	Converts a Unicode character into a Unicode decimal number. 'Ä' becomes 196.
UPPER	Returns a text string in upper case.
URLENCODE	Converts a given text into one that conforms to a valid URL. If no particular standard is specified, ISO-8859-1 is followed..
Information functions	
CHOOSE	The first argument is an index, followed by a list of values. The value represented by the index is returned. CHOOSE(2;"Apple";"Pear";"Banana") returns Pear. CHOOSE([age_level_field];"Milk";"Cola";"Beer") returns a possible drink for the given 'age_level_field' .
COUNT	Only fields containing a number or a date are counted. COUNT([time];[number]) returns 2, if both fields contain a value (non-NULL) or else 1 or 0.
COUNTA	Includes also fields containing text. Even NULL is counted, along with boolean fields.

COUNTBLANK	Counts the empty fields in a region.
HASCHANGED	Checks if the named column has changed. However no information about the column is provided.
INDEX	Works with regions (since LO 3.5).
ISBLANK	Tests if the field is NULL (empty).
ISERR	Returns TRUE if the entry has an error other than NA. **ISERR(1/0)** gives **TRUE**
ISERROR	Like ISERR, except that NA also returns TRUE.
ISEVEN	Tests if a number is even.
ISLOGICAL *(ISTLOG)*	Tests if this is a Yes/No value. **ISLOGICAL(TRUE())** or **ISLOGICAL(FALSE())** yield **TRUE**, Text values such as **ISLOGICAL("TRUE")** yield **FALSE**.
ISNA	Tests if the expression is an error of type NA.
ISNONTEXT	Tests if the value is not text.
ISNUMBER	Tests if something is numeric. **ISNUMBER(1)** yields **TRUE**, **ISNUMBER("1")** yields **FALSE**
ISODD	Tests if a number is an odd number.
ISREF	Tests if something is a field reference. **ISREF([Fieldname])** yields **TRUE**, **ISREF(1)** yields **FALSE**.
ISTEXT	Tests if the content of the field is text.
NA *(NV)*	Returns the error code **NA**.
VALUE	(since LO 3.5)
User defined	
CSVARRAY	Converts CSV text into an array. (since LO 3.5)
CSVTEXT	Converts an array into CSV text. (since LO 3.5)
NORMALIZEARRAY	(since LO 3.5)
NULL	Returns NULL.
PARSEDATE	Converts text into a date. Uses the SimpleDateFormat. Requires a date in text as described in this date format. Example: PARSEDATE("9.10.2012";"dd.MM.yyyy") yields the internally usable number for the date. (since LO 3.5)
Document information	
AUTHOR	Author, as read from the **Tools → Options → LibreOffice → User data**. This is not therefore the actual author but the current user of the database.
TITLE	Returns the title of the report.

User-defined functions

You can use user-defined functions to return specific intermediate results for a group of records. In the above example, a function of this sort was used to calculate the fines in the *Reader_Name_Footer* area.

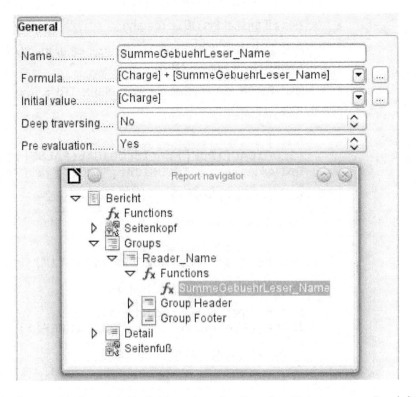

In the Report Navigator the function is displayed under *Reader_Name* group. By right-clicking on this function, you can define additional functions by name.

The properties of the function *SummeGebuehrLeser_Name* are shown above. The formula adds the field *Charge* to the value already stored in the function itself. The initial value is the value of the *Charge* field on the first traverse of the group. This value is stored in the function under the function name and is reused in the formula, until the loop is ended and the group footer is written.

Deep traversing seems to have no function for now, unless charts are being treated here as subreports.

If *Pre evaluation* is activated for the function, the result can also be placed in the group header. Otherwise the group header contains only the corresponding value of the first field of the group.

User-defined functions can also reference other user-defined functions. In that case you must ensure that the functions used have already been created. Pre-calculation in functions that refer to other functions must be excluded.

```
[SumMarksClass] / ([ClassNumber]+1)
```

refers to the *Class* group. The content of the *Marks* field is summed and the sum for all the records is returned. The sum of the marks is divided by the sum of the records. To get the correct number, 1 must be added as shown with *[ClassNumber]*. This will then yield the average marks.

Formula entry for a field

Using **Data > Data field** you can enter formulas that affect only one field in the Details area.

```
IF([boolean_field];"Yes";"No")
```

sets the allowable values to "Yes" or "No" instead of TRUE and FALSE.

Conditional print

The general properties of group headers, group footers, and fields include a *Conditional Print Expression* field. Formulas that are written in this field influence the content of a field or the display of an entire region. Here, too, you can make use of the Function Wizard.

```
[Fieldname]="true"
```

causes the content of the named field to be displayed only if it is true.

Many forms of conditional display are not fully determined by the specified properties. For instance, if a graphical separator line is to be inserted after the tenth place of a list of competition results, you cannot simply use the following conditional display command for the graphic:

```
[Place]=10
```

This command does not work. Instead the graphic will continue to appear in the *Details* section after each subsequent record.

It is safer to bind the conditional display to a *group footer* rather than to the graphic, if this is not otherwise needed. The line is positioned in the *group footer*. Then the line does actually appear after the 10th place, when formulated as above. But in that case the content that would previously have appeared in the *Details* section must be stored in the *group header*.

Conditional formatting

Conditional formatting can be used, for example, to format a calender so that weekends are shown differently. Choose **Format > Conditional formatting** and enter:

```
WEEKDAY([Date])=1
```

and the corresponding formatting for Sundays.

If you use 'Expression is' in conditional formatting, you can enter a formula. As is usual in Calc, several conditions can be formulated and are evaluated sequentially. In the above example, first Sunday is tested for, then Saturday. Finally there might be a query about the content of the field. So for example the content 'Holiday' would lead to a different format.

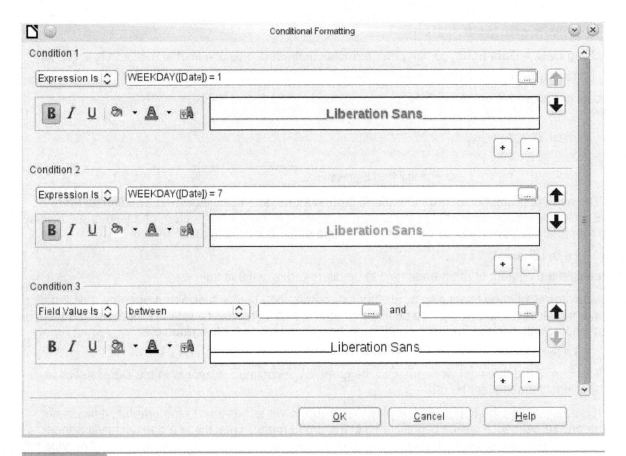

Note	The Report Builder is a plug-in. If additional uncorrectable errors occur (formulas not implemented, too long text shown as an empty field, and so on), it is sometimes necessary to delete parts of the report or simply create it afresh.

Chapter 7
Linking to Databases

General notes on database linkage

Base allows you to use documents in LibreOffice Writer and Calc in various ways as data sources. This means that the use of Base is not necessarily tied to the registration of databases in the configuration of LibreOffice. External forms can also interact directly with Base, provided that the path to the data sources is supplied.

Registration of databases

Many functions, such as printing labels or using data for form letters, require the registration of a database in the configuration of LibreOffice.

Using **Tools > Options > LibreOffice Base > Databases > New**, a database can be registered for subsequent use by other LibreOffice components.

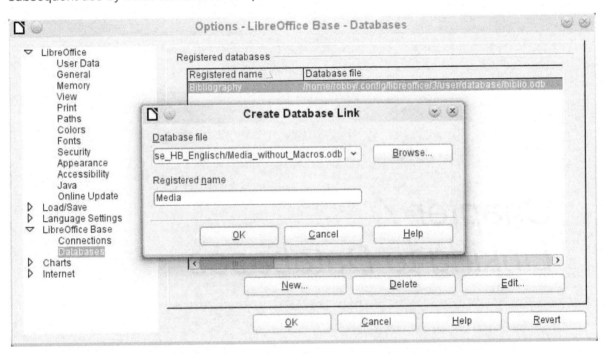

The database is found using the file browser and connected to LibreOffice in a similar way as for a simple form. The database itself must be given a suitably informative name, for which you can simply use the name of the database file. The name serves as an alias, which can also be used in queries to the database.

Data source browser

The data source browser allows you access to tables and queries of all registered databases under their registered names. The browser can be opened using **View > Data sources**, or by pressing the *F4* key, or by using the corresponding symbol in the standard toolbar.

Registered data sources are shown on the left side of the data source browser. The Bibliography data source is included in LibreOffice by default. The other data sources are listed by their registered names.

A click on the expansion sign in front of the database name opens the database and shows a sub-folder for queries and another for tables. Other sub-folders of the database are not made available here. Internal forms and reports can only be accessed by opening the database itself.

Only when you click on the Tables folder is the database actually accessed. For databases protected by a password, the password must be entered at this point.

To the right of the name tree, you can see the table you have selected. It can be edited just as in Base. However direct entry into tables should be carried out with caution in very complex relational databases, as the tables are linked together with foreign keys. For example, the database shown below has separate tables for street names, postcodes and towns.

For a proper view of the data (but without the ability to edit), queries or views are more suitable.

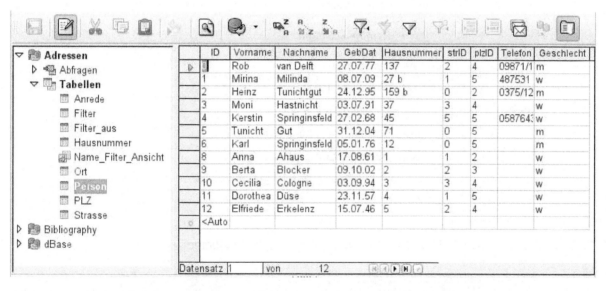

Of the icons in the toolbar, many will be familiar from data entry into tables. The main new ones are those in the last section: *Data to Text, Data to Fields, Mail Merge, Data Source of Current Document, Explorer on/off*.

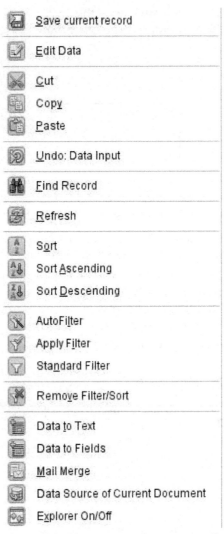

Figure 51: Data source browser toolbar

Data to Text

The *Data to Text* function is available as soon as a record is selected.

Figure 52: Selecting a data record

If you now choose Data to Text, a Wizard appears to carry out the necessary formatting.

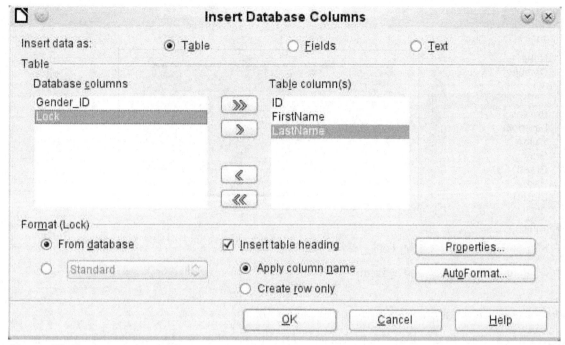

Figure 53: Data entry as table

There are several possibilities for entering data as text: as a table, as single fields, or as ordinary text.

The figure above shows the option **Insert Data as Table**. In the case of numeric and date fields, the database format can be changed to a chosen format. Otherwise, formatting is carried out automatically when the table fields are selected. The sequence of fields is adjusted by using the arrow keys.

As soon as table columns have been selected, the Properties button for the table is activated. This allows you to set the usual table properties for Writer (table width, column width, and so on).

The checkbox determines if a table header is required. If it is not checked, no separate row will be reserved for headings.

The row chosen for the table headings can be taken from the column names, or the record may be written out with space left for the headings to be edited in later.

The AutoFormat button provides several pre-formatted table views. Apart from the suggested *Default* format, all the formats can be renamed.

To add an autoformat, a table in this format must first be created. This is then selected and can be added to the list by using the *Add* button.

The table is finally created with the selected columns.

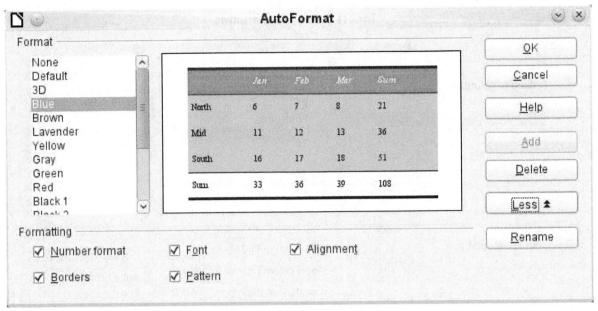

Figure 54: AutoFormat provides a choice of table formats

Insert data as Fields provides the possibility of using a mini-editor to position the various table fields successively in the text. The text created in this way can also be provided with a paragraph style. In this case too, the formatting of dates and numbers can be specified separately, or can be read directly from the table settings in the database.

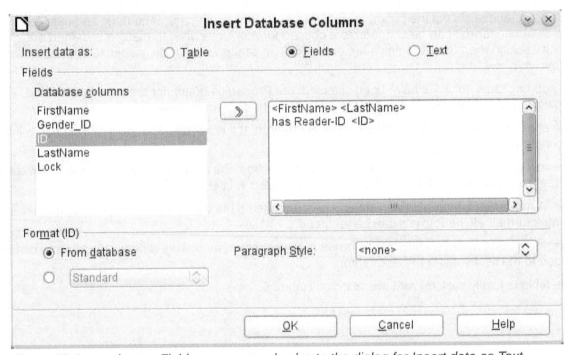

Figure 55: Insert data as Fields – corresponds also to the dialog for Insert data as Text

The fields inserted into the text in this way can subsequently be deleted singly or used for a mail merge.

If you choose **Insert data as Text**, the only difference from using fields is that fields remain linked to the database. When you insert as text, only the content of the specified fields is transferred and not the link to the actual database. That explains why the dialog for this option is the same as for the previous one.

The results of the two procedures are compared below.

Input data as fields	Input data as text
Bert Lederstrumpf has Reader-ID 🖙	Bert Lederstrumpf has Redaer-ID 0

Media.Reader.ID

Figure 56: Comparison of Data as Fields and Data as Text

The fields have a gray background. If the mouse is hovered over the fields, it shows that the fields are linked to the *Media* database, to the table *Reader* and, within this table, to the field *ID*.

So, for example, a double-click on the field *ID* opens the following overview. This makes it clear which field was created through the *Insert Data as Fields* procedure. It is the same field type that is shown by **Insert > Fields > Other > Database**.

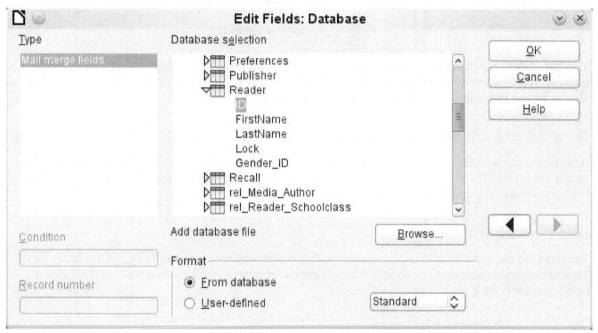

Figure 57: Double-click on an inserted field to show the properties of the Mail Merge fields

It is simpler to create such a field by selecting the column header of the table in the data source browser and dragging it into the document with the mouse. You can create a form letter directly in this way.

Data to Fields

Data as Fields, as described in the previous section, is used to create mail merge fields in a Writer document. If now you select a different record in the data source browser and then choose *Data as Fields*, the previously inserted data are replaced by the new data.

Here another record has been selected. While the *Insert data as Fields* option leads to the previous values being changed to the values for the new record, in the case of *Insert data as Text*, the existing text remains unchanged.

Mail merge

The *Mail Merge* button launches the Mail Merge Wizard. As the form letter in the above example assembles its data from different tables, you need first to launch the database. In the database, you then create a new query to make the required data available.

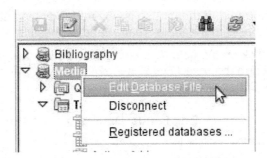

The database is launched through a right-click on the database itself or on one of its tables or queries, which immediately refreshes the display in the data source browser. After that the Mail Merge Wizard can be called up by using the corresponding button.

Data source of current document

A click on the *Data Source of Current Document* button opens a direct view on the table which forms the basis for the data inserted into the document. In the above example, the *Person* table from the *Addresses* database *appears*.

Explorer on/off

Toggling the *Explorer On/Off* button shows or hides the directory tree to the left of the table view. This allows more space, if necessary, for a display of the data. To access another table, you will need to switch the Explorer back on.

Creating mail merge documents

The Mail Merge Wizard is also accessible from the database browser. This Wizard allows the address field and the salutation to be constructed from a data source in small steps. In principle you can create these fields without using the Wizard. Here we will work through the steps of the Wizard as an example.

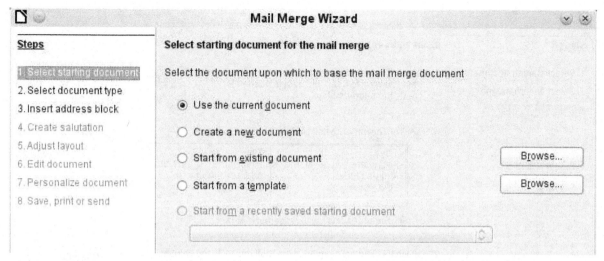

The **Starting document** for the form letter is the document to which the **database fields are linked**.

The **Merged document** is the one containing the data for the various people who are to receive the form letters. In the merged document there is **no linkage** to the data source. It is similar to the output of *Insert Data as Text*.

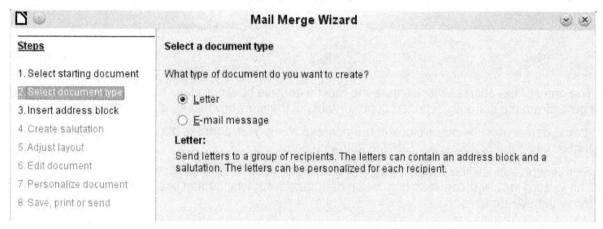

The Mail Merge Wizard can produce either letters or emails using records from the database.

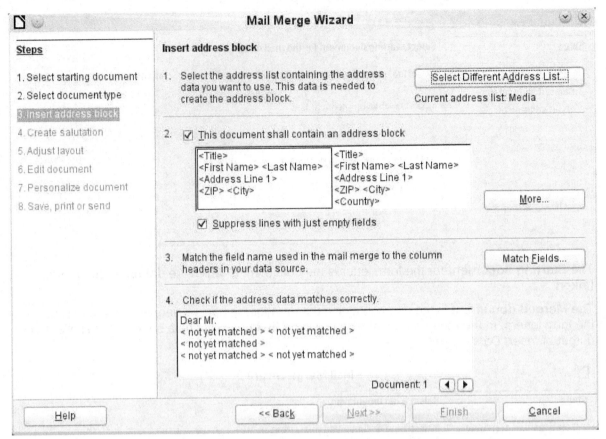

The entry of the address block allows the most extensive configuration. The suggested address list comes from the currently selected query or table in the currently selected database.

Step 2 determines the overall look of the address block. This address block can be customized further using the *More* button. See the following figure.

Step 3 serves to link the named fields in the address block to the correct fields in the database. The Wizard initially recognizes only those database fields which have exactly the same names as those the Wizard uses.

In Step 4, the addresses are displayed. You can choose which addresses to take from the database by using the arrow keys. In the displayed addresses two elements require further editing:

- There is no salutation.
- Apart from the first name, all the other fields are < *not yet allocated* > , because the field names in the database are different from the names that the Wizard initially uses.

To correct these errors, the address block from Step 2 must be made editable.

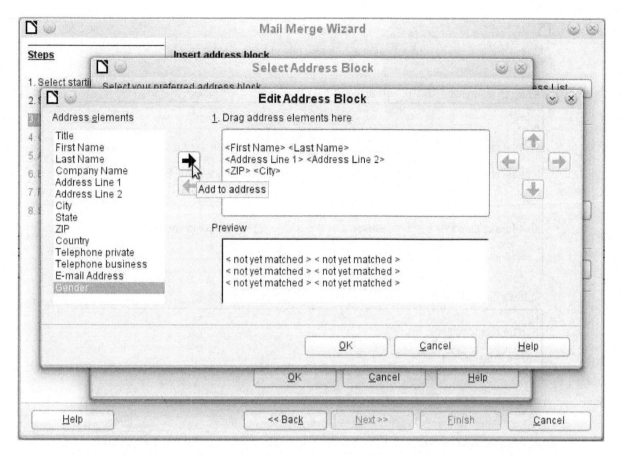

You can see in the background that, when you choose to edit, you are first presented with an enlarged list of address blocks. Here you can select the most suitable address block to start with, and then edit it.

The address block cannot be edited directly. Instead, the arrangement of the fields is carried out by using the arrow buttons visible to the right to move fields into or out of the address block

For the salutation the *Salutation* field is inserted. All the other fields except FirstName must now be entered appropriately.

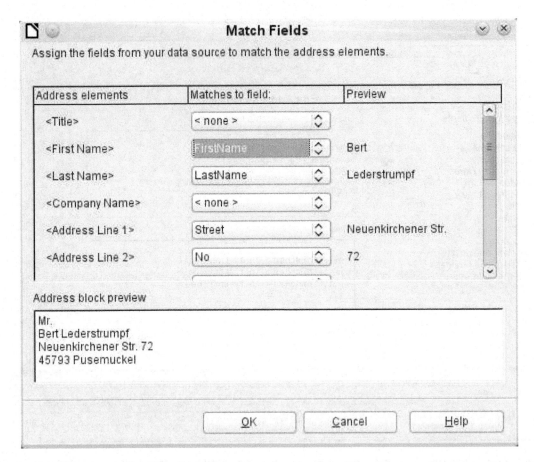

Here the address elements are associated with the corresponding elements from the query of the database successfully transferred by the Mail Merge Wizard. Again the first record in the query is used for the preview.

The database settings are essentially ended with Step 4. Here, it is just a matter of choosing which field the gender of the recipient should be taken from. This field has already been named, so that only the field content for a female recipient still needs to be specified.

Three different salutations are to be produced. All records with a 'w' start with *Dear Ms...*, all those with 'm' with *Dear Mr...* If there is no gender given, *Dear Sir/Madam* is selected.

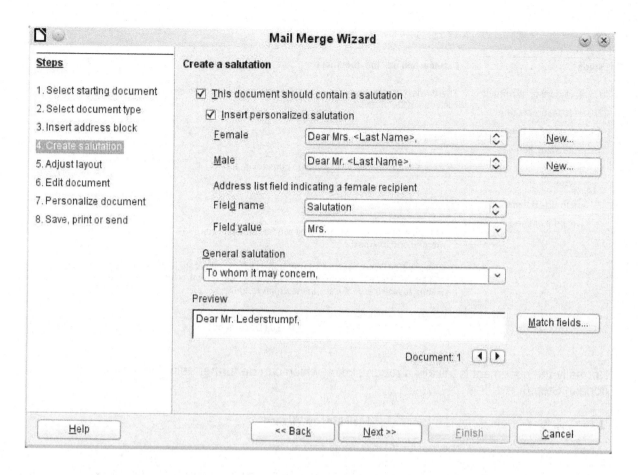

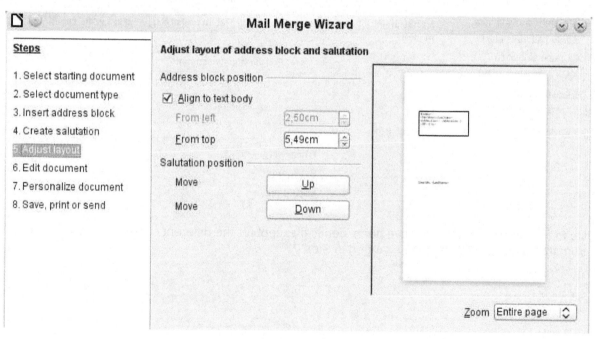

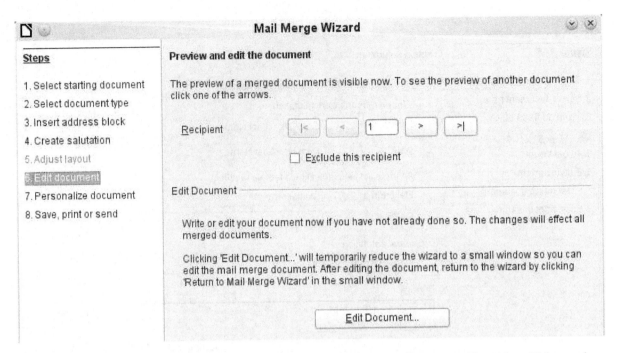

Normally the document is initially a rough sketch which can be further edited in Writer. This can be done in Step 6.

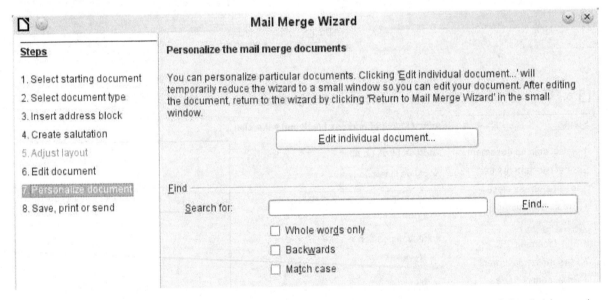

Up to now all the documents have been identical except for the different content of the fields read from the database. This can be changed in Step 7.

The **Starting document** is the document in which the **field properties** and the **linkage to the database** are stored. In the background meanwhile, you can see the original document with the contents of the first record that is to be converted into the form letter. This is called the Mail Merge document.

Only when one of the options is actually carried out (in the above example to save the starting document) does the Mail Merge Wizard terminate.

Label printing

Files > New > Labels launches the Label Printing Wizard. It opens a dialog, which includes all questions of formating and content for labels, before the labels themselves are produced. The settings in this dialog are saved in the personal settings for the user.

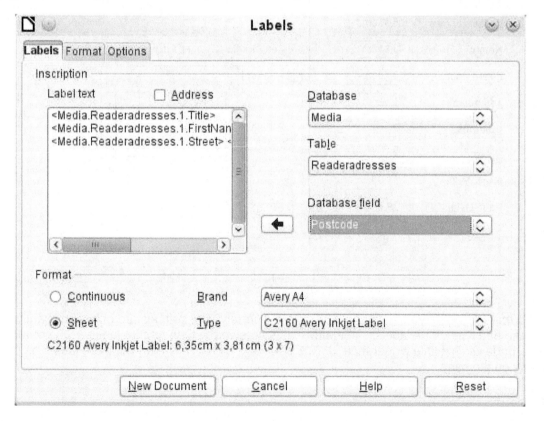

The basic settings for the content are in the *Labels* tab. If for Label text you check the Address box, all the labels will have the same content, taken from the LibreOffice settings for the user of the program.

As an example we will again use the *Addresses* database. Although the next selection field is headed *Tables*, **Tables and Queries** are both listed here, just as in the data source browser.

The arrow buttons are used to insert individual database fields into the editor. The name for the database field *Surname* is set here to *<Addresses.MailMergeQuery.1.Surname>*. The sequence is thus *<database.Table.1.database field>*.

You can work with the keyboard in the editor. So for example, it is possible to insert a line break at the beginning, so that the labels will not be printed directly on the top edge but the content can be printed as completely and clearly visible.

The format can be selected in the tab *Labels*. Here many label brands are incorporated so that most other settings in the tab *Format* are not necessary.

| Note | In versions 3.4.x to 3.5.2, due to a change in the basic settings in the label wizard, display errors occurred when the labels were the same width as the page width. Under these conditions, the last label simply slides down one line. |
| | In version 3.5.3 page settings were added in the *Format* tab. |

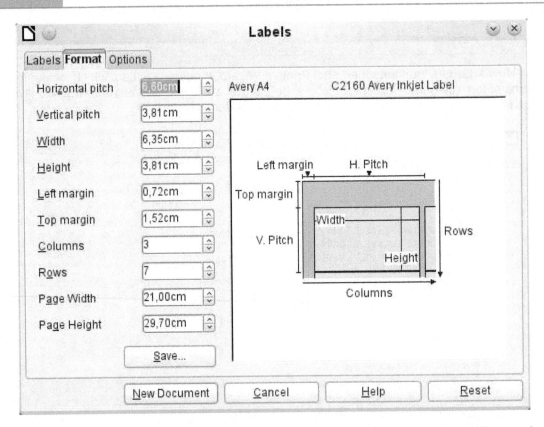

The *Format* tab allows you to set the label size accurately. The settings are only significant when the make and type of the labels is not known. It is noteworthy that, to print labels 7.00 cm wide, you need a page width a little bigger than 3*7.00 cm = 21.00 cm. Only then will three labels be printed in a row on the page.

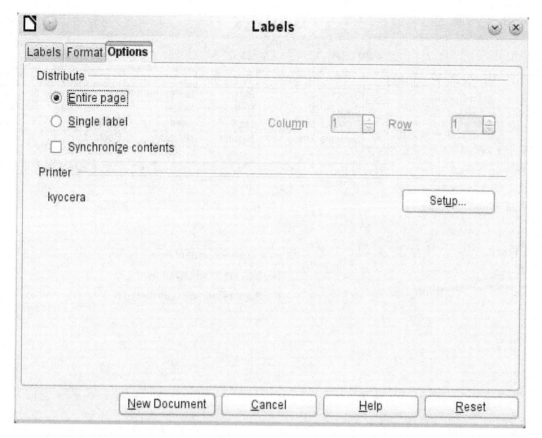

Under the *Options* tab you can specify whether only a single label or a whole page of labels will be produced. The page will then be filled with data from successive records of the database, beginning with the first record. If there are more records than will fit on the page, the next page will automatically be filled with the next set of records.

The *Synchronize contents* checkbox links all the labels together so that subsequent changes in layout of any label will be applied to all the others. To transfer the edited content, just use the included button labelled *Synchronize*, which appears during label production if you have selected this checkbox.

Finally the **New Document** button is used to create a document containing the selected fields.

When you initiate the printing process, the following question appears:

Choose **Yes** to fill the address database fields with the corresponding content.

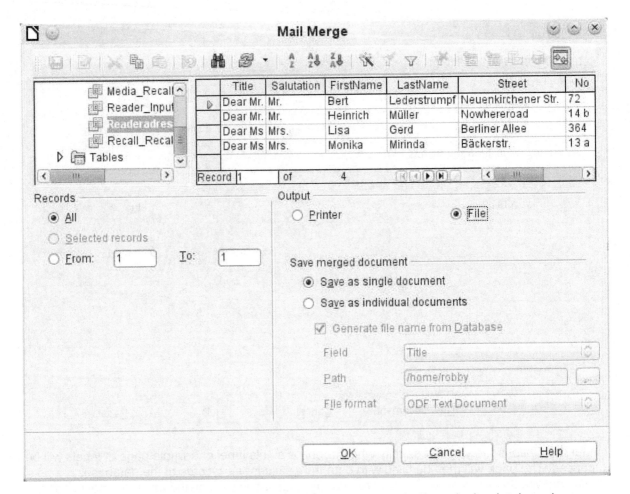

The source of the data for the label printing is not found automatically; only the database is pre-selected. The actual query must be specified by the user, because in this case we are not dealing with a table.

When the query is selected and the corresponding records chosen (in this case *All*), the printing can begin. It is advisable, especially for the first tests, to choose *Output* to a *File*, which will save the labels as a document. The option to save in several documents is not appropriate for label printing but rather for letters to different recipients which can then be worked on subsequently.

Direct creation of mail merge and label documents

Instead of using the Wizard, you can of course produce mail merge and label documents directly.

Mail merge using the mouse

Mail merge fields can be taken from the database browser using the mouse:

Select the table header with the left mouse button. Hold the button down and drag the cursor through the text document. The cursor changes its shape to an insert symbol. The MailMerge field is inserted into the text document, here shown in the complete description which is made visible using **View > Field names**.

Creating form letters by selecting fields

Mail merge fields can be inserted using **Insert > Fields > Other > Database**.

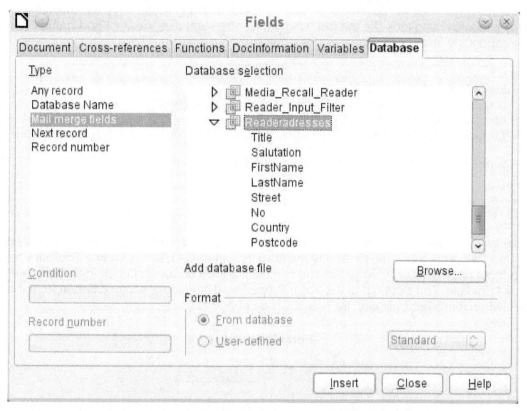

Here all tables and queries in the selected database are available. Using the '*Insert*' button, the various fields can be inserted one after another directly into the text at the current cursor position.

If you want to create a salutation, which is usual in form letters, you can use a hidden paragraph or hidden text: **Insert > Fields > Other > Functions > Hidden paragraph**. For both variants take care that the condition you formulate will **not** be fulfilled, since you want the paragraph to be visible.

For the formula *Dear Mrs <Surname>,* to appear only when the person is female, a sufficient condition is:

[Addresses.Mailmergequery.Gender] != "f"

Now the only remaining problem is that there may be no surname. Under these circumstances, "*Dear Sir/Madam,*" should appear so this is the condition you must insert. The overall condition is:

**[Addresses.MailMergeQuery.Gender] != "w" OR NOT
[Addresses.MailMergeQuery.Surname]**

That excludes the possibility of this paragraph appearing when the person is not female or there is no entered surname.

In the same way you can create entries for the masculine gender and for missing entries for the two remaining types of salutation.

Naturally you can create a salutation in the address field in exactly the same way, wherever the gender is specified.

Further information is given in the LibreOffice Help under *Hidden Text* and *Conditional Text*.

Of course it would be still simpler if someone who understands databases were to put the whole salutation right into the query. This can be done using a correlated subquery (see the chapter on Queries in this Handbook).

Particularly interesting for labels is the field type Next record. If this field type is chosen at the end of a label, the next label will be filled with data from the following record. Typical labels for sequential label printing look like the following figure when you use **View > Field names** to make the corresponding field designations visible:

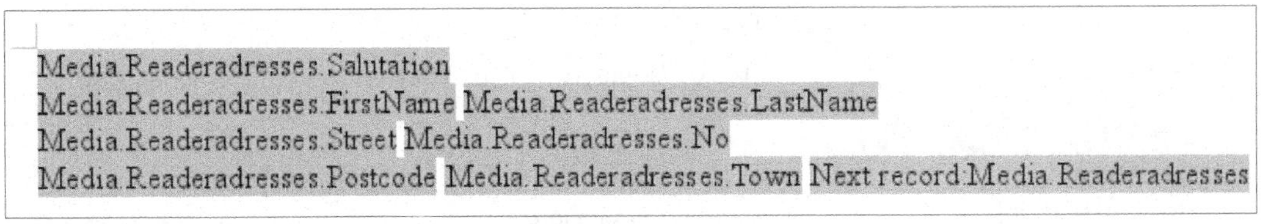

Media.Readeradresses.Salutation
Media.Readeradresses.FirstName Media.Readeradresses.LastName
Media.Readeradresses.Street Media.Readeradresses.No
Media.Readeradresses.Postcode Media.Readeradresses.Town Next record:Media.Readeradresses

Figure 58: Field selection for labels with sequential content

External forms

If simple form properties available in LibreOffice are to be used in other program modules such as Writer and Calc, you only need to display the form design toolbar, using **View > Toolbars > Form design**, then open the *Form navigator*. You can build a form or, as described in the Forms chapter, create a form field. The *Data* tab of the Form Properties dialog looks a little different from the one you see when forms are built directly in an ODB database file:

Form Properties
General
Data
Events
Data source
Content type
Table
Content

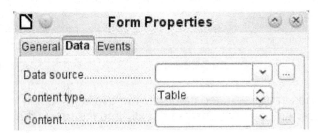

Figure 59: Form with an external data source

Form Properties
General
Data
Events
Content type
Table
Content

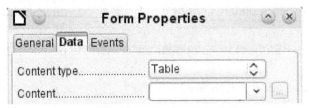

Figure 60: Form with an internal data source.

The *Data source* must be selected separately when using an external form. Use the button to the right of the data source listbox to open the file browser. Any ODB file can be selected. In addition, the field for the data source contains a link, beginning with file:///.

If instead you look in the listbox contents, you will see databases already registered in LibreOffice under their registered names.

The forms are created in exactly the same way as in Base itself.

Advantages of external forms

Base need not be opened first in order to work with the database. Therefore you do not need an extra open window in the background.

In a database that is already complete, existing database users can subsequently be sent the improved form without problems. They can continue to use the database during the development of further forms, and do not need to copy complicated external forms from one database into another.

Forms for a database can be varied to suit the user. Users who do not have the authority to correct data or make new entries can be sent a current data set by other users, and simply replace their *.odb file to have an up-to-date view. This could, for example, be useful for a database for an association where all committee members get the database but only one person can edit the data; the others can still view the addresses for their respective departments.

Disadvantages of external forms

Users must always install forms and Base with the same directory structure. That is the only way that access to the database can be free from errors. As the links are stored relative to the form, it is sufficient to store the database and its forms in a common directory.

Only forms can be created externally, not queries or reports. A simple glance at a query therefore must go through a form. A report on the other hand requires the opening of the database. Alternatively it might be possible to create it, at least partially, using mail merge.

Database use in Calc

Data can be used in Calc for calculation purposes. For this purpose it is first necessary to make the data accessible in a Calc worksheet.

Entering data into Calc

There are various ways of inserting data into Calc.

Select a table with the left mouse button and drag it into a Calc worksheet. The cursor sets the left upper corner of the table. The table is created complete with field names. The data source browser in this case does not offer the options of *Data into Text* or *Data into Fields*.

Data dragged into Calc in this way shows the following properties:
Not only the data are imported, but the field properties too are read and acted on during the import. Fields such as house numbers, which were declared as text fields, are formatted as text after insertion into Calc.

The import becomes a Calc range, which by default is assigned the name Import1. The data can later be accessed using this range. **Data > Refresh range** allows the range, where appropriate, to be supplied with new data from the database.

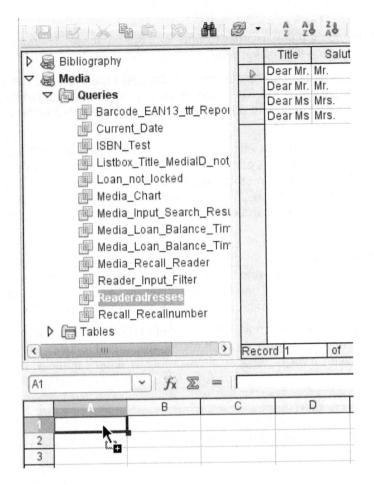

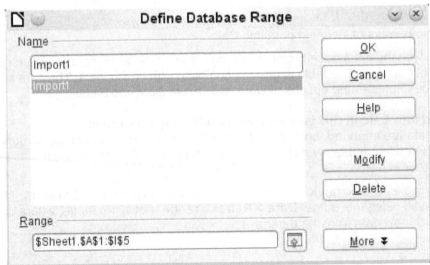

The imported data is not formatted except as the properties of the database fields require.

You can also use the context menu of a table to make a copy of the data. In this case, however, there is no import but merely a copy. The properties of the data fields are not read with them but are determined by Calc. In addition the field names are formatted as table headers.

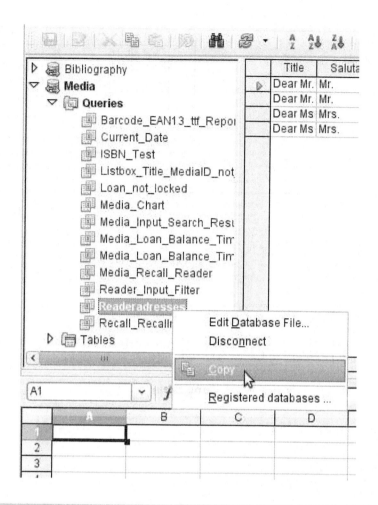

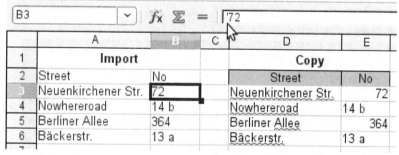

You see the difference especially in database fields that are formatted as text. On import, Calc turns these into text fields and precedes numbers, which would otherwise be interpreted as such, with a single quote (`'137`). These numbers can then no longer be used in calculations.

If you export them again, the single quote is removed, so that the data remain as they were.

Exporting data from Calc into a database

Select the data in the Calc worksheet. Hold the left mouse button down and drag the data that you want to turn into a database into the table area of the database browser.

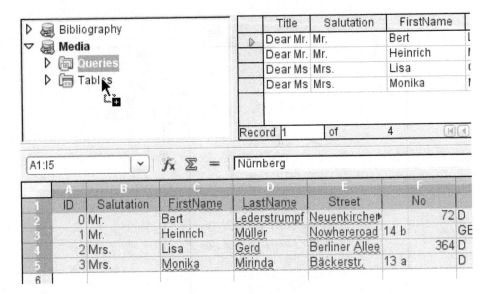

	Title	Salutation	FirstName	
▷	Dear Mr.	Mr.	Bert	L
	Dear Mr.	Mr.	Heinrich	I
	Dear Ms	Mrs.	Lisa	(
	Dear Ms	Mrs.	Monika	I

Record 1   of   4

A1:I5   *fx* Σ =   Nürnberg

	A	B	C	D	E	F	
1	ID	Salutation	FirstName	LastName	Street	No	
2	0	Mr.	Bert	Lederstrumpf	Neuenkirchen	72	D
3	1	Mr.	Heinrich	Müller	Nowhereroad	14 b	GE
4	2	Mrs.	Lisa	Gerd	Berliner Allee	364	D
5	3	Mrs.	Monika	Mirinda	Bäckerstr.	13 a	D
6							

The cursor changes its appearance, showing that something can be inserted.

The *Copy Table* dialog appears. In the above case a new table is created. The table name is "Names". *Definition and Data* are to be transferred. The first line contains the column headers.

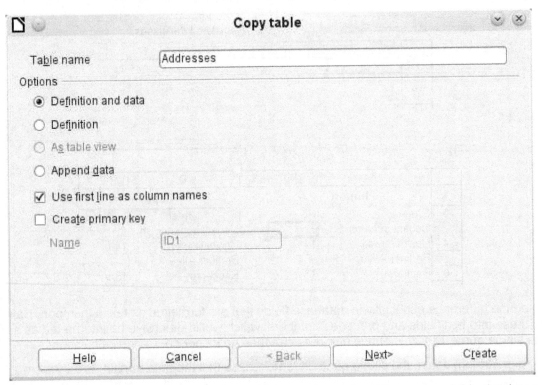

At this point you can create a new additional field for a primary key. The name of this database field must not be one that already exists as a column header in the Calc sheet. Otherwise you get the error message:

The following fields are already set as primary key: ID

Unfortunately this message does not describe the problem quite correctly.

If you want an existing field to be used as the key, do *not* check the *Create primary key* box. In such cases the primary key is set using the third dialog in the Wizard.

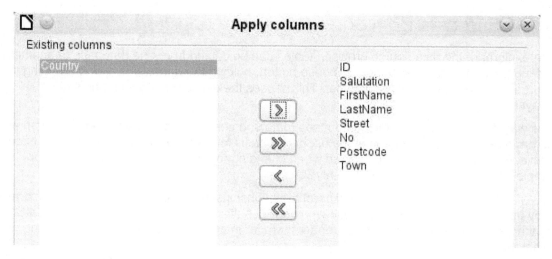

The appropriate fields are selected.

The formatting of the columns needs to be checked, especially for numeric fields. Other fields should also be checked for size. It just so happens that the test table contains only first names with a maximum length of 10 characters, so that it can become a field of type *Varchar* with a length of 10 characters.

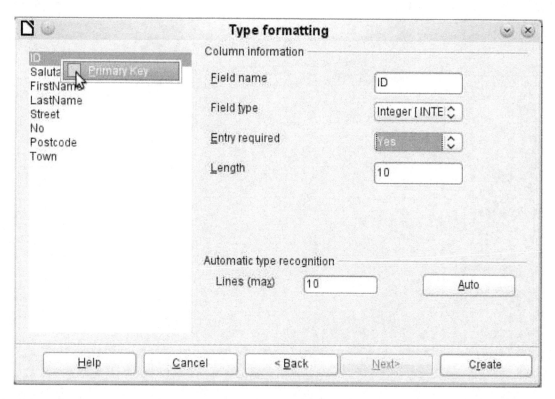

Here the ID field, which is to be the primary key, is formatted. The primary key must be set by using the context menu of its field name, in cases where it has not been created by the Wizard in the *Copy Table* dialog as an additional field. After you click the *Finish* button, the table is created.

The new primary key is not an *Auto-Value* key. To create such a key, you must open the database for editing. There you can carry out further formatting of the table.

Converting data from one database to another

In the explorer of the data source browser, tables can be copied from one database to another by selecting the source table with the left mouse button, holding the button down, and dragging it into the target database in the table container. This causes the dialog for copying tables to be displayed.

In this way, for example, read-only databases (data sources such as address books from an email program or a spreadsheet table) can be used as a basis for a database in which the data become editable. Also data can be directly copied when changing to another database program (for example changing from PostgreSQL to MySQL).

If you wish the new database to have different relationships from the original one, you can arrange this by using appropriate queries. Those who are not sufficiently expert can instead use Calc. Just drag the data into a spreadsheet and prepare them for import into the target database using the facilities that Calc provides.

For the cleanest possible import into a new database, the tables should be prepared in advance. This allows problems of formatting and those involving the creation of primary keys to be recognized well in advance.

Chapter 8
Database tasks

General remarks on database tasks

This chapter describes some solutions for problems that arise for many datsbase users.

Data filtering

Data filtering using the GUI is described in the chapter on data entry into tables. Here we describe a solution to a problem which many users have raised: how to use listboxes to search for the content of fields in tables, which then appear filtered in the underlying form section and can be edited.

The basis for this filtering is an editable query (see the chapter on queries) and an additional table, in which the data to be filtered are stored. The query shows from its underlying table only the records that correspond to the filter values. If no filter value is given, the query shows all records.

The following example starts from a **MediaExample** table that includes, among others, the following fields: **ID** (primary key), **Title**, **Category**. The field types are **INTEGER**, **VARCHAR**, and **VARCHAR** respectively.

First we require a **FilterExample** table. This table contains a primary key and 2 filter fields (of course you can have more if you want): **"ID"** (primary key), **Filter_1**, **Filter_2**. As the fields of the **MediaExample** table, which is to be filtered, are of the type **VARCHAR**, the fields **Filter_1** and **Filter_2** are also of this type. **ID** can be the smallest numeric type, **TINYINT** because the **Filter** table will never contain more than one record.

You can also filter fields that occur in the **MediaExample** table only as foreign keys. In that case, you must give the corresponding fields in the **FilterExample** table the type appropriate for the foreign keys, usually **INTEGER**.

The following query is certainly editable:

```
SELECT * FROM "MediaExample"
```

All records from the **MediaExample** table are displayed, including the primary key.

```
SELECT * FROM "MediaExample" WHERE "Title" = IFNULL( ( SELECT
"Filter_1" FROM "FilterExample" ), "Title" )
```

If the field **Filter_1** is not **NULL**, those records are displayed for which the **Title** is the same as **Filter_1**. If the field **Filter_1** is **NULL**, the value of the **Title** field is used instead. As **Title** is the same as **"Title"**, all records are displayed. This assumption does not hold however if the **Title** field of any record is empty (contains **NULL**). That means that those records will never be displayed that have no title entry. Therefore we need to improve the query:

```
SELECT * , IFNULL( "Title", '' ) AS "T" FROM "MediaExample" WHERE "T"
= IFNULL( ( SELECT "Filter_1" FROM "FilterExample" ), "T" )
```

Tip	**IFNULL(expression, value)** requires the **expression** has the same field type as the **value**. • If the **expression** has the field type **VARCHAR**, use two single quotes ` '' ` as the value. • If it has **DATE** as its field type, enter a date as the value that is not contained in the field of the table to be filtered. Use this format: **{D 'YYYY-MM-DD'}**. • If it is any of the numerical field types, use the **NUMERIC** field type for the value. Enter a number that does not appear in the field of the table to be filtered.

This variant will lead to the desired goal. Instead of filtering **Title** directly, a field is filtered which carries the alias **T**. This field has no content either but it is not **NULL**. In the conditions only the field **T** is considered. All records are therefore displayed even if **Title** is **NULL**.

Unfortunately you cannot do this using the GUI. This command is available only directly with SQL. To make it editable in the GUI, further modification is required:

```
SELECT "MediaExample".* , IFNULL( "MediaExample"."Title", '' ) AS "T"
FROM "MediaExample" WHERE "T" = IFNULL( ( SELECT "Filter_1" FROM
"FilterExample" ), "T" )
```

If the relationship of the table to the fields is now set up, the query becomes editable in the GUI.

As a test, you can put a title into **"Filter"."Filter_1"**. As **"Filter"."ID"** set the value **'0'**. The record is saved and the filtering can be comprehended. If **"Filter"."Filter_1"** is emptied, the GUI treats that as **NULL**. A new test yields a display of all the media. In any case, before a form is created and tested, just one record with a primary key should be entered into the **Filter** table. It must be only one record, since sub-queries as shown above can only transmit one value.

The query can now be enlarged to filter two fields:

```
SELECT "MediaExample".* , IFNULL( "MediaExample"."Title", '' ) AS "T",
IFNULL( "MediaExample"."Category", '' ) AS "K" FROM "MediaExample"
WHERE "T" = IFNULL( ( SELECT "Filter_1" FROM "FilterExample" ), "T" )
AND "K" = IFNULL( ( SELECT "Filter_2" FROM "FilterExample" ), "K" )
```

This concludes the creation of the editable query. Now for the basic query for the two listboxes:

```
SELECT DISTINCT "Title", "Title" FROM "MediaExample" ORDER BY "Title"
ASC
```

The listbox should show the **Title** and then also transmit that **Title** to the **Filter_1** field in the **Filter** table that underlies the form. Also no duplicate values should be shown (**'DISTINCT'** condition). And the whole thing should of course be sorted into the correct order.

A corresponding query is then created for the **Category** field, which is to write its data into the **Filter_2** field in the **Filter** table.

If one of these fields contains a foreign key, the query is adapted so that the foreign key is passed to the underlying **Filter** table.

The form consists of two parts. Form 1 is the form based on the **Filter** table. Form 2 is the form based on the query. Form 1 has **no navigation bar** and the cycle is set to **Current record**. In addition, the **Allow additions** property is set to **No**. The first and only record for this form already exists.

Form 1 contains two listboxes with appropriate labels. Listbox 1 returns values for **Filter_1** and is linked to the query for the **Title** field. Listbox 2 returns values for **Filter_2** and relates to the query for the **Category** field.

Form 2 contains a table control field, in which all fields from the query can be listed except for the fields **T** und **K**. The form would still work if these fields were present; they are omitted to avoid a confusing duplication of field contents. In addition form 2 contains a button, linked to the **Update form** function. An additional navigation bar can be built in to prevent screen flicker every time the form changes, due to the navigation bar being present in one form and not in the other.

Once the form is finished, the test phase begins. When a listbox is changed, the button on form 2 is used to store this value and update Form 2. This now relates to the value which the listbox provides. The filtering can be made retrospective by choosing an empty field in the listbox.

Searching for data

The main difference between searching for data and filtering data is in the query technique. The aim is to deliver, in response to free language search terms, a resulting list of records that may only partially contain these actual terms. First the similar approaches to the table and form are described.

The table for the search content may be the same one that already contains the filter values. The **Filter** table is simply expanded to include a field named **Searchterm**. So, if required, the same table can be accessed and, using the forms, simultaneously filtered and searched. **Searchterm** has the field type **VARCHAR**.

The form is built just as for filtering. Instead of a listbox, we need a text entry field for the search term, and also perhaps a label field with the title Search. The field for the search term can stand alone in the form or together with the fields for filtering, if both functions are desired.

The difference between filtering and searching lies in the query technique. While filtering uses a term that already occurs in the underlying table, searching uses arbitrary entries. (After all, the listbox is constructed from the table content.)

```
SELECT * FROM "MediaExample" WHERE "Title" = ( SELECT "Searchterm"
FROM "FilterExample" )
```

This query normally leads to an empty result list for these reasons:

8) When entering search terms , people seldom know completely and accurately what the title is. Therefore the correct title does not get displayed. To find the book "Per Anhalter through the Galaxy" it should be sufficient to put "Anhalter" into the Search field or even just "Anh".

9) If the field "Searchterm" is empty, only records are displayed in which there is no title. The field "Searchterm" is empty, the **Title** field must be empty also. This only happens in one of two possibilities: the item does not have a title, or someone did not enter its title.

The last condition can be removed if the filtering condition is:

```
SELECT * FROM "MediaExample" WHERE "Title" = IFNULL( ( SELECT
"Searchterm" FROM "FilterExample" ), "Title" )
```

With this refinement of the filtering (what happens if the title is **NULL**?) we get a result more in line with expectations. But the first condition is still not fulfilled. Searching should work well when only fragmentary knowledge is available. The query technique must therefore use the **LIKE** condition:

```
SELECT * FROM "MediaExample" WHERE "Title" LIKE ( SELECT '%' ||
"Searchterm" ||'%' FROM "FilterExample" )
```

or better still:

```
SELECT * FROM "MediaExample" WHERE "Title" LIKE IFNULL( ( SELECT '%'
|| "Searchterm" ||'%' FROM "FilterExample" ), "Title" )
```

LIKE, coupled with %, means that all records are displayed which have the search term anywhere within them. % is a wildcard for any number of characters before or after the search term. Various projects still remain after this version of the query has been built:

- It is common to use lower case letters for search terms. So how do I get a result if I type "anhalter" instead of "Anhalter"?

- What other conventions in writing need to be considered?

- What about fields that are not formatted as text fields? Can you search for dates or numbers with the same search field?

- And what if, as in the case of the filter, you want to prevent **NULL** values in the field from causing all the records to being displayed?

The following variant covers one or two of these possibilities:

```
SELECT * FROM "MediaExample" WHERE
LOWER("Title") LIKE IFNULL( ( SELECT '%' || LOWER("Searchterm") ||'%'
FROM "FilterExample" ), LOWER("Title") )
```

The condition changes the search term and the field content to lower case. This also allows whole sentences to be compared.

```
SELECT * FROM "MediaExample" WHERE
LOWER("Title") LIKE IFNULL( ( SELECT '%' || LOWER("Searchterm") ||'%'
FROM "FilterExample" ), LOWER("Title") ) OR
LOWER("Category") LIKE ( SELECT '%' || LOWER("Searchterm") ||'%' FROM
"FilterExample" )
```

The **IFNULL** function must occur only once, so that when the **Searchterm** is **NULL**, **LOWER("Title") LIKE LOWER("Title")** is queried. And as the title should be a field that cannot be **NULL**, in such cases all records are displayed. Of course, for multiple field searches, this code becomes correspondingly longer. In such cases it is better to use a macro, to allow the code to cover all the fields in one go.

But does the code still work with fields that are not text? Although the LIKE condition is really tailored to text, it also works for numbers, dates, and times without needing any alterations. So in fact text conversion need not take place. However, a time field that is a mixture of text and numbers cannot interact with the search results – unless the query is broadened, so that a single search term is subdivided across all the spaces between the text and numbers. This, however, will significantly bloat the query.

Code snippets

These code snippets come from queries to mailing lists. Particular problems arise that might perhaps be useful as solutions for your own database experiments.

Getting someone's current age

A query needs to calculate a person's actual age from a birth date. See also the functions in the appendix to this Base Handbook.

```
SELECT DATEDIFF('yy',"Birthdate",CURDATE()) AS "Age" FROM "Person"
```

This query gives the age as a difference in years. But, the age of a child born on 31 December 31 2011 would be given as 1 year on 1 January 2012. So we also need to consider the position of the day within the year. This is accessible using the **'DAYOFYEAR()'** function. Another function will carry out the comparison.

```
SELECT CASEWHEN
( DAYOFYEAR("Birthdate") > DAYOFYEAR(CURDATE()) ,
DATEDIFF ('yy',"Birthdate",CURDATE())-1,
DATEDIFF ('yy',"Birthdate",CURDATE()))
AS "Age" FROM "Person"
```

Now we get the correct current age in years.

CASEWHEN can also be used to make the text **Birthday today** appear in another field, if **DAYOFYEAR("Birthdate") = DAYOFYEAR(CURDATE())**.

A subtle objection might now arise: "What about leap years?". For persons born after 28 February, there will be an error of one day. Not a serious problem in everyday use, but should we not strive for accuracy?

```
CASEWHEN (
(MONTH("Birthdate") > MONTH(CURDATE())) OR
((MONTH("Birthdate") = MONTH(CURDATE())) AND (DAY("Birthdate") >
DAY(CURDATE()))) ,
DATEDIFF('yy',"Birthdate",CURDATE())-1,
DATEDIFF('yy',"Birthdate",CURDATE()))
```

The code above achieves this goal. As long as the month of the birth date is greater than the current month, the year difference function will subtract one year. Equally one year will be subtracted when the two months are the same, but the day of the month for the birth date is greater than the day in the current date. Unfortunately this formula is not comprehensible to the GUI. Only **'Direct SQL-Command'** will handle this query successfully and that would prevent our query from being edited. But the query needs to be editable, so here is how to trick the GUI:

```
CASE
WHEN MONTH("Birthdate") > MONTH(CURDATE())
THEN DATEDIFF('yy',"Birthdate",CURDATE())-1
WHEN (MONTH("Birthdate") = MONTH(CURDATE()) AND DAY("Birthdate") >
DAY(CURDATE()))
THEN DATEDIFF('yy',"Birthdate",CURDATE())-1
ELSE DATEDIFF('yy',"Birthdate",CURDATE())
END
```

With this formulation, the GUI no longer reacts with an error message. The age is now given accurately even in leap years and the query still remains editable.

Getting a running balance by categories

Instead of using a household book, a database on a PC can simplify the tiresome business of adding up expenses for food, clothing, transport and so on. We want most of these details to be immediately visible in the database, so our example assumes that income and expenditure will be stored as signed values in one field called Amount. In principle, the whole thing can be expanded to cover separate fields and a relevant summation for each.

```
SELECT "ID", "Amount", ( SELECT SUM( "Amount" ) FROM "Cash" WHERE "ID"
<= "a"."ID" ) AS "Balance" FROM "Cash" AS "a" ORDER BY "ID" ASC
```

This query causes for each new record a direct calculation of the current account balance. At the same time the query remains editable because the "Balance" field is created through a correlating sub-query. The query depends on the automatically created primary key "ID" to calculate the state of the account. However balances are usually calculated on a daily basis. So we need a date query.

```
SELECT "ID", "Date", "Amount", ( SELECT SUM( "Amount" ) FROM "Cash"
WHERE "Date" <= "a"."Date" ) AS "Balance" FROM "Cash" AS "a" ORDER BY
"Date", "ID" ASC
```

The expenditure now appears sorted and summed by date. There still remains the question of the category, since we want corresponding balances for the individual categories of expenditure.

```
SELECT "ID", "Date", "Amount", "Acct_ID",
( SELECT "Acct" FROM "Acct" WHERE "ID" = "a"."Acct_ID" ) AS
"Acct_name",
( SELECT SUM( "Amount" ) FROM "Cash" WHERE "Date" <= "a"."Date" AND
"Acct_ID" = "a"."Acct_ID" ) AS "Balance",
( SELECT SUM( "Amount" ) FROM "Cash" WHERE "Date" <= "a"."Date" ) AS
"Total_balance"
FROM "Cash" AS "a" ORDER BY "Date", "ID" ASC
```

This creates an editable query in which, in addition to the entry fields (Date, Amount, Acct_ID), the account name, the relevant balance, and the total balance appear together. As the correlating subqueries are partially based on previous entries ("Date" <= "a"."Date") only new entries will go through smoothly. Alterations to a previous record are initially detectable only in that record. The query must be updated if later calculations dependent on it are to be carried out.

Line numbering

Automatically incrementing fields are fine. However, they do not tell you definitely how many records are present in the database or are actually available to be queried. Records are often deleted and many users try in vain to determine which numbers are no longer present in order to make the running number match up.

```
SELECT "ID", ( SELECT COUNT( "ID" ) FROM "Table" WHERE "ID" <=
"a"."ID" ) AS "Nr." FROM "Table" AS "a"
```

The ID field is read, and the second field is determined by a correlating sub-query, which seeks to determine how many field values in ID are smaller than or equal to the current field value. From this a running line number is created.

Each record to which you want to apply this query contains fields. To apply this query to the records, you must first add these fields to the query. You can place them in whatever order you desire in the **SELECT** clause. If you have the records in a form, you need to modify the form so that the data for the form comes from this query.

For example the record contains field1, field2, and field3. The complete query would be:

```
SELECT "ID", "field1", "field2", "field3", ( SELECT COUNT( "ID" ) FROM
"Table" WHERE "ID" <= "a"."ID" ) AS "Nr." FROM "Table" AS "a"
```

A numbering for a corresponding grouping is also possible:

```
SELECT "ID", "Calculation", ( SELECT COUNT( "ID" ) FROM "Table" WHERE
"ID" <= "a"."ID" AND "Calculation" = "a"."Calculation" ) AS "Nr." FROM
"Table" AS "a" ORDER BY "ID" ASC, "Nr." ASC
```

Here one table contains different calculated numbers. ("Calculation"). For each calculated number, **"Nr."** is separately expressed in ascending order after sorting on the ID field. This produces a numbering from 1 upwards.

If the actual sort order within the query is to agree with the line numbers, an appropriate type of sorting must be mapped out. For this purpose the sort field must have a unique value in all records. Otherwise two place numbers will have the same value. This can actually be useful if, for example, the place order in a competition is to be depicted, since identical results will then lead to a joint position. In order for the place order to be expressed in such a way that, in case of joint positions, the next value is omitted, the query needs to be be constructed somewhat differently:

```
SELECT "ID", ( SELECT COUNT( "ID" ) + 1 FROM "Table" WHERE "Time" <
"a"."Time" ) AS "Place" FROM "Table" AS "a"
```

All entries are evaluated for which the "Time" field has a smaller value. That covers all athletes who reached the winning post before the current athlete. To this value is added the number 1. This determines the place of the current athlete. If the time is identical with that of another athlete, they are placed jointly. This makes possible place orders such as 1st Place, 2nd Place, 2nd Place, 4. Place.

It would be more problematic, if line numbers were required as well as a place order. That might be useful if several records needed to be combined in one line.

```
SELECT "ID", ( SELECT COUNT( "ID" ) + 1 FROM "Table" WHERE "Time" <
"a"."Time" ) AS "Place",
CASE WHEN
( SELECT COUNT( "ID" ) + 1 FROM "Table" WHERE "Time" = "a"."Time" ) = 1
```

```
THEN ( SELECT COUNT( "ID" ) + 1 FROM "Table" WHERE "Time" < "a"."Time" )
ELSE (SELECT ( SELECT COUNT( "ID" ) + 1 FROM "Table" WHERE "Time" <
"a"."Time" ) + COUNT( "ID" ) FROM "Table" WHERE "Time" = "a"."Time" "ID"
< "a"."ID"
END
AS "LineNumber" FROM "Table" AS "a"
```

The second column still gives the place order. The third column checks first if only one person crossed the line with this time. If so, the place order is converted directly into a line number. Otherwise a further value is added to the place order. For the same time (**"Time" = "a"."Time"**) at least 1 is added, if there is a further person with the primary key ID, whose primary key is smaller than the primary key in the current record (**"ID" < "a"."ID"**). This query therefore yields identical values for the place order so long as no second person with the same time exists. If a second person with the same time does exist, the ID determines which person has the lesser line number.

Incidentally, this sorting by line number can serve whatever purpose the users of the database want. For example, if a series of records are sorted by name, records with the same name are not sorted randomly but according to their primary key, which is of course unique. In this way too, numbering can lead to a sorting of records.

Line numbering is also a good prelude to the combining of individual records into a single record. If a line-numbering query is created as a view, a further query can be applied to it without creating any problem. As a simple example here once more is the first numbering query with one extra field:

```
SELECT "ID", "Name", ( SELECT COUNT( "ID" ) FROM "Table" WHERE "ID" <=
"a"."ID" ) AS "Nr." FROM "Table" AS "a"
```

This query is turned into the view 'View1'. The query can be used, for example, to put the first three names together in one line:

```
SELECT "Name" AS "Name_1", ( SELECT "Name" FROM "View1" WHERE "Nr." =
2 ) AS "Name_2", ( SELECT "Name" FROM "View1" WHERE "Nr." = 3 ) AS
"Name_3" FROM "View1"  WHERE "Nr." = 1
```

In this way several records can be converted into adjacent fields. This numbering simply runs from the first to the last record.

If all these individuals are to be assigned the same surname, this can be carried out as follows:

```
SELECT "ID", "Name", "Surname", ( SELECT COUNT( "ID" ) FROM "Table"
WHERE "ID" <= "a"."ID" AND "Surname" = "a"."Surname") AS "Nr." FROM
"Table" AS "a"
```

Now that the view has been created, the family can be assembled.

```
SELECT "Surname", "Name" AS "Name_1", ( SELECT "Name" FROM "View1"
WHERE "Nr." = 2  AND "Surname" = "a"."Surname") AS "Name_2", ( SELECT
"Name" FROM "View1" WHERE "Nr." = 3  AND "Surname" = "a"."Surname") AS
"Name_3" FROM "View1" AS "a" WHERE "Nr." = 1
```

In this way, in an address book, all members of one family ("Surname") can be collected together so that each address need be considered only once when sending a letter, but everyone who should receive the letter is listed.

We need to be careful here, as we do not want an endlessly looping function. The query in the above example limits the parallel records that are to be converted into fields to 3. This limit was chosen deliberately. No further names will appear even if the value of *"Nr."* is greater than 3.

In a few cases such a limit is clearly understandable. For example, if we are creating a calendar, the lines might represent the weeks of the year and the columns the weekdays. As in the original calendar only the date determines the field content, line numbering is used to number the days of each week continuously and then the weeks in the year become the records. This does require that the table contains a date field with continuous dates and a field for the events. Also the earliest date will always create an "Nr." = 1. So, if you want the calendar to begin on Monday, the earliest date must be on Monday. Column 1 is then Monday, column 2 Tuesday and so on. The subquery then ends at *"Nr."* = 7. In this way all seven days of the week can be shown alongside each other and a corresponding calendar view created.

Getting a line break through a query

Sometimes it is useful to assemble several fields using a query and separate them by line breaks, for example when reading a complete address into a report.

The line break within the query is represented by **'Char(13)'**. Example:

```
SELECT "Firstname"||' '||"Surname"||Char(13)||"Road"||Char(13)||"Town"
FROM "Table"
```

This yields:

```
Firstname Surname
Road
Town
```

Such a query, with a line numbering up to 3, allows you to print address labels in three columns by creating a report. The numbering is necessary in this connection so that three addresses can be placed next to one another in one record. That is the only way they will remain next to each other when read into the report.

Grouping and summarizing

For other databases, and for newer versions of HSQLDB, the **Group_Concat()** command is available. It can be used to group individual fields in a record into one field. So, for example, it is possible to store first names and surnames in one table, then to present the data in such a way that one field shows the surnames as family names while a second field contains all the relevant first names sequentially, separated by commas.

This example is similar in many ways to line numbering. The grouping into a common field is a kind of supplement to this.

Surname	Firstname
Müller	Karin
Schneider	Gerd
Müller	Egon
Schneider	Volker
Müller	Monika
Müller	Rita

is converted by the query to:

Surname	Firstnames
Müller	Karin, Egon, Monika, Rita
Schneider	Gerd, Volker

This procedure can, within limits, be expressed in HSQLDB. The following example refers to a table called Name with the fields ID, Firstname and Surname. The following query is first run on the table and saved as a view called View_Group.

```
SELECT "Surname", "Firstname", ( SELECT COUNT( "ID" ) FROM "Name"
WHERE "ID" <= "a"."ID" AND "Surname" = "a"."Surname" ) AS "GroupNr"
FROM "Name" AS "a"
```

You can read in the Queries chapter how this query accesses the field content in the same query line. It yields an ascending numbered sequence, grouped by *Surname*. This numbering is necessary for the following query, so that in the example a maximum of 5 first names is listed.

```
SELECT "Surname",
( SELECT "Firstname" FROM "View_Group" WHERE "Surname" = "a"."Surname"
AND "GroupNr" = 1 ) ||
IFNULL( ( SELECT ', ' || "Firstname" FROM "View_Group" WHERE "Surname"
= "a"."Surname" AND "GroupNr" = 2 ), '' ) ||
IFNULL( ( SELECT ', ' || "Firstname" FROM "View_Group" WHERE "Surname"
= "a"."Surname" AND "GroupNr" = 3 ), '' ) ||
IFNULL( ( SELECT ', ' || "Firstname" FROM "View_Group" WHERE "Surname"
= "a"."Surname" AND "GroupNr" = 4 ), '' ) ||
IFNULL( ( SELECT ', ' || "Firstname" FROM "View_Group" WHERE "Surname"
= "a"."Surname" AND "GroupNr" = 5 ), '' )
AS "Firstnames"
FROM "View_Group" AS "a"
```

Using sub-queries, the first names of the group members are searched for one after another and combined. From the second sub-query onward you must ensure that **'NULL'** values do not set the whole combination to **'NULL'**. That is why a result of **''** rather than **'NULL'** is shown.

Chapter 9
Macros

In principle a database in Base can manage without macros. At times, however, they may become necessary for:

- More effective prevention of input errors
- Simplifying certain processing tasks (changing from one form to another, updating data after input into a form, and so on)
- Allowing certain SQL commands to be called up more easily than with the separate SQL editor.

You must decide for yourself how intensively you wish to use macros in Base. Macros can improve usability but are always associated with small reductions in the speed of the program, and sometimes with larger ones (when coded poorly). It is always better to start off by fully utilizing the possibilities of the database and the provisions for configuring forms before trying to provide additional functionality with macros. Macros should always be tested on larger databases to determine their effect on performance.

Macros are created using **Tools > Macros > Organize macros > LibreOffice Basic**. A window appears which provides access to all macros. For Base, the important area corresponds to the filename of the Base file.

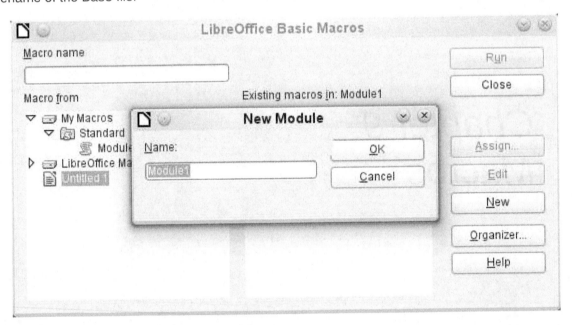

The **New** button in the LibreOffice Basic Macros dialog opens the New Module dialog, which asks for the module name (the folder in which the macro will be filed). The name can be altered later if desired.

As soon as this is given, the macro editor appears. Its input area already contains the Start and the End for a subroutine:

```
REM  *****  BASIC  *****

Sub Main

End Sub
```

If macros are to be usable, the following steps are necessary:

- Under **Tools > Options > Security > Macro security** the security level should be reduced to Medium. If necessary you can additionally use the Trusted sources tab to set the path to your own macro files to prevent later queries about the activation of macros.
- The database file must be closed and then reopened after the creation of the first macro module.

Some basic principles for the use of Basic code in LibreOffice:

- Lines have no line numbers and must end with a hard return.
- Functions, reserved expressions, and similar elements are not case-sensitive. So "String" is the same as "STRING" or "string" or any other combination of upper and lower case. Case should be used only to improve legibility. Names for constants and enumerations, however, are case sensitive the first time that they are seen by the macro compiler, so it is best to always write those using the proper case.
- There is a basic difference between subroutines (beginning with SUB) and functions (beginning with FUNCTION). Subroutines are program segments without return values. Functions return a value.

For further details see Chapter 13, Getting Started with Macros, in the *Getting Started* guide.

Note	Macros in the PDF and ODT versions of this chapter are colored according to the rules of the LibreOffice macro editor:
	
	`Macro designation`
	`Macro comment`
	`Macro operator`
	`Macro reserved expression`
	`Macro number`
	`Macro character string`

Improving usability

For this first category of macro use, we show various possibilities for improving the usability of Base forms.

Automatic updating of forms

Often something is altered in a form and this alteration is required to appear in a second form on the same page. The following code snippet calls the reload method on the second form, causing it to refresh.

```
SUB Update
```

First the macro is named. The default designation for a macro is **SUB**. This may be written in upper or lower case. **SUB** allows a subroutine to run without returning a value. Further down by contrast a function is described, which does return a value.

The macro has the name *Update*. You do not need to declare variables because LibreOffice Basic automatically creates variables when they are used. Unfortunately, if you misspell a variable, LibreOffice Basic silently creates a new variable without complaint. Use **Option Explicit** To prevent LibreoOffice Basic from automatically creating variables; this is recommended by most programmers.

Therefore we usually start by declaring variables. All the variables declared here are objects (not numbers or text), so we add **AS OBJECT** to the end of the declaration. To remind us later of the type of the variables, we preface their names with an "o". In principle, though, you can choose almost any variable names you like.

```
DIM oDoc AS OBJECT
DIM oDrawpage AS OBJECT
DIM oForm AS OBJECT
```

The form lies in the currently active document. The container, in which all forms are stored, is named **drawpage**. In the form navigator this is the top-level concept, to which all the forms are subsidiary.

In this example, the form to be accessed is named Display. Display is the name visible in the form navigator. So, for example, the first form by default is called Form1.

```
oDoc = thisComponent
oDrawpage = oDoc.drawpage
oForm = oDrawpage.forms.getByName("Display")
```

Since the form has now been made accessible and the point at which it can be accessed is saved in the variable **oForm**, it is now reloaded (refreshed) with the **reload()** command.

```
    oForm.reload()
END SUB
```

The subroutine begins with **SUB** so it must end with **END SUB**.

This macro can now be selected to run when another form is saved. For example, on a cash register (till), if the total number of items sold and their stock numbers (read by a barcode scanner) are entered into one form, another form in the same open window can show the names of all the items, and the total cost, as soon as the form is saved.

Filtering records

The filter itself can function perfectly well in the form described in Chapter 8, Database Tasks. The variant shown below replaces the Save button and reads the listboxes again, so that a chosen filter from one listbox can restrict the choices available in the other listbox.

```
SUB Filter
    DIM oDoc AS OBJECT
    DIM oDrawpage AS OBJECT
    DIM oForm1 AS OBJECT
    DIM oForm2 AS OBJECT
    DIM oFieldList1 AS OBJECT
    DIM oFieldList2 AS OBJECT
    oDoc = thisComponent
    oDrawpage = oDoc.drawpage
```

First the variables are defined and set to access the set of forms. This set comprises the two forms "Filter" and "Display". The listboxes are in the "Filter" form and have the names "List_1" and "List_2".

```
    oForm1 = oDrawpage.forms.getByName("Filter")
    oForm2 = oDrawpage.forms.getByName("Display")
    oFieldList1 = oForm1.getByName("List_1")
    oFieldList2 = oForm1.getByName("List_2")
```

First the contents of the listboxes are transferred to the underlying form using **commit()**. The transfer is necessary, because otherwise the change in a listbox will not be recognized when saving. The **commit()** instruction need only be applied to the listbox that has just been accessed. After that the record is saved using **updateRow()**. In principle, our filter table contains only one record, which is written once at the beginning. This record is therefore overwritten continuously using an update command.

```
oFieldList1.commit()
oFieldList2.commit()
oForm1.updateRow()
```

The listboxes are meant to influence each other. For example, if one listbox is used to restrict displayed media to CDs, the other listbox should not include all the writers of books in its list of authors. A selection in the second listbox would then all too often result in an empty filter. That is why the listboxes must be read again. Strictly speaking, the **refresh()** command only needs to be carried out on the listbox that has not been accessed.

After this, form2, which should display the filtered content, is read in again.

```
oFieldList1.refresh()
oFieldList2.refresh()
oForm2.reload()
END SUB
```

Listboxes that are to be influenced using this method can be supplied with content using various queries.

The simplest variant is to have the listbox take its content from the filter results. Then a single filter determines which data content will be further filtered.

```
SELECT "Field_1" || ' - ' || "Count" AS "Display", "Field_1"
FROM ( SELECT COUNT( "ID" ) AS "Count", "Field_1" FROM
"Table_Filter_result" GROUP BY "Field_1" )
ORDER BY "Field_1"
```

The field content and the number of hits is displayed. To get the number of hits, a sub-query is used. This is necessary as otherwise only the number of hits, without further information from the field, will be shown in the listbox.

The macro creates listboxes quite quickly by this action; they are filled with only one value. If a listbox is not NULL, it is taken into account by the filtering. After activation of the second listbox, only the empty fields and one displayed value are available to both listboxes. That may seem practical for a limited search. But what if a library catalog shows clearly the classification for an item, but does not show uniquely if this is a book, a CD or a DVD? If the classification is chosen first and the second listbox is then set to "CD", it must be reset to NULL in order to carry out a subsequent search that includes books. It would be more practical if the second listbox showed directly the various media types available, with the corresponding hit counts.

To achieve this aim, the following query is constructed, which is no longer fed directly from the filter results. The number of hits must be obtained in a different way.

```
SELECT
IFNULL( "Field_1" || ' - ' || "Count", 'empty - ' || "Count" ) AS
"Display",
"Field_1"
FROM
( SELECT COUNT( "ID" ) AS "Count", "Field_1" FROM "Table" WHERE "ID"
IN
( SELECT "Table"."ID" FROM "Filter", "Table" WHERE "Table"."Field_2" =
IFNULL( "Filter"."Filter_2", "Table"."Field_2" ) )
GROUP BY "Field_1" )
ORDER BY "Field_1"
```

This very complex query can be broken down. In practice it is common to use a **VIEW** for the sub-query. The listbox receives its content from a query relating to this **VIEW.**

The query in detail: The query presents two columns. The first column contains the view seen by a person who has the form open. This view shows the content of the field and, separated by a hyphen, the hits for this field content. The second column transfers its content to the underlying table of the form. Here we have only the content of the field. The listboxes thus draw their content from the query, which is presented as the filter result in the form. Only these fields are available for further filtering.

The table from which this information is drawn is actually a query. In this query the primary key fields are counted (**SELECT COUNT("ID") AS "Count"**). This is then grouped by the search term in the field (**GROUP BY "Field_1"**). This query presents the term in the field itself as the second column. This query in turn is based on a further sub-query:

```
SELECT "Table"."ID" FROM "Filter", "Table" WHERE "Table"."Field_2" =
IFNULL( "Filter"."Filter_2", "Table"."Field_2" )
```

This sub-query deals with the other field to be filtered. In principle, this other field must also match the primary key. If there are further filters, this query can be extended:

```
SELECT "Table"."ID" FROM "Filter", "Table" WHERE
"Table"."Field_2" = IFNULL( "Filter"."Filter_2", "Table"."Field_2" )
AND
"Table"."Field_3" = IFNULL( "Filter"."Filter_3", "Table"."Field_3" )
```

This allows any further fields that are to be filtered to control what finally appears in the listbox of the first field, "Field_1".

Finally the whole query is sorted by the underlying field.

What the final query underlying the displayed form, actually looks like, can be seen from Chapter 8, Database Tasks.

The following macro can control through a listbox which listboxes must be saved and which must be read in again.

The following subroutine assumes that the "Additional information" property for each listbox contains a comma-separated list of all listbox names with no spaces. The first name in the list must be the name of that listbox.

```
SUB Filter_more_info(oEvent AS OBJECT)
    DIM oDoc AS OBJECT
    DIM oDrawpage AS OBJECT
    DIM oForm1 AS OBJECT
    DIM oForm2 AS OBJECT
    DIM oFieldList1 AS OBJECT
    DIM oFieldList2 AS OBJECT
    DIM sTag AS String
    sTag = oEvent.Source.Model.Tag
```

An array (a collection of data accessible via an index number) is established and filled with the field names of the listboxes. The first name in the list is the name of the listbox linked to the event.

```
    aList() = Split(sTag, ",")
    oDoc = thisComponent
    oDrawpage = oDoc.drawpage
    oForm1 = oDrawpage.forms.getByName("Filter")
    oForm2 = oDrawpage.forms.getByName("Display")
```

The array is run through from its lower bound (**'Lbound()'**) to its upper bound (**'Ubound()'**) in a single loop. All values which were separated by commas in the additional information, are now transferred successively.

```
    FOR i = LBound(aList()) TO UBound(aList())
        IF i = 0 THEN
```

The listbox that triggered the macro must be saved. It is found in the variable **aList(0)**. First the information for the listbox is carried across to the underlying table, and then the record is saved.

```
            oForm1.getByName(aList(i)).commit()
            oForm1.updateRow()
        ELSE
```

The other listboxes must be refreshed, as they now contain different values depending on the first listbox.

```
            oForm1.getByName(aList(i)).refresh()
      END IF
   NEXT
   oForm2.reload()
END SUB
```

The queries for this more usable macro are naturally the same as those already presented in the previous section.

Searching data records

You can search database records without using a macro. However, the corresponding query that must be set up can be very complicated. A macro can solve this problem with a loop.

The following subroutine reads the fields in a table, creates a query internally, and finally writes a list of primary key numbers of records in the table that are retrieved by this search term. In the following description, there is a table called Searchtmp, which consists of an auto-incrementing primary key field (ID) and a field called Nr. that contains all the primary keys retrieved from the table being searched. The table name is supplied initially to the subroutine as a variable.

To get a correct result, the table must contain the content you are searching for as text and not as foreign keys. If necessary, you can create a VIEW for the macro to use.

```
SUB Search(stTable AS STRING)
   DIM oDataSource AS OBJECT
   DIM oConnection AS OBJECT
   DIM oSQL_Statement AS OBJECT
   DIM stSql AS STRING
   DIM oQuery_Result AS OBJECT
   DIM oDoc AS OBJECT
   DIM oDrawpage AS OBJECT
   DIM oForm AS OBJECT
   DIM oForm2 AS OBJECT
   DIM oField AS OBJECT
   DIM stContent AS STRING
   DIM arContent() AS STRING
   DIM inI AS INTEGER
   DIM inK AS INTEGER
   oDoc = thisComponent
   oDrawpage = oDoc.drawpage
   oForm = oDrawpage.forms.getByName("Searchform")
   oField = oForm.getByName("Searchtext")
   stContent = oField.getCurrentValue()
   stContent = LCase(stContent)
```

The content of the search text field is initially converted into lower case so that the subsequent search function need only compare lower case spellings.

```
   oDataSource = ThisComponent.Parent.DataSource
   oConnection = oDataSource.GetConnection("","")
   oSQL_Statement = oConnection.createStatement()
```

First it must be determined if a search term has actually been entered. If the field is empty, it will be assumed that no search is required. All records will be displayed without further searching.

If a search term has been entered, the column names are read from the table being searched, so that the query can access the fields.

```
   IF stContent <> "" THEN
```

```
    stSql = "SELECT ""COLUMN_NAME"" FROM
""INFORMATION_SCHEMA"".""SYSTEM_COLUMNS"" WHERE ""TABLE_NAME"" = '" + stTable
+ "' ORDER BY ""ORDINAL_POSITION"""
    oQuery_Result = oSQL_Statement.executeQuery(stSql)
```

Note	SQL formulas in macros must first be placed in double quotes like normal character strings. Field names and table names are already in double quotes inside the SQL formula. To create final code that transmits the double quotes properly, field names and table names must be given two sets of these quotes.

```
    stSql = "SELECT ""Name"" FROM ""Table"";"
```

becomes, when displayed with the command `msgbox stSql`,

SELECT "Name" FROM "Table"

The index of the array, in which the field names are written is initially set to 0. Then the query begins to be read out. As the size of the array is unknown, it must be adjusted continuously. That is why the loop begins with **'ReDim Preserve arContent(inI)'** to set the size of the array and at the same time to preserve its existing contents. Next the fields are read and the array index incremented by 1. Then the array is dimensioned again and a further value can be stored.

```
    InI = 0
    IF NOT ISNULL(oQuery_Result) THEN
        WHILE oQuery_result.next
            ReDim Preserve arContent(inI)
            arContent(inI) = oQuery_Result.getString(1)
            inI = inI + 1
        WEND
    END IF
    stSql = "DROP TABLE ""Searchtmp"" IF EXISTS"
    oSQL_Statement.executeUpdate (stSql)
```

Now the query is put together within a loop and subsequently applied to the table defined at the beginning. All case combinations are allowed for, since the content of the field in the query is converted to lower case.

The query is constructed such that the results end up in the Searchtmp table. It is assumed that the primary key is the first field in the table (**arContent(0)**).

```
    stSql = "SELECT """+arContent(0)+""" INTO ""Searchtmp"" FROM """ + stTable
    + """ WHERE "
    FOR inK = 0 TO (inI - 1)
        stSql = stSql+"LCase("""+arContent(inK)+""") LIKE '%"+stContent+"%'"
        IF inK < (inI - 1) THEN
            stSql = stSql+" OR "
        END IF
    NEXT
    oSQL_Statement.executeQuery(stSql)
ELSE
    stSql = "DELETE FROM ""Searchtmp"""
    oSQL_Statement.executeUpdate (stSql)
END IF
```

The display form must be reloaded. Its data source is a query, in this example Searchquery.

```
    oForm2 = oDrawpage.forms.getByName("Display")
    oForm2.reload()
End Sub
```

This creates a table that is to be evaluated by the query. As far as possible, the query should be constructed so that it can subsequently be edited. A sample query is shown:

```
SELECT * FROM "Searchtable" WHERE "Nr." IN ( SELECT "Nr." FROM
"Searchtmp" ) OR "Nr." = CASE WHEN ( SELECT COUNT( "Nr." ) FROM
"Searchtmp" ) > 0 THEN '0' ELSE "Nr." END
```

All elements of the **Searchtable** are included, including the primary key. No other table appears in the direct query; therefore no primary key from another table is needed and the query result remains editable.

The primary key is saved in this example under the name **Nr.** The macro reads precisely this field. There is an initial check to see if the content of the **Nr.** field appears in the **Searchtmp** table. The **IN** operator is compatible with multiple values. The sub-query can also yield several records.

For larger amounts of data, value matching by using the **IN** operator quickly slows down. Therefore it is not a good idea to use an empty search field simply to transfer all primary key fields from **Searchtable** into the **Searchtmp** table and then view the data in the same way. Instead an empty search field creates an empty **Searchtmp** table, so that no records are available. This is the purpose of the second half of the condition:

```
OR "Nr." = CASE WHEN ( SELECT COUNT( "Nr." ) FROM "Searchtmp" ) > 0
THEN '-1' ELSE "Nr." END
```

If a record is found in the Searchtmp table, it means that the result of the first query is greater than 0. In this case: **"Nr." = '-1'** (here we need a number which cannot occur as a primary key, so **'-1'**is a good value). If the query yields precisely 0 (which will be the case if no records are present), then **"Nr." = "Nr."**. This will list every record which has a **Nr.** As **Nr.** is the primary key, this means all records.

Comboboxes as listboxes with an entry option

A table with a single record can be directly created by using comboboxes and invisible numeric fields and the corresponding primary key entered into another table.

In previous versions of LibreOffice or OpenOffice.org, it was necessary to make the numeric fields invisible by using a macro. This is no longer necessary in LibreOffice as the 'visible' property is now contained in the GUI.

The Combobox control treats form fields for combined entry and choice of values (comboboxes) as listboxes with an entry option. For this purpose, in addition to the comboboxes in the form, the key field values which are to be transferred to the underlying table are stored in separate numeric fields. These fields, prior to OpenOffice.org 3.3, had to have the 'invisible' switch set, as the function was not accessible from form design. This is no longer necessary in LibreOffice and OpenOffice.org 3.3. Fields can now be declared as invisible. The keys from these fields are read in when the form is loaded and the combobox is set to show the corresponding content. If the content of the combobox is changed, it is saved and the new primary key is transferred into the corresponding numeric field to be stored in the main table.

The original of this module is in the example database, as expanded with macros.

Text display in comboboxes

This subroutine is to show text in the combobox according to the value of the invisible foreign key fields from the main form. It can also be used for listboxes which refer to two different tables. This might happen if, for example, the postcode in a postal address is stored separately from the town. In that case the postcode might be read from a table that contains only a foreign key for the town. The listbox should show postcode and town together.

```
SUB TextDisplay(NameForm AS STRING, NameSubform AS STRING, NameSubSubform AS
STRING, NameField AS STRING, NameIDField AS STRING, NameTableField1 AS
STRING, NameTableField2 AS STRING, Fieldseparator AS STRING, NameTable1 AS
```

```
STRING, OPTIONAL NameTable2 AS STRING, OPTIONAL NameTab12ID AS STRING,
OPTIONAL Position AS INTEGER )
```

This macro should be bound to the following form events: 'When loading' and 'After record change'.

The following parameters are optional and need not be given when the subroutine is called. To prevent a runtime error, default values must be predefined.

```
IF isMissing(NameTable2) THEN NameTable2 = ""
IF isMissing(NameTab12ID) THEN NameTab12ID = ""
IF isMissing(Position) THEN Position = 2
```

The **IF** condition here is only one line, so it does **not** require an **END IF**.

After this, the variables are declared. Some variables have already been declared globally in a separate module and are not declared here again.

```
DIM oForm AS OBJECT
DIM oSubForm AS OBJECT
DIM oSubSubForm AS OBJECT
DIM oField AS OBJECT
DIM oFieldList AS OBJECT
DIM stFieldValue AS STRING
DIM inID AS INTEGER
DIM oCtlView AS OBJECT
oDoc = thisComponent
oDrawpage = oDoc.Drawpage
oForm = oDrawpage.forms.getByName(NameForm)
```

The position of the field in the corresponding form is determined. All forms are held on the **Drawpage** of the current document **thisComponent**. This subroutine uses arguments to cover the possibility that the field is contained in a subform of a subform, that is two levels down from the actual form. The field that contains the foreign key is named **oField**. The combobox, which now exists instead of a listbox is named **oFieldList**.

```
IF NameSubform <> "" THEN
    oSubForm = oForm.getByName(NameSubform)
    IF NameSubSubform <> "" THEN
        oSubSubForm = oSubForm.getByName(NameSubSubform)
        oField = oSubSubForm.getByName(NameIDField)
        oFieldList = oSubSubForm.getByName(NameField)
    ELSE
        oField = oSubForm.getByName(NameIDField)
        oFieldList = oSubForm.getByName(NameField)
    END IF
ELSE
    oField = oForm.getByName(NameIDField)
    oFieldList = oForm.getByName(NameField)
END IF
oFieldList.Refresh()
```

The combobox is read in again using **Refresh()**. It might be that the content of the field has been changed by the entry of new data. This must be made possible.

After this, the value of the foreign key is read. Only if a value is entered here will a connection be made to the data source.

```
IF NOT IsEmpty(oField.getCurrentValue()) THEN
    inID = oField.getCurrentValue()
    oDataSource = ThisComponent.Parent.CurrentController
    IF NOT (oDataSource.isConnected()) Then
        oDataSource.connect()
    End IF
    oConnection = oDataSource.ActiveConnection()
```

```
        oSQL_Statement = oConnection.createStatement()
```

The SQL statement is formulated according to the fields used in the combobox. This requires the testing of various combinations. The most general is that the combobox must be provided with a query that refers to two table fields from different tables. This subroutine is not designed for further possibilities. The test begins with this most important possibility.

```
        IF NameTableField2 <> "" THEN
```

If a second table field exists,

```
        IF NameTable2 <> "" THEN
```

... and if a second table exists, the following SQL code will be produced:

```
    IF Position = 2 THEN
        stSql = "SELECT """ + NameTable1 + """.""" + NameTableField1 + """'||'" +
    Fieldseparator + "'||""" + NameTable2 + """.""" + NameTablenField2 + """ FROM
    """ + NameTable1 + """,""" + NameTable2 + """ WHERE ""ID""'='" +inID+ "' AND
    """ + NameTable1 + """.""" + NameTab12ID + """'=""" + NameTable2 + """.""ID"""
    ELSE
        stSql = "SELECT """ + NameTable2 + """.""" + NameTableField2 + """'||'" +
    Fieldseparator + "'||""" + NameTable1 + """.""" + NameTableField1 + """ FROM
    """ + NameTable1 + """,""" + NameTable2 + """ WHERE ""ID""'='" + inID + "' AND
    """ + NameTable1 + """.""" + NameTab12ID + """'=""" + NameTable2 + """.""ID"""
    END IF
```

When written out in the form required by Basic, this SQL command is pretty incomprehensible. Each field and each table name must be written into the SQL input with two sets of double quotes as shown above. As double quotes are normally interpreted by Basic as indicating text, they disappear when the code is transferred. Only when a second set of double quotes is used are terms passed on in simple quotes. **""ID""** therefore means that the **"ID"** field (with a single set of quotation marks for the SQL relationship) is accessed in the query. A partial simplification for this subroutine is that all primary keys in this database carry the name ID.

The code is further complicated by the fact that, as well as requiring duplicate quotation marks, some of the included table fields are entered as variables. These are not text; they are simply concatenated with the preceding text by using + . But these variables must also be masked. That is why these variables are shown above with three sets of quotation marks: **"""+NameTable1+""".""" +NameTableField1+"""** finally translates into the familiar query language **"Table1"."Field1"**. Fortunately when we create the macro, the coloring of the code shows if any double quotes have been omitted. The quotation marks change their color immediately if they are not recognised by the macro as string delimiters.

```
        ELSE
```

... and if the second table does not exist, the following SQL code is created:

```
    IF Position = 2 THEN
        stSql = "SELECT """ + NameTableField1 + """'||'" + Fieldseparator +
    "'||""" + NameTableField2 + """ FROM """ + NameTable1 + """ WHERE ""ID""'='" +
    inID + "'"
    ELSE
        stSql = "SELECT """ + NameTableField2 + """'||'" + Fieldseparator +
    "'||""" + NameTableField1 + """ FROM """ + NameTable1 + """ WHERE ""ID""'='" +
    inID + "'"
    END IF
    END IF
ELSE
```

If a second table field does not exist there can be only one table. This yields the following query:

```
    stSql = "SELECT """ + NameTableField1 + """ FROM """ + NameTable1 +
    """ WHERE ""ID""'='" + inID + "'"
END IF
```

The query stored in the variable **stSql** is now run and the result of the query is stored in the variable **oQuery_result**.

```
oQuery_result = oSQL_Statement.executeQuery(stSql)
```

The query result is read in a loop. Here, as in GUI queries, several fields and records can be created. But the construction of this query will produce only one result. This result will be found in the first column **(1)** of the query. It is the record which provides the content which the combobox is to display. The content is a text string (**'getString()'**), so here we see **'oQuery_result.getString(1)'**.

```
IF NOT IsNull(oQuery_result) THEN
    WHILE oQuery_result.next
        stFieldValue = oQuery_result.getString(1)
    WEND
```

The combobox must now be set to the text values resulting from the query. This requires access to the Controller.

```
    oDocCrl = ThisComponent.getCurrentController()
    oCtlView = oDocCrl.GetControl(oFieldList)
    oCtlView.setText(stFieldValue)
END IF
END IF
```

If there is no value in the field for the foreign key 'oField', it means that the query has failed. The combobox is then set to an empty display.

```
IF IsEmpty(oField.getCurrentValue()) THEN
    oDocCrl = ThisComponent.getCurrentController()
    oCtlView = oDocCrl.GetControl(oFieldList)
    oCtlView.setText("")
END IF
END SUB
```

This subroutine handles the contact between the foreign keys in a hidden field and the combobox. This is sufficient for the display of the correct values in the combobox. To store a new value requires a further subroutine.

Transfering a foreign key value from a combobox to a numeric field

If a new value is entered into the combobox (and this after all is the purpose for which this macro was constructed), the corresponding primary key must be entered into the form's underlying table as a Foreign key.

```
SUB TextChoiceValueSave(NameForm AS STRING, NameSubform AS STRING,
NameSubSubform AS STRING, NameField AS STRING, NameIDField AS STRING,
NameTableField1 AS STRING, NameTableField2 AS STRING, FieldSeparator AS
STRING, NameTable1 AS STRING, OPTIONAL NameTable2 AS STRING, OPTIONAL
NameTab12ID AS STRING, OPTIONAL Position AS INTEGER )
```

This macro should be bound to the following form event: 'Before record action'.

The start of this function corresponds in principle with the previously described subroutine. Here too there are optional variables.

```
IF isMissing(NameTable2) THEN NameTable2 = ""
IF isMissing(NameTab12ID) THEN NameTab12ID = ""
IF isMissing(Position) THEN Position = 2
```

After this the other variables are declared, those that have not yet been declared outside the subroutine or function. Then the form is loaded and the relevant fields are allocated to variables. The field **oField** contains the foreign key and **oFieldList** shows the corresponding text.

```
DIM oForm AS OBJECT
DIM oSubForm AS OBJECT
```

```
DIM oSubSubForm AS OBJECT
DIM oField AS OBJECT
DIM oFieldList AS OBJECT
DIM stContent AS STRING
DIM stContentField2 AS STRING
DIM a_stPart() AS STRING
DIM stmsgbox1 AS STRING
DIM stmsgbox2 AS STRING
DIM inID1 AS INTEGER
DIM inID2 AS INTEGER
DIM Field1Length AS INTEGER
DIM Field2Length AS INTEGER
```

The maximum length allowed for an entry is determined using the function Columnsize, described below. Just setting a limit on the size of the combobox is not safe here, as we need to include the possibility of entering two fields together.

```
Field1Length = Columnsize(NameTable1,NameTableField1)
IF NameTableField2 <> "" THEN
   IF NameTable2 <> "" THEN
      Feld2Length = Columnsize(NameTable2,NameTableField2)
   ELSE
      Feld2Length = Columnsize(NameTable1,NameTableField2)
   END IF
ELSE
   Feld2Length = 0
END IF
```

The form is loaded, and the comobox is read.

```
oDoc = thisComponent
oDrawpage = oDoc.Drawpage
oForm = oDrawpage.Forms.getByName(NameForm)
IF NameSubform <> "" THEN
   oSubForm = oForm.getByName(NameSubform)
   IF NameSubSubform <> "" THEN
      oSubSubForm = oSubForm.getByName(NameSubSubform)
      oField = oSubSubForm.getByName(NameIDField)
      oFieldList = oSubSubForm.getByName(NameField)
   ELSE
      oField = oSubForm.getByName(NameIDField)
      oFieldList = oSubForm.getByName(NameField)
   END IF
ELSE
   oField = oForm.getByName(NameIDField)
   oFieldList = oForm.getByName(NameField)
END IF
stContent = oFieldList.getCurrentValue()
```

The displayed content of the combobox is read. Leading and trailing spaces and non-printing characters are removed if necessary.

```
StContent = Trim(stContent)
IF stContent <> "" THEN
   IF NameTableField2 <> "" THEN
```

If a second table field exists, the content of the combobox must be split. To determine where the split is to occur, we use the field separator provided to the function as an argument.

```
a_stPart = Split(stContent, FieldSeparator, 2)
```

The last parameter signifies that the maximum number of parts is 2.

Depending on which entry corresponds to field 1 and which to field 2, the content of the combobox is now allocated to the individual variables. "Position = 2" serves here as a sign that the second part of the content stands for Field 2.

```
            IF Position = 2 THEN
                stContent = Trim(a_stPart(0))
                IF UBound(a_stPart()) > 0 THEN
                    stContentField2 = Trim(a_stPart(1))
                ELSE
                    stContentField2 = ""
                END IF
                stContentField2 = Trim(a_stPart(1))
            ELSE
                stContentField2 = Trim(a_stPart(0))
                IF UBound(a_stPart()) > 0 THEN
                    stContent = Trim(a_stPart(1))
                ELSE
                    stContent = ""
                END IF
                stContent = Trim(a_stPart(1))
            END IF
        END IF
```

It can happen that with two separable contents, the installed size of the combobox (text length) does not fit the table fields to be saved. For comboboxes that represent a single field, this is normally handled by suitably configuring the form control. Here by contrast, we need some way of catching such errors. The maximum permissible length of the relevant field is checked.

```
    IF (Field1Length > 0 AND Len(stContent) > Field1Length) OR (Field2Length >
0 AND Len(stContentField2) > Field2Length) THEN
```

If the field length of the first or second part is too big, a default string is stored in one of the variables. The character **CHR(13)** is used to put in a line break .

```
    stmsgbox1 = "The field " + NameTableField1 + " must not exceed " +
Field1Length + "characters in length." + CHR(13)
    stmsgbox2 = "The field " + NameTableField2 + " must not exceed " +
Field2Length + "characters in length." + CHR(13)
```

If both field contents are too long, both texts are displayed.

```
    IF (Field1Length > 0 AND Len(stContent) > Field1Length) AND
(Field2Length > 0 AND Len(stContentField2) > Field2Length) THEN
        msgbox ("The entered text is too long." + CHR(13) + stmsgbox1 +
stmsgbox2 + "Please shorten it.",64,"Invalid entry")
```

The display uses the **msgbox()** function. This expects as its first argument a text string, then optionally a number (which determines the type of message box displayed), and finally an optional text string as a title for the window. The window will therefore have the title "Invalid entry" and the number '64' provides a box containing the Information symbol.

The following code covers any further cases of excessively long text that might arise.

```
    ELSEIF (Field1Length > 0 AND Len(stContent) > Field1Length) THEN
        msgbox ("The entered text is too long." + CHR(13) + stmsgbox1 +
"Please shorten it.",64,"Invalid entry")
    ELSE
        msgbox ("The entered text is too long." + CHR(13) + stmsgbox2 +
"Please shorten it.",64,"Invalid entry")
    END IF
ELSE
```

If there is no excessively long text, the function can proceed. Otherwise it exits here.

First variables are preallocated which can subsequently be altered by the query. The variables inID1 and inID2 store the content of the primary key fields of the two tables. If a query yields no results, Basic assigns these integer variable a value of 0. However this value could also indicate a successful query returning a primary key value of 0; therefore the variable is preset to -1. HSQLDB cannot set this value for an autovalue field.

Next the database connection is set up, if it does not already exist.

```
inID1 = -1
inID2 = -1
oDataSource = ThisComponent.Parent.CurrentController
If NOT (oDataSource.isConnected()) Then
   oDataSource.connect()
End If
oConnection = oDataSource.ActiveConnection()
oSQL_Statement = oConnection.createStatement()
IF NameTableField2 <> "" AND NOT IsEmpty(stContentField2) AND
NameTable2 <> "" THEN
```

If a second table field exists, a second dependency must first be declared.

```
stSql = "SELECT ""ID"" FROM """ + NameTable2 + """ WHERE """ +
NameTableField2 + """='" + stContentField2 + "'"
oQuery_result = oSQL_Statement.executeQuery(stSql)
IF NOT IsNull(oQuery_result) THEN
   WHILE oQuery_result.next
      inID2 = oQuery_result.getInt(1)
   WEND
END IF
IF inID2 = -1 THEN
   stSql = "INSERT INTO """ + NameTable2 + """ (""" +
NameTableField2 + """) VALUES ('" + stContentField2 + "') "
   oSQL_Statement.executeUpdate(stSql)
   stSql = "CALL IDENTITY()"
```

If the content within the combobox is not present in the corresponding table, it is inserted there. The primary key value which results is then read. If it is present, the existing primary key is read in the same way. The function uses the automatically generated primary key fields (**IDENTITY**).

```
      oQuery_result = oSQL_Statement.executeQuery(stSql)
      IF NOT IsNull(oQuery_result) THEN
         WHILE oQuery_result.next
            inID2 = oQuery_result.getInt(1)
         WEND
      END IF
END IF
```

The primary key for the second value is temporarily stored in the variable **inID2** and then written as a foreign key into the table corresponding to the first value. According to whether the record from the first table was already available, the content is freshly saved (**INSERT**) or altered (**UPDATE**):

```
IF inID1 = -1 THEN
   stSql = "INSERT INTO """ + NameTable1 + """ (""" +
NameTableField1 + """,""" + NameTab12ID + """) VALUES ('" + stContent + "','"
+ inID2 + "') "
   oSQL_Statement.executeUpdate(stSql)
```

And the corresponding ID directly read out:

```
stSql = "CALL IDENTITY()"
oQuery_result = oSQL_Statement.executeQuery(stSql)
IF NOT IsNull(oQuery_result) THEN
   WHILE oQuery_result.next
      inID1 = oQuery_result.getInt(1)
   WEND
END IF
```

The primary key for the first table must finally be read again so that it can be transferred to the form's underlying table.

```
ELSE
```

```
            stSql = "UPDATE """ + NameTable1 + """ SET """ + NameTab12ID +
"""='" + inID2 + "' WHERE """ + NameTableField1 + """ = '" + stContent + "'"
            oSQL_Statement.executeUpdate(stSql)
         END IF
      END IF
```

In the case where both the fields underlying the combobox are in the same table (for example Surname and Firstname in the Name table), a different query is needed:

```
IF NameTableField2 <> "" AND NameTable2 = "" THEN
         stSql = "SELECT ""ID"" FROM """ + NameTable1 + """ WHERE """ +
NameTableField1 + """='" + stContent + "' AND """ + NameTableField2 + """='"
+ stContentField2 + "'"
         oQuery_result = oSQL_Statement.executeQuery(stSql)
         IF NOT IsNull(oAbfrageergebnis) THEN
            WHILE oQuery_result.next
               inID1 = oQuery_result.getInt(1)
            WEND
         END IF
         IF inID1 = -1 THEN
```

... and a second table does not exist:

```
         stSql = "INSERT INTO """ + NameTable1 + """ (""" + NameTableField1 +
""","""" + NameTableField2 + """) VALUES ('" + stContent + "','" +
stContentField2 + "') "
            oSQL_Statement.executeUpdate(stSql)
```

Then the primary key is read again.

```
         stSql = "CALL IDENTITY()"
         oquery_result = oSQL_Statement.executeQuery(stSql)
         IF NOT IsNull(oQuery_result) THEN
            WHILE oQuery_result.next
               inID1 = oQuery_result.getInt(1)
            WEND
         END IF
      END IF
   END IF
   IF NameTableField2 = "" THEN
```

Now we consider the simplest case: The second table field does not exist and the entry is not yet present in the table. In other words, a single new value has been entered into the combobox.

```
      stSql = "SELECT ""ID"" FROM """ + NameTable1 + """ WHERE """ +
NameTableField1 + """='" + stContent + "'"
      oQuery_result = oSQL_Statement.executeQuery(stSql)
      IF NOT IsNull(oQuery_result) THEN
         WHILE oQuery_result.next
            inID1 = oQuery_result.getInt(1)
         WEND
      END IF
      IF inID1 = -1 THEN
```

If there is no second field, the content of the box is inserted as a new record.

```
         stSql = "INSERT INTO """ + NameTable1 + """ (""" + NameTableField1 +
""") VALUES ('" + stContent + "') "
            oSQL_Statement.executeUpdate(stSql)
```

… and the resulting ID directly read out.

```
         stSql = "CALL IDENTITY()"
         oQuery_result = oSQL_Statement.executeQuery(stSql)
         IF NOT ISNULL(oQuery_result) THEN
            WHILE oQuery_result.next
               inID1 = oQuery_result.getInt(1)
```

```
            WEND
        END IF
      END IF
    END IF
```

The value of the primary key field must be determined, so that it can be transferred to the main part of the form.

Next the primary key value that has resulted from all these loops is transferred to the invisible field in the main table and the underlying database. The table field linked to the form field is reached by using **'BoundField'**. **'updateInt'** places an integer (see under numerical type definitions) in this field.

```
            oField.BoundField.updateInt(inID)
          END IF
      ELSE
```

If no primary key is to be entered, because there was no entry in the combobox or that entry was deleted, the content of the invisible field must also be deleted. **updateNull()** is used to fill the field with the database-specific expression for an empty field, **NULL**.

```
            oField.BoundField.updateNull()
      END IF
END SUB
```

Function to measure the length of the combobox entry

The following function gives the number of characters in the respective table column, so that entries that are too long do not just get truncated. A **FUNCTION** is chosen here to provide return values. A **SUB** has no return value that can be passed on and processed elsewhere.

```
FUNCTION ColumnSize(Tablename AS STRING, Fieldname AS STRING) AS INTEGER
    oDataSource = ThisComponent.Parent.CurrentController
    If NOT (oDataSource.isConnected()) Then
        oDataSource.connect()
    End If
    oConnection = oDataSource.ActiveConnection()
    oSQL_Statement = oConnection.createStatement()
    stSql = "SELECT ""COLUMN_SIZE"" FROM
""INFORMATION_SCHEMA"".""SYSTEM_COLUMNS"" WHERE ""TABLE_NAME"" = '" +
Tablename + "' AND ""COLUMN_NAME"" = '" + Fieldname + "'"
    oQuery_result = oSQL_Statement.executeQuery(stSql)
    IF NOT IsNull(oQuery_result) THEN
        WHILE oQuery_result.next
            i = oQuery_result.getInt(1)
        WEND
    END IF
    Columnsize = i
END FUNCTION
```

Calling the subroutine for displaying texts

The subroutine for creating the combobox is called each time a record is changed. The following example shows this for the sample database.

```
SUB Form_Reader_Input_Load
    REM TextDisplay(NameForm AS STRING, NameSubForm AS STRING, NameSubSubForm
AS STRING, NameField AS STRING, NameIDField AS STRING, NameTableField1(from
Table 1) AS STRING, NameTableField2(from Table 1 or from Table 2) AS STRING,
FieldSeparator AS STRING, NameTable1 AS STRING, OPTIONAL NameTable2 AS
STRING, OPTIONAL NameIDFromTable2InTable1 AS STRING, OPTIONAL Field Position
from the table2 in the Combobox AS INTEGER [1 or 2] )
    TextDisplay ("Filter", "Form", "Address", "comStr", "numStrID", "Street",
"", "", "Street")
```

```
    TextDisplay ("Filter", "Form", "Address", "comPlcTown", "numPlcTownID",
"Postcode", "Town", " ", "Postcode", "Town", "Town_ID", 2)
    END SUB
```

The comment lines show the list of parameters that need to be provided for the subroutine. An empty parameter is represented by a pair of double quotes. The last three parameters are optional as they are covered where necessary by default values in the subroutine.

The **TextDisplay** subroutine is called. The form that contains the fields is **Filter > Form > Address**. We are therefore dealing with the subform of a subform.

The first combobox, in which the street is entered, is called **comStr**, the hidden foreign key field in the table underlying the form is called **numStrID**. In this first combobox the field **Street** is displayed. The table, which will contain the entries from the combobox, is also called **Street**.

The town and postcode are entered into the second combobox. This is called **comPlcTown**. The hidden foreign key field is called **numPlcTownID**. This second combobox contains the **Postcode** and **Town**, separated by a space (" "). The first table has the name **Postcode**, the second table the name **Town**. In the first table the foreign key for the second table is called **Town_ID**. The field for the second table is the second element in the combobox, that is position **2**.

Calling the subroutine for text storage

To store the entry, we use the subroutine TextChoiceValueSave.

```
    SUB Form_Reader_Output_Save
        REM TextChoiceValueSave(NameForm AS STRING, NameSubForm AS STRING,
NameSubSubForm AS STRING, NameField AS STRING, NameIDField AS STRING,
NameTableField1(from Table 1) AS STRING, NameTableField2(from table 1 or
table 2) AS STRING, FieldSeparator AS STRING,NameTable1 AS STRING, OPTIONAL
NameTable2 AS STRING, OPTIONAL NameIDFromTable2InTable1 AS STRING, OPTIONAL
Position of the field from Table2 in the Combobox AS INTEGER [1 or 2] )
```

The comment is similar to the one in the previous subroutine. The variables being passed are also the same.

```
        TextChoiceValueSave ("Filter", "Form", "Address", "comStr", "numStrID",
"Street", "", "", "Street", "", "")
        TextChoiceValueSave ("Filter", "Form", "Address", "comPlcTown",
"numPlcTownID", "Postcode", "Town", " ", "Postcode", "Town", "Town_ID", 2)
    END SUB
```

To safely store the value, the form must be informed about changes. As far as the user is concerned, the change takes place only to the text inside the combobox to which the form has no further connection. Rather it is the numeric field containing the foreign key that is the link to the database. So the foreign key is simply assigned the value -1, which an autovalue field cannot legally have. This ensures a change in the field content. This field content is then copied over by the normal operation of the listbox.

```
    SUB RecordAction_produce(oEvent AS OBJECT)
```

This macro should be bound to the following event for the listbox: 'On focus'. It is necessary so that the save operation takes place in all cases where the listbox content changes. Without this macro there will be no change in the table, that Base can recognise, since the combobox is not linked to the form.

```
        DIM oForm AS OBJECT
        DIM oSubForm AS OBJECT
        DIM oSubSubForm AS OBJECT
        DIM oField AS OBJECT
        DIM stTag AS String
        stTag = oEvent.Source.Model.Tag
        aForms() = Split(stTag, ",")
```

An array is populated; the field name comes first and then the form names, with the main form preceding the subform.

```
oDoc = thisComponent
oDrawpage = oDoc.Drawpage
oForm = oDrawpage.Forms.getByName(aForms(1))
IF UBound(aForms()) > 1 THEN
    oForm = oForm.getByName(aForms(2))
    IF UBound(aForms()) > 2 THEN
        oForm = oForm.getByName(aForms(3))
    END IF
END IF
oField = oForm.getByName(aForms(0))
oField.BoundField.updateInt(-1)
END SUB
```

Navigation from one form to another

A form is to be opened when a particular event occurs.

In the form control properties, on the line "Additional information" (tag), enter the name of the form. Further information can also be entered here, and subsequently separated out by using the **Split()** function.

```
SUB From_form_to_form(oEvent AS OBJECT)
    DIM stTag AS String
    stTag = oEvent.Source.Model.Tag
    aForm() = Split(stTag, ",")
```

The array is declared and filled with the form names, first the form to be opened and secondly the current form, which will be closed after the other has been opened.

```
    ThisDatabaseDocument.FormDocuments.getByName( Trim(aForm(0)) ).open
    ThisDatabaseDocument.FormDocuments.getByName( Trim(aForm(1)) ).close
END SUB
```

If instead, the other form is only to be opened when the current one is closed, for example where a main form exists and all other forms are controlled from it using buttons, the following macro should be bound to the form with **Tools > Customize > Events > Document closed**:

```
SUB Mainform_open
    ThisDatabaseDocument.FormDocuments.getByName( "Mainform" ).open
END SUB
```

If the form documents are sorted within the ODB file into directories, the macro for changing the form needs to be more extensive:

```
SUB From_form_to_form_with_folders(oEvent AS OBJECT)
    REM The form to be opened is given first.
    REM If a form is in a folder, use "/" to define the relationship
    REM so that the subfolder can be found.
    DIM stTag AS STRING
    stTag = oEvent.Source.Model.Tag 'Tag is entered in the additional
information
    aForms() = Split(stTag, ",")    'Here the form name for the new form
comes first, then the one for the old form
    aForms1() = Split(aForms(0),"/")
    aForms2() = Split(aForms(1),"/")
    IF UBound(aForms1()) = 0 THEN
        ThisDatabaseDocument.FormDocuments.getByName( Trim(aForms1(0)) ).open
    ELSE
        ThisDatabaseDocument.FormDocuments.getByName(
Trim(aForms1(0)) ).getByName( Trim(aForms1(1)) ).open
    END IF
```

```
IF UBound(aForms2()) = 0 THEN
    ThisDatabaseDocument.FormDocuments.getByName( Trim(aForms2(0)) ).close
ELSE
    ThisDatabaseDocument.FormDocuments.getByName(
Trim(aForms2(0)) ).getByName( Trim(aForms2(1)) ).close
    END IF
END SUB
```

Form documents that lie in a directory are entered into the Additional Information field as directory/form. This must be converted to:

`...getByName("Directory").getByName("Form")`.

Removing distracting elements from forms

Toolbars have no function in forms. They are more likely to irritate the normal user, as the form is not being edited while data is input. These macros allow toolbars to be removed and subsequently reinstated. However, depending on the LibreOffice version, menu bars in text form can only be temporarily removed and then reappear.

```
Sub Toolbar_remove
    DIM oFrame AS OBJECT
    DIM oLayoutMng AS OBJECT
    oFrame = thisComponent.CurrentController.Frame
    oLayoutMng = oFrame.LayoutManager
    oLayoutMng.visible = false
    oLayoutMng.showElement("private:Resource/menubar/menubar")
End Sub

Sub Toolbar_restore
    DIM oFrame AS OBJECT
    DIM oLayoutMng AS OBJECT
    oFrame = thisComponent.CurrentController.Frame
    oLayoutMng = oFrame.LayoutManager
    oLayoutMng.visible = true
End Sub
```

When a toolbar is removed, all bars are affected. However as soon as a form control is clicked, the menu bar reappears. This is a safety precaution so that the user does not end up in a jam. To prevent constant toggling, the menu bar reappears.

Database tasks expanded using macros

Making a connection to a database

```
oDataSource = ThisComponent.Parent.DataSource
IF NOT oDataSource.IsPasswordRequired THEN
    oConnection = oDataSource.GetConnection("","")
```

Here it would be possible to provide a username and a password, if one were necessary. In that case the brackets would contain ("Username","Password"). Instead of including the username and a password in clear text, the dialog for password protection is called up:

```
ELSE
    oAuthentication = createUnoService("com.sun.star.sdb.InteractionHandler")
    oConnection = oDataSource.ConnectWithCompletion(oAuthentication)
END IF
```

If however a form within the same Base file is accessing the database, you only need:

```
oDataSource = ThisComponent.Parent.CurrentController
```

```
IF NOT (oDataSource.isConnected()) Then
    oDataSource.connect()
End IF
oConnection = oDataSource.ActiveConnection()
```

Here the database is known so a username and a password are not necessary, as these are already switched off in the basic HSQLDB configuration for internal version.

For forms outside Base, the connection is made through the first form:

```
oDataSource = Thiscomponent.Drawpage.Forms(0)
oConnection = oDataSource.activeConnection
```

Securing your database

It can sometimes happen, especially when a database is being created, that the ODB file is unexpectedly truncated. Frequent saving after editing is therefore useful, especially when using the Reports module.

When the database is in use, it can be damaged by operating system failure, if this occurs just as the Base file is being terminated. This is when the content of the database is being written into the file.

In addition, there are the usual suspects for files that suddenly refuse to open, such as hard drive failure. It does no harm therefore to have a backup copy which is as up-to-date as possible. The state of the data does not change as long as the ODB file remains open. For this reason, safety subroutines can be directly linked to the opening of the file. You simply copy the file using the backup path given in **Tools > Options > LibreOffice > Paths**. This macro begins to overwrite the oldest version after five copies have been made.

```
SUB Databasebackup
    REM The database file *.odb is copied into the Backup directory.
    REM The maximum number of copies is set to 5. After that, the oldest copy
is replaced.
    REM This method does not cover:
    REM - data entry into a database that is already open as the data are
written into the *.odb file only when it is closed.
    DIM oPath AS OBJECT
    DIM oDoc AS OBJECT
    DIM sTitle AS STRING
    DIM sUrl_end AS STRING
    DIM sUrl_start AS STRING
    DIM i AS INTEGER
    DIM k AS INTEGER
    oDoc = ThisComponent
    sTitle = oDoc.Title
    sUrl_start = oDoc.URL
    oPath = createUnoService("com.sun.star.util.PathSettings")
    FOR i = 1 TO 6
        IF NOT FileExists(oPath.Backup & "/" & i & "_" & sTitle) THEN
            IF i > 5 THEN
                FOR k = 1 TO 4
                IF FileDateTime(oPath.Backup & "/" & k & "_" & sTitle) <=
FileDateTime(oPath.Backup & "/" & k+1 & "_" & sTitle) THEN
                    i = k
                    EXIT FOR
                END IF
                NEXT
            END IF
            EXIT FOR
        END IF
```

```
        NEXT
        sUrl_end = oPath.Backup & "/" & i &"_" & sTitle
        FileCopy(sUrl_start,sUrl_end)
    END SUB
```

You can also do a backup while Base is running, provided that the data can be written back out of the cache into the file before the Databasebackup subroutine is carried out. It might be useful to do this, perhaps after a specific elapsed time or when an on-screen button is pressed. This cache-clearing is handled by the following subroutine:

```
    SUB Write_data_out_of_cache
        REM Writes the data out of the table directly to disk while Base is
    running.
        DIM oData AS OBJECT
        DIM oDataSource AS OBJECT
        oData = ThisDatabaseDocument.CurrentController
        IF NOT ( oData.isConnected() ) THEN oData.connect()
        oDataSource = oData.DataSource
        oDataSource.flush
    END SUB
```

Database compaction

This is simply a SQL command (**SHUTDOWN COMPACT**), which should be carried out now and again, especially after a lot of data has been deleted. The database stores new data, but still reserves the space for the deleted data. In cases where the data have been substantially altered, you therefore need to compact the database.

Once compaction is carried out, the tables are no longer accessible. The file must be reopened. Therefore this macro closes the form from which it is called. Unfortunately you cannot close the document itself without causing a recovery when it is opened again. Therefore this function is commented out.

```
    SUB Database_compaction
        DIM stMessage AS STRING
        oDataSource = ThisComponent.Parent.CurrentController    ' Accessible from
    the form
        IF NOT (oDataSource.isConnected()) THEN
            oDataSource.connect()
        END IF
        oConnection = oDataSource.ActiveConnection()
        oSQL_Statement = oConnection.createStatement()
        stSql = "SHUTDOWN COMPACT" ' The database is being compacted and shut down
        oSQL_Statement.executeQuery(stSql)
        stMessage = "The database is being compacted." + CHR(13) + "The form will
    now close."
        stMessage = stMessage + CHR(13) + "Following this, the database file
    should be closed."
        stMessage = stMessage + CHR(13) + "The database can only be accessed after
    reopening the database file."
        msgbox stMessage
        ThisDatabaseDocument.FormDocuments.getByName( "Maintenance" ).close
        REM The closing of the database file causes a recovery operation when you
    open it again.
    '   ThisDatabaseDocument.close(True)
    END SUB
```

Decreasing the table index for autovalue fields

If a lot of data is deleted from a table, users are often concerned that the sequence of automatically generated primary keys simply continues upwards instead of starting again at the highest current value of the key. The following subroutine reads the currently highest value of the "ID" field in a table and sets the next initial key value 1 higher than this maximum.

If the primary key field is not called ID, the macro must be edited accordingly.

```
SUB Table_index_down(stTable AS STRING)
   REM This subroutine sets the automatically incrementing primary key field
mit the preset name of "ID" to the lowest possible value.
   DIM inCount AS INTEGER
   DIM inSequence_Value AS INTEGER
   oDataSource = ThisComponent.Parent.CurrentController    ' Accessible
through the  form
   IF NOT (oDataSource.isConnected()) THEN
      oDataSource.connect()
   END IF
   oConnection = oDataSource.ActiveConnection()
   oSQL_Statement = oConnection.createStatement()
   stSql = "SELECT MAX(""ID"") FROM """+stTable+"""" ' The highest value in
"ID" is determined
   oQuery_result = oSQL_Statement.executeQuery(stSql)' Query is launched and
the return value stored in the variable oQuery_result
   IF NOT ISNULL(oQuery_result) THEN
      WHILE oQuery_result.next
      inCount = oQuery_result.getInt(1)  ' First data field is read
      WEND  ' next record, in this case none as only one record exists
      IF inCount = "" THEN    ' If the highest value is not a value, meaning
the table is empty, the highest value is set to -1
          inCount = -1
      END IF
      inSequence_Value = inCount+1 ' The highrst value is increased by 1
      REM A new command is prepared for the database. The ID will start
afresh from inCount+1.
      REM This statement has no return value, as no record is being read
      oSQL_statement = oConnection.createStatement()
      oSQL_statement.executeQuery("ALTER TABLE """ + stTable + """ ALTER
COLUMN ""ID"" RESTART WITH " + inSequence_Value + "")
   END IF
END SUB
```

Dialogs

Input errors in fields are often only noticed later. Often it is necessary to modify identical entries in several records at the same time. It is awkward to have to do this in normal table view, especially when several records must be edited, as each record requires an individual entry to be made.

Forms can use macros to do this kind of thing, but to do it for several tables, you would need identically constructed forms. Dialogs can do the job. A dialog can be supplied at the beginning with the necessary data for appropriate tables and can be called up by several different forms.

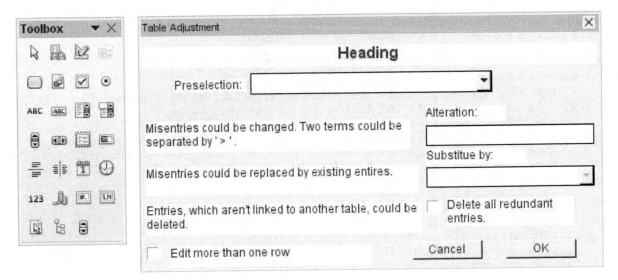

Dialogs are saved along with the modules for macros. Their creation is similar to that of a form. Very similar control fields are available. Only the table control of forms is absent as a special entry possibility.

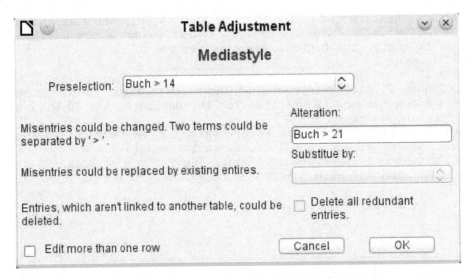

The appearance of dialog controls is determined by the settings for the graphical user interface.

The dialog shown above serves in the example database to edit tables which are not used directly as the basis of a form. So, for example, the media type is accessible only through a listbox (in the macro version it becomes a combobox). In the macro version, the field contents can be expanded by new content but an alteration of existing content is not possible. In the version without macros, alterations are carried out using a separate table control.

While alterations in this case are easy to carry out without macros, it is quite difficult to change the media type of many media at once. Suppose the following types are available: "Book, bound", "Book, hard-cover", "Paperback" and "Ringfile". Now it turns out, after the database has been in use for a long time, that more active contemporaries foresaw similar additional media types for printed works. The task of differentiating them has become excessive. We therefore wish to reduce them, preferably to a single term. Without macros, the records in the media table would have to be found (using a filter) and individually altered. If you know SQL, you can do it much better using a SQL command. You can change all the records in the Media table with a single entry. A second SQL command then removes the now surplus media types which no longer have any link to the

Media table. Precisely this method is applied using this dialog's Replace With box – only the SQL command is first adapted to the Media Type table using a macro that can also edit other tables.

Often entries slip into a table which with hindsight can be changed in the form, and so are no longer needed. It does no harm simply to delete such orphaned entries, but they are quite hard to find using the graphical user interface. Here again a suitable SQL command is useful, coupled with a delete instruction. This command for affected tables is included in the dialog under *Delete all superfluous entries*.

If the dialog is to be used to carry out several changes, this is indicated by the *Edit multiple records* checkbox. Then the dialog will not simply terminate when the OK button is clicked.

The macro code for this dialog can be seen in full in the example database. Only excerpts are explained below.

```
SUB Table_purge(oEvent AS OBJECT)
```

The macro should be launched by entering into the *Additional information* section for the relevant buttons:

```
0: Form, 1: Subform, 2: SubSubform, 3: Combobox or table control, 4: Foreign
key field in a form, empty for a table control, 5: Table name of auxiliary
table, 6: Table field1 of auxiliary table, 7: Table field2 of auxiliary
table, or 8: Table name of auxiliary table for table field2
```

The entries in this area are listed at the beginning of the macro as comments. The numbers bound to them are transferred and the relevant entry is read from an array. The macro can edit listboxes, which have two entries, separated by **">"**. These two entries can also come from different tables and be brought together using a query, as for instance in the Postcode table, which has only the foreign key field Town_ID for the town, requiring the Town table to display the names of towns.

```
DIM aForeignTable(0, 0 to 1)
DIM aForeignTable2(0, 0 to 1)
```

Among the variables defined at the beginning are two arrays. While normal arrays can be created by the **Split()** command during execution of the subroutine, two-dimensional arrays must be defined in advance. Two-dimensional arrays are necessary to store several records from one query when the query itself refers to more than one field. The two arrays declared above must be able to interpret queries that refer to two table fields. Therefore they are defined for two different contents by using *0 to 1* for the second dimension.

```
stTag = oEvent.Source.Model.Tag
aTable() = Split(stTag, ", ")
FOR i = LBound(aTable()) TO UBound(aTable())
   aTable(i) = trim(aTable(i))
NEXT
```

The variables provided are read. The sequence is that set up in the comment above. There is a maximum of nine entries, and you need to declare if an eighth entry for the table field2 and a nineth entry for a second table exist.

If values are to be removed from a table, it is first necessary to check that they do not exist as foreign keys in some other table. In simple table structures a given table will have only one foreign key connection to another table. However, in the given example database, there is a Town table which is used for both the place of publication of media and the town for addresses. Thus the primary key of the Town table is entered twice into different tables. These tables and foreign key names can naturally also be entered using the Additional Information field. It would be nicer though if they could be provided universally for all cases. This can be done using the following query.

```
stSql = "SELECT ""FKTABLE_NAME"", ""FKCOLUMN_NAME"" FROM
""INFORMATION_SCHEMA"".""SYSTEM_CROSSREFERENCE"" WHERE ""PKTABLE_NAME"" = '"
+ aTable(5) + "'"
```

In the database, the INFORMATION_SCHEMA area contains all information about the tables of the database, including information about foreign keys. The tables that contain this information can be accessed using "INFORMATION_SCHEMA"."SYSTEM_CROSSREFERENCE". KTABLE_NAME" gives the table that provides its primary key for the connection. FKTABLE_NAME gives the table that uses this primary key as a foreign key. Finally FKCOLUMN_NAME gives the name of the foreign key field.

The table that provides its primary key for use as a foreign key is in the previously created array at position 6. A the count begins with 0, the value is read from the array using **aTable(5)**.

```
inCount = 0
stForeignIDTab1Tab2 = "ID"
stForeignIDTab2Tab1 = "ID"
stAuxiltable = aTable(5)
```

Before the reading of the arrays begins, some default values must be set. These are the index for the array in which the values from the auxiliary table will be written, the default primary key if we do not need the foreign key for a second table, and the default auxiliary table, linked to the main table, for postcode and town, the Postcode table.

When two fields are linked for display in a listbox, they can, as described above, come from two different tables. For the display of Postcode and town the query is:

SELECT "Postcode"."Postcode" || ' > ' || "Town"."Town" FROM "Postcode", "Town" WHERE "Postcode"."Town_ID" = "Town"."ID"

The table for the first field (Postcode), is linked to the second table by a foreign key. Only the information from these two tables and the Postcode and Town fields is passed to the macro. All primary keys are by default called ID in the example database. The foreign key of Town in Postcode must therefore be determined using the macro.

In the same way the macro must access each table with which the content of the listbox is connected by a foreign key.

```
oQuery_result = oSQL_Statement.executeQuery(stSql)
IF NOT ISNULL(oQuery_result) THEN
    WHILE oQuery_result.next
        ReDim Preserve aForeignTable(inCount,0 to 1)
```

The array must be freshly dimensioned each time. In order to preserve the existing contents, they are backed up using (Preserve).

```
aForeignTables(inCount,0) = oQuery_result.getString(1)
```

Reading the first field with the name of the table which contains the foreign key. The result for the Postcode table is the Address table.

```
aForeignTables(inCount,1) = oQuery_result.getString(2)
```

Reading the second field with the name of the foreign key field. The result for the Postcode table is the field Postcode_ID in the Address table.

In cases where a call to the subroutine includes the name of a second table, the following loop is run. Only when the name of the second table occurs as the foreign key table for the first table is the default entry changed. In our case this does not occur, as the Town table has no foreign key from the Postcode table. The default entry for the auxiliary table therefore remains Postcode; finally the combination of postcode and town is a basis for the Address table, which contains a foreign key from the Postcode table.

```
IF UBound(aTable()) = 8 THEN
    IF aTable(8) = aForeignTable(inCount,0) THEN
        stForeignIDTab2Tab1 = aForeignTable(inCount,1)
        stAuxiltable = aTable(8)
    END IF
END IF
inCount = inCount + 1
```

As further values may need to be read in, the index is incremented to redimension the arrays. Then the loop ends.

```
        WEND
    END IF
```

If, when the subroutine is called, a second table name exists, the same query is launched for this table:

```
    IF UBound(aTable()) = 8 THEN
```

It runs identically except that the loop tests whether perhaps the first table name occurs as a foreign key table name. That is the case here: the Postcode table *contains* the *foreign* key Town_ID from the Town table. This foreign key is now assigned to the variable stForeignIDTab1Tab2, so that the relationship between the tables can be defined.

```
        IF aTable(5) = aForeignTable2(inCount,0) THEN
            stForeignIDTab1Tab2 = aForeignTable2(inCount,1)
        END IF
```

After a few further settings to ensure a return to the correct form after running the dialog (determining the line number of the form, so that we can jump back to that line number after a new read), the loop begins, which recreates the dialog when the first action is completed but the dialog is required to be kept open for further actions. The setting for repetition takes place using the corresponding checkbox

```
    DO
```

Before the dialog is launched, first of all the content of the listboxes is determined. Care must be taken if the listboxes represent two table fields and perhaps even are related to two different tables.

```
    IF UBound(aTable()) = 6 THEN
```

The listbox relates to only one table and one field, as the argument array ends at Tablefield1 of the auxiliary table.

```
        stSql = "SELECT """ + aTable(6) + """ FROM """ + aTable(5) + """
    ORDER BY """ + aTable(6) + """"
        ELSEIF UBound(aTable()) = 7 THEN
```

The listbox relates to two table fields but only one table, as the argument array ends at Tablefield2 of the auxiliary table.

```
        stSql = "SELECT """ + aTable(6) + """||' > '||""" + aTable(7) + """
    FROM """ + aTable(5) + """ ORDER BY """ + aTable(6) + """"
        ELSE
```

The listbox is based on two table fields from two tables. This query corresponds to the example with the postcode and the town.

```
        stSql = "SELECT """ + aTable(5) + """.""" + aTable(6) + """||' >
    '||""" + aTable(8) + """.""" + aTable(7) + """ FROM """ + aTable(5) + """,
    """ + aTable(8) + """ WHERE """ + aTable(8) + """.""" + stForeignIDTab2Tab1 +
    """ = """ + aTable(5) + """.""" + stForeignIDTab1Tab2 + """ ORDER BY """ +
    aTable(6) + """"
        END IF
```

Here we have the first evaluation to determine the foreign keys. The variables stForeignIDTab2Tab1 and stForeignIDTab1Tab2 start with the value ID. For stForeignIDTab1Tab2 evaluation of the previous query yields a different value, namely the value of Town_ID. In this way the previous query construction yields exactly the content already formulated for postcode and town – only enhanced by sorting.

Now we must make contact with the listboxes, to supply them with the content returned by the queries. These listboxes do not yet exist, since the dialog itself has not yet been created. This dialog is created first in memory, using the following lines, before it is actually drawn on the screen.

```
DialogLibraries.LoadLibrary("Standard")
oDlg = CreateUnoDialog(DialogLibraries.Standard.Dialog_Table_purge)
```

Next come the settings for the fields of the dialog. Here, for example, is the listbox which is to be supplied with the results of the above query:

```
oCtlList1 = oDlg.GetControl("ListBox1")
oCtlList1.addItems(aContent(),0)
```

Access to the fields of the dialog is accomplished by using **GetControl** with the appropriate name. In dialogs it is not possible for two fields to use the same name as this would create problems when evaluating the dialog.

The listbox is supplied with the contents of the query, which have been stored in the array aContent() . The listbox contains only the content to be displayed as a field, so only the position 0 is filled.

After all fields with the desired content have been filled, the dialog is launched.

```
Select Case oDlg.Execute()
Case 1'Case 1 means the "OK" button has been clicked
Case 0'If it was the "Cancel" button
    inRepetition = 0
End Select
LOOP WHILE inRepetition = 1
```

The dialog runs repeatedly as long as the value of "inRepetition" is 1. This is set by the corresponding checkbox.

Here, in brief, is the content after the "OK" button is clicked:

```
Case 1
    stInhalt1 = oCtlList1.getSelectedItem() 'Read value from Listbox1 ...
    REM ... and determine the corresponding ID-value.
```

The ID value of the first listbox is stored in the variable "inLB1".

```
    stText = oCtlText.Text  ' Read the field value.
```

If the text field is not empty, the entry in the text field is handled. Neither the listbox for a replacement value nor the checkbox for deleting all orphaned records are considered. This is made clear by the fact that text entry sets these other fields to be inactive.

```
    IF stText <> "" THEN
```

If the text field is not empty, the new value is written in place of the old one using the previously read ID field in the table. There is the possibility of two entries, as is also the case in the listbox. The separator is >. For two entries in different tables, two UPDATE-commands must be launched, which are created here simultaneously and forwarded, separated by a semicolon.

```
    ELSEIF oCtlList2.getSelectedItem() <> "" THEN
```

If the text field is empty and the listbox 2 contains a value, the value from listbox 1 must be replaced by the value in listbox 2. This means that all records in the tables for which the records in the listboxes are foreign keys must be checked and, if necessary, written with an altered foreign key.

```
    stInhalt2 = oCtlList2.getSelectedItem()
    REM Read value from listbox.
    REM Determine ID for the value of the listbox.
```

The ID value of the second listbox is stored in the variable inLB2. Here too, things develop differently depending on whether one or two fields are contained in the listbox, and also on whether one or two tables are the basis of the listbox content.

The replacement process depends on which table is defined as the table which supplies the foreign key for the main table. For the obove example, this is the Postcode table, as the Postcode_ID is the foreign key which is forwarded through Listbox 1 and Listbox 2.

```
IF stAuxilTable = aTable(5) THEN
    FOR i = LBound(aForeignTables()) TO UBound(aForeignTables())
```

Replacing the old ID value by the new ID value becomes problematic in n:m-relationships, as in such cases, the same value can be assigned twice. That might be what you want, but it must be prevented when the foreign key forms part of the primary key. So in the table rel_Media_Author a medium cannot have the same author twice because the primary key is constructed from Media_ID and Author_ID. In the query, all key fields are searched which collectively have the property UNIQUE or were defined as foreign keys with the UNIQUE property using an index.

So if the foreign key has the UNIQUE property and is already represented there with the desired future inLB2, that key cannot be replaced.

```
stSql = "SELECT ""COLUMN_NAME"" FROM
""INFORMATION_SCHEMA"".""SYSTEM_INDEXINFO"" WHERE ""TABLE_NAME"" = '" +
aForeignTables(i,0) + "' AND ""NON_UNIQUE"" = False AND ""INDEX_NAME"" =
(SELECT ""INDEX_NAME"" FROM ""INFORMATION_SCHEMA"".""SYSTEM_INDEXINFO"" WHERE
""TABLE_NAME"" = '" + aForeignTables(i,0) + "' AND ""COLUMN_NAME"" = '" +
aForeignTables(i,1) + "')"
```

' **"NON_UNIQUE" = False** ' gives the names of columns that are UNIQUE. However not all column names are needed but only those which form an index with the foreign key field. This is handled by the Subselect with the same table names (which contain the foreign key) and the names of the foreign key fields.

If now the foreign key is present in the set, the key value can only be replaced if other fields are used to define the corresponding index as UNIQUE. You must take care when carrying out replacements that the uniqueness of the index combination is not compromised.

```
IF aForeignTables(i,1) = stFieldname THEN
    inUnique = 1
ELSE
    ReDim Preserve aColumns(inCount)
    aColumns(inCount) = oQuery_result.getString(1)
    inCount = inCount + 1
END IF
```

All column names, apart from the known column names for foreign key fields as Index with the UNIQUE property, are stored in the array. As the column name of the foreign key field also belongs to the group, it can be used to determine whether uniqueness is to be checked during data modification.

```
IF inUnique = 1 THEN
    stSql = "UPDATE """ + aForeignTables(i,0) + """ AS ""a"" SET """ +
aForeignTables(i,1) + """='" + inLB2 + "' WHERE """ + aForeignTables(i,1) +
"""='" + inLB1 + "' AND ( SELECT COUNT(*) FROM """ + aForeignTables(i,0) +
""" WHERE """ + aForeignTables(i,1) + """='" + inLB2 + "' )"
    IF inCount > 0 THEN
        stFieldgroup = Join(aColumns(), """|| ||""")
```

If there are several fields, apart from the foreign key field, which together form a 'UNIQUE' index, they are combined here for a SQL grouping. Otherwise only "aColumns(0)" appears as "stFieldgroup".

```
        stFieldname = ""
        FOR ink = LBound(aColumns()) TO UBound(aColumns())
            stFieldname = stFieldname + " AND """ + aColumns(ink) + """ =
""a"".""" + aColumns(ink) + """ "
```

The SQL parts are combined for a correlated subquery.

```
        NEXT
    stSql = Left(stSql, Len(stSql) - 1)
```

The previous query ends with a bracket. Now further content is to be added to the subquery, so this closure must be removed again. After that, the query is expanded with the additional conditions.

```
    stSql = stSql + stFeldbezeichnung + "GROUP BY (""" + stFeldgruppe + """) ) < 1"
END IF
```

If the foreign key has no connection with the primary key or with a UNIQUE index, it does not matter if content is duplicated.

```
ELSE
    stSql = "UPDATE """ + aForeignTables(i,0) + """ SET """ +
aForeignTables(i,1) + """='" + inLB2 + "' WHERE """ + aForeignTables(i,1) +
"""='" + inLB1 + "'"
END IF
oSQL_Statement.executeQuery(stSql)
NEXT
```

The update is carried out for as long as different connections to other tables occur; that is, as long as the current table is the source of a foreign key in another table. This is the case twice over for the Town table: in the Media table and in the Postcode table.

Afterwards the old value can be deleted from listbox 1, as it no longer has any connection to other tables.

```
stSql = "DELETE FROM """ + aTable(5) + """ WHERE ""ID""='" + inLB1 + "'"
oSQL_Statement.executeQuery(stSql)
```

In some cases, the same method must now be carried out for a second table that has supplied data for the listboxes. In our example, the first table is the Postcode table and the second is the Town table.

If the text field is empty and listbox 2 also contains nothing, we check if the relevant checkbox indicates that all surplus entries are to be deleted. This means the entries which are not bound to other tables by a foreign key.

```
ELSEIF oCtlCheck1.State = 1 THEN
    stCondition = ""
    IF stAuxilTable = aTable(5) THEN
        FOR i = LBound(aForeignTables()) TO UBound(aForeignTables())
            stCondition = stCondition + """ID"" NOT IN (SELECT """ +
aForeignTables(i,1) + """ FROM """ + aForeignTables(i,0) + """) AND "
        NEXT
    ELSE
        FOR i = LBound(aForeignTables2()) TO UBound(aForeignTables2())
            stCondition = stCondition + """ID"" NOT IN (SELECT """ +
aForeignTables2(i,1) + """ FROM """ + aForeignTables2(i,0) + """) AND "
        NEXT
    END IF
```

The last AND must be removed, since otherwise the delete instruction would end with AND.

```
    stCondition = Left(stCondition, Len(stCondition) - 4)    '
    stSql = "DELETE FROM """ + stAuxilTable + """ WHERE " + stCondition + ""
    oSQL_Statement.executeQuery(stSql)
```

As the table has already been purged once, the table index can be checked and optionally corrected downwards. See the subroutine described in one of the previous sections.

```
Table_index_down(stAuxilTable)
```

Afterwards, if necessary the listbox in the form from which the Table_purge dialog was called can be updated. In some cases, the whole form needs to be reread. For this purpose, the current record is determined at the beginning of the subroutine so that after the form has been refreshed, the current record can be reinstated.

```
oDlg.endExecute() 'End dialog ...
```

```
    oDlg.Dispose() '... and remove from storage
  END SUB
```

Dialogs are terminated with the endExecute() command and completely removed from memory with Dispose().

Chapter 10
Database Maintenance

General remarks on maintaining databases

Frequent alteration of the data in a database, in particular many deletions, has two effects. First, the database grows steadily even though it may not actually contain more data. Second, the automatically created primary key continues to increment regardless of what value for the next key is actually necessary. Important maintenance is described in this chapter.

Compacting a database

The behavior of HSQLDB is to preserve storage space for deleted records. Databases that are filled with test data, especially if this includes images, retain the same size even if all these records are subsequently deleted.

To free this storage space, the database records must be rewritten (tables, table descriptions, etc).

On the main Base interface, using **Tools > SQL**, you can directly enter a simple command (which on server databases is only available to the system administrator):

    SHUTDOWN COMPACT

The database is taken down and freed from all accumulated waste space. After this is done, Base must be restarted in order to access the database.

Resetting autovalues

A database is created, all possible functions tested with examples, and corrections made until everything works. By this time, on average, many primary key values will have risen to over 100. Bad luck if the primary key has been set to auto-increment, as is commonplace! If the tables are emptied in preparation for normal usage or prior to handing the database on to another person, the primary key continues to increment from its current position instead of resetting itself to zero.

The following SQL command, again entered using **Tools > SQL**, lets you reset the initial value:

    ALTER TABLE "Table_name" ALTER COLUMN "ID" RESTART WITH 'New value'

This assumes that the primary key field has the name "ID" and has been defined as an autovalue field. The new value should be the one that you want to be automatically created for the next new record. So, for example, if current records go up to 4, the new value should be 5.

Querying database properties

All information on the tables of the database is stored in table form in a separate part of HSQLDB. This separate area can be reached using the name "INFORMATION_SCHEMA".

The following query can be used to find out field names, field types, column sizes, and default values. Here an example is given for a table named Searchtable.

    SELECT "COLUMN_NAME", "TYPE_NAME", "COLUMN_SIZE", "COLUMN_DEF" AS "Default Value" FROM "INFORMATION_SCHEMA"."SYSTEM_COLUMNS" WHERE "TABLE_NAME" = 'Searchtable' ORDER BY "ORDINAL_POSITION"

All special tables in HSQLDB are described in the appendix to this handbook. Information on the content of these tables is most easily obtained by direct queries:

    SELECT * FROM "INFORMATION_SCHEMA"."SYSTEM_PRIMARYKEYS"

The asterisk ensures that all available columns of the table are shown. The table searched for above gives essential information on the primary keys of the various tables.

This information is useful above all for macros. Instead of having to provide detailed information on each freshly created table or database, procedures are written to fetch this information directly out of the database and are therefore universally applicable. The example database shows this, among other things, in one of the maintenance modules, where foreign keys are determined.

Testing tables for unnecessary entries

A database consists of one or more main tables, which contain foreign keys from other tables. In the example database, these are the Media and Address tables. In the Address table the primary key of the postcode occurs as a foreign key. If a person moves home, the address gets changed. The result may be that no foreign key Postcode_ID corresponding to this postcode exists any longer. In principle therefore, the postcode itself could be deleted. However, it is not apparent during normal usage that the record is no longer needed. There are various ways to prevent this sort of problem arising.

Testing entries using relationship definition

The integrity of the data can be ensured while defining relationships. In other words, you can prevent the deletion or alteration of keys from leading to errors in the database.

The following dialog is accessible through **Tools > Relationships**, followed by a right-click on the connector between two tables.

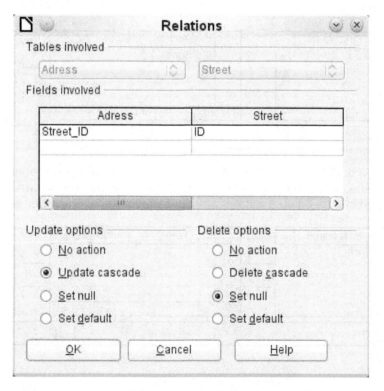

Here the tables Address and Street are considered. **All specified actions apply to the Address table**, which contains the foreign key Street_ID. Update options refer to an update of the ID field in the Street table. If the numeric key in the "Street"."ID" field is altered, "No action" means that the database resists this change if a "Street"."ID" with that key number occurs as a foreign key in the Address table.

"Update cascade" means that the key number is simply carried over. If the street 'Burgring' in the Street table has the ID '3' and is also represented in "Address"."Street_ID", the ID can be safely altered, for example, to '67' – the corresponding *"Address"."Street_ID"* values will be automatically be changed to '67'.

If *Set null* is chosen, altering the ID makes "Address"."Street_ID" an empty field.

The delete options are handled similarly.

For both options, the GUI currently does not allow the possibility *Set default*, as the GUI default settings are different from those of the database. See Chapter 3, Tables.

Defining relationships helps keep the relationships themselves clean, but it does not remove unnecessary records that provide their primary key as a foreign key in the relationship. There may be any number of streets without corresponding addresses.

Editing entries using forms and subforms

In principle the whole interrelationship between tables can be displayed within forms. This is easiest of course when a table is related to only one other table. Thus in the following example, the author's primary key becomes the foreign key in the table rel_Media_Author; rel_Media_Author also contains a foreign key from Media, so that the following arrangement shows a n:m-relationship with three forms. Each is presented through a table.

The first figure shows that the title *I hear you knocking* belongs to the author *Dave Edmunds*. Therefore *Dave Edmunds* must not be deleted – otherwise information required for the media *I hear you knocking* will be missing. However the listbox allows you to choose a different record instead of *Dave Edmunds*.

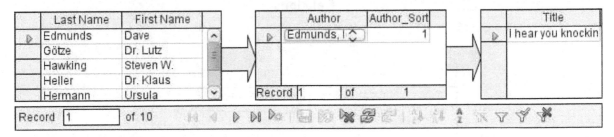

In the form there is a built-in filter whose activation can tell you which categories are not needed in the Media table. In the case just described, almost all the example authors are in use. Only the *Erich Kästner* record can be deleted without any consequences for any other record in *Media*.

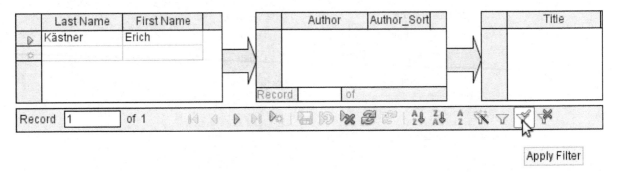

The filter is hard-coded in this case. It is found in the form properties. Such a filter is activated automatically when the form is launched. It can be switched off and on. If it is deleted, it can be accessed again by a complete reload of the form. This means more than just updating the data; the whole form document must be closed and then reopened.

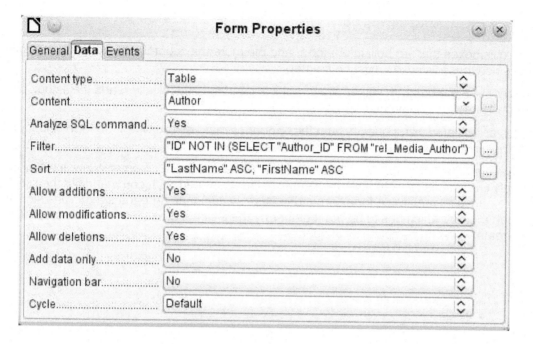

Queries for finding orphan entries

The above filter is part of a query which can be used to find orphaned entries.

SELECT "Surname", "Firstname" FROM "Author" WHERE "ID" NOT IN (SELECT "Author_ID" FROM "rel_Media_Author")

If a table contains foreign keys from several other tables, the query needs to be extended accordingly. This affects, for example, the Town table, which has foreign keys in both the Media table and the Postcode table. Therefore, records in the Town table which are to be deleted should not be referenced in either of these tables. This is determined by the following query:

SELECT "Town" FROM "Town" WHERE "ID" NOT IN (SELECT "Town_ID" FROM "Media") AND "ID" NOT IN (SELECT "Town_ID" FROM "Postcode")

Orphaned entries can then be deleted by selecting all the entries that pass the set filter, and using the Delete option in the context menu of the record pointer, called up by right-clicking.

Database search speed

Effect of queries

It is just these queries, used in the previous section to filter data, that prove unsatisfactory in regard to the maximum speed of searching a database. The problem is that in large databases, the subquery retrieves a correspondingly large amount of data with which each single displayable record must be compared. Only comparisons with the relationship IN make it possible to compare a single value with a set of values. The query

... WHERE "ID" NOT IN (SELECT "Author_ID" FROM "rel_Media_Author")

can contain a large number of possible foreign keys from the rel_Media_Author table, which must first be compared with the primary keys in the table Authors for each record in that table. Such a query is therefore not suitable for daily use but may be required for database maintenance. For daily use, search functions need to be constructed differently so that the search for data is not excessively long and does not damage day-to-day work with the database.

Effect of listboxes and comboboxes

The more listboxes that are built into a form, and the more they contain, the longer the form takes to load, since these listboxes must be created.

The better the Base program sets up the graphical interface and initially reads the listbox contents only partially, the less delay there will be.

Listboxes are created using queries, and these queries must be run when the form is loaded for each listbox.

The same query structure for more listboxes is better done using a common View, instead of repeatedly creating fields with the same syntax using the stored SQL commands in the listboxes. Views are above all preferable for external database systems, as here the server runs significantly faster than a query which has to be put together by the GUI and freshly put to the server. The server treats Views as complete local queries.

Appendix

Barcodes

To be able to use the barcode print function, the font `ean13.ttf` must be installed. This font is freely available.

EAN13 barcodes can be created using `ean13.ttf` as follows:

1	2	3	4	5	6	7	8	9	10	11	12	13	14	15
Number	Upper case, A=0 B=1 etc.						*	Lower case, a=0 b=1 etc.						+

See also the query **Barcode_EAN13_ttf_command** in the example database Media_without_Macros.

Data types for the table editor

Integers

Type	Option	HSQLDB	Range	Storage space
Tiny Integer	TINYINT	TINYINT	$2^8 = 256$ | - 128 bis + 127	1 Byte
Small Integer	SMALLINT	SMALLINT	$2^{16} = 65536$ | - 32768 bis + 32767	2 Byte
Integer	INTEGER	INTEGER | INT	$2^{32} = 4294967296$ | - 2147483648 bis + 2147483647	4 Byte
BigInt	BIGINT	BIGINT	2^{64}	8 Byte

Floating-point numbers

Type	Option	HSQLDB	Range	Storage space
Decimal	DECIMAL	DECIMAL	Unlimited, up to 50 places in the GUI, fixed decimal point, perfect accuracy	variable
Number	NUMERIC	NUMERIC	Unlimited, up to 50 places in the GUI, fixed decimal point, perfect accuracy	variable
Float	FLOAT	(DOUBLE used instead)		
Real	REAL	REAL		
Double	DOUBLE	DOUBLE [PRECISION] | FLOAT	Adjustable, not exact, 15 decimal places maximum	8 Byte

Text

Type	Option	HSQLDB	Range	Storage space
Text	VARCHAR	VARCHAR	Adjustable	variable
Text	VARCHAR_ IGNORECASE	VARCHAR_ IGNORECASE	Adjustable, range affects sorting	variable
Text (fix)	CHAR	CHAR | CHARACTER	Adjustable, rest of actual text replaced with spaces	fixed
Memo	LONGVARCHAR	LONGVARCHAR		variable

Time

Type	Option	HSQLDB	Range	Storage space
Date	DATE	DATE		4 Byte
Time	TIME	TIME		4 Byte
Date/Time	TIMESTAMP	TIMESTAMP | DATETIME	Adjustable (0.6 – 6 means with milliseconds)	8 Byte

Other

Type	Option	HSQLDB	Range	Storage space
Yes/No	BOOLEAN	BOOLEAN | BIT		
Binaryfield (fix)	BINARY	BINARY	Like Integer	fixed
Binary field	VARBINARY	VARBINARY	Like Integer	variable
Image	LONGVARBINARY	LONGVARBINARY	Like Integer	variable, intended for larger images
OTHER	OTHER	OTHER | OBJECT		

Numeric

As we are dealing here with floating point numbers, be sure to take care with the settings of the fields in queries. Mostly the display of decimal places is restricted, so that in some cases there may be unexpected results. For example, column 1 might show 0.00 but actually contain 0.001, and column 2, 1000. If column 3 is set to show Column 1 * Column 2, it would actually show 1.

ABS(d)	Returns the absolute value of a number, removing a minus sign where necessary.
ACOS(d)	Returns the arc-cosine.
ASIN(d)	Returns the arc-sine.
ATAN(d)	Returns the arc-tangent.
ATAN2(a,b)	Returns the arc-tangent using coordinates. a is the value of the x-axis, b the value of the y-axis
BITAND(a,b)	Both the binary form of a and the binary form of b must have 1 at the same position to yield 1 in the result. BITAND(3,5) yields 1; 0011 AND 0101 = 0001
BITOR(a,b)	Either the binary form of a or the binary form of b must have 1 at the same position to yield 1 in the result. BITAND(3,5) yields 7; 0011 OR 0101 = 0111
CEILING(d)	Returns the smallest whole number that is not smaller than d.
COS(d)	Returns the cosine.
COT(d)	Returns the cotangent.
DEGREES(d)	Converts radians to degrees.
EXP(d)	Returns e^d (e: (2.718...)).
FLOOR(d)	Returns the largest whole number that is not greater than d.
LOG(d)	Returns the natural logarithm to base e.
LOG10(d)	Returns the logarithm to base 10.
MOD(a,b)	Returns the remainder as a whole number, in the division of 2 whole numbers. MOD(11,3) ergibt 2, weil 3*3+2=11
PI()	Returns π (3.1415...).
POWER(a,b)	a^b , POWER(2,3) = 8, since $2^3 = 8$
RADIANS(d)	Converts degrees to radians.
RAND()	Returns a random number greater than or equal to 0.0 and less than 1.0.

ROUND(a,b)	Rounds a to b decimal places.
ROUNDMAGIC(d)	Solves rounding problems, that arise from using floating point numbers. 3.11-3.1-0.01 is not exactly 0, but is shown as 0 in the GUI. ROUNDMAGIC makes it an actual zero value.
SIGN(d)	Returns –1, if d is less than 0, 0 if d==0 and 1 if d is greater than 0.
SIN(A)	Returns the sine of an angle in radians.
SQRT(d)	Returns the square root.
TAN(A)	Returns the tangent of an angle in radians.
TRUNCATE(a,b)	Truncates a to b decimal places. TRUNCATE(2.37456,2) = 2.37

Text

ASCII(s)	Returns the ASCII code of the first letter of the string.
BIT_LENGTH(str)	Returns the length of the text string str in bits.
CHAR(c)	Returns the letter corresponding to the ASCII code c.
CHAR_LENGTH(str)	Returns the length of the text in characters.
CONCAT(str1,str2)	Concatenates str1 and str2.
'str1'||'str2'||'str3' or 'str1'+'str2'+'str3'	Concatenates str1 + str2 + str3, simpler alternative to CONCAT.
DIFFERENCE(s1,s2)	Returns the sound difference between s1 and s2. Only a whole number is output. 0 means they sound the same. So 'for' and 'four' yield 0, 'king' and 'wing' yield 1, 'see' and 'sea' yield 0.
HEXTORAW(s1)	Translates hexadecimal code to other characters.
INSERT(s,start,len,s2)	Returns a text string, with part of the text replaced. Beginning with start, a length len is cut out of the text s and replaced by the text s2. INSERT(Bundesbahn, 3, 4, mmel) converts Bundesbahn into Bummelbahn, where the length of the inserted text can be greater than that of the deleted text without causing any problems. So INSERT(Bundesbahn, 3, 5, s und B) yields 'Bus und Bahn'.
LCASE(s)	Converts a string to lower case.
LEFT(s,count)	Returns the first count characters from the beginning of the text s.
LENGTH(s)	Returns the length of text in characters.
LOCATE(search,s,[start])	Returns the first match for the term search in the text s. The match is given as an offset number: (1=left, 0=not found) Setting a starting point within the text string is optional.
LTRIM(s)	Removes leading spaces and non-printing characters from the beginning of a text string.

OCTET_LENGTH(str)	Returns the length of a text string in bytes. This corresponds to twice the length in characters.
RAWTOHEX(s1)	Converts to hexadecimals, reverse of HEXTORAW().
REPEAT(s,count)	Repeats the text string s count times.
REPLACE(s,replace,s2)	Replaces all existing occurrences of replace in the text string s by the text s2.
RIGHT(s,count)	Opposite of LEFT; returns the last count characters at the end of a text string.
RTRIM(s)	Removes all spaces and non-printing characters from the end of a text string.
SOUNDEX(s)	Returns a 4-character code, corresponding to the sound of s – matches the function DIFFERENCE().
SPACE(count)	Returns count spaces.
SUBSTR(s,start[,len])	Abbreviation for SUBSTRING.
SUBSTRING(s,start[,len])	Returns the text s from the start position (1=left). If length is left out, the whole string is returned.
UCASE(s)	Converts a string to upper case.
LOWER(s)	As LCASE(s)
UPPER(s)	As UCASE(s)

Date/Time

CURDATE()	Returns the current date.
CURTIME()	Returns the current time.
DATEDIFF(string, datetime1, datetime2)	Date difference between two dates- compares date/time values. The entry in string determines the units in which the difference is returned: ms=millisecond, ss=second, mi=minute, hh=hour, dd=day, mm=month, yy = year. Both the long and the short forms can be used for string.
DAY(date)	Returns the day of the month (1-31).
DAYNAME(date)	Returns the English name of the day.
DAYOFMONTH(date)	Returns the day of the month (1-31). Synonym for DAY()
DAYOFWEEK(date)	Returns the weekday as a number (1 represents Sunday).
DAYOFYEAR(date)	Returns the day of the year (1-366).
HOUR(time)	Returns the hour (0-23).
MINUTE(time)	Returns the minute (0-59).

MONTH(date)	Returns the month (1-12).
MONTHNAME(date)	Returns the English name of the month.
NOW()	Returns the current date and the current time together as a timestamp. Alternatively CURRENT_TIMESTAMP can be used.
QUARTER(date)	Returns the quarter of the year (1-4).
SECOND(time)	Returns the seconds part of the time (0-59).
WEEK(date)	Returns the week of the year (1-53).
YEAR(date)	Returns the year part of a date entry.
CURRENT_DATE	Synonym for CURDATE(), SQL-Standard, *Base gives the message: Access is denied.*
CURRENT_TIME	Synonym for CURTIME(), SQL-Standard.
CURRENT_TIMESTAMP	Synonym for NOW(), SQL-Standard.

Database connection

Except for IDENTITY(), which has no meaning in Base, all these can be carried out using **Direct SQL Command**.

DATABASE()	Returns the name of the database to which this connection belongs.
USER()	Returns the username of this connection.
CURRENT_USER	SQL standard function, synonym for USER().
IDENTITY()	Returns the last value for an autovalue field, which was created in the current connection. This is used in macro coding to transfer a primary key in one table to become a foreign key for another table.

System

IFNULL(exp,value)	If exp is NULL, value is returned, otherwise exp. Alternatively as an extension COALESCE() can be used. Exp and value must have the same data type.
CASEWHEN(exp,v1,v2)	If exp is true, v1 is returned, otherwise v2. Alternatively CASE WHEN can be used. CASE WHEN works better with the GUI.
CONVERT(term,type)	Converts term into another data type.
CAST(term AS type)	Synonym for CONVERT().
COALESCE(expr1,expr2, expr3,...)	If expr1 is not NULL, returns expr1, otherwise expr2 is checked, then expr3 and so on.
NULLIF(v1,v2)	If v1 is equal to v2, NULL is returned, otherwise v1.
CASE v1 WHEN v2 THEN v3 [ELSE v4] END	If v1 is equal to v2, v3 is returned. Otherwise v4 is returned or NULL, if there is no ELSE clause.

CASE WHEN expr1 THEN v1[WHEN expr2 THEN v2] [ELSE v4] END	If expr1 is true, v1 is returned [optionally further conditions can be set]. Otherwise v4 is returned or NULL if there is no ELSE condition.
EXTRACT ({YEAR | MONTH | DAY | HOUR | MINUTE | SECOND} FROM <date or time>)	Can replace many of the date and time functions. Returns the year, the month, the day, etc. from a date or date/time value.
POSITION(<string expression> IN <string expression>)	If the first string is contained in the second one, the offset of the first string is given, otherwise 0 is returned.
SUBSTRING(<string expression> FROM <numeric expression> [FOR <numeric expression>])	Yields part of a text string from the position specified in FROM, optionally up to the length given in FOR.
TRIM([{LEADING | TRAILING | BOTH}] FROM <string expression>)	Non-printing special characters and spaces are removed.

Information tables for HSQLDB

Inside a database, information on all table properties and their connections to one another are stored in the *INFORMATION_SCHEMA* area. This information allows Base macros to be created that require very few arguments for their procedures. An application is to be found in the example database in the *Maintenance* module—the *Table_purge* procedure for the control of dialogs.

In a query, individual pieces of information and all the fields that belong can be provided in the following way:

```
SELECT * FROM "INFORMATION_SCHEMA"."SYSTEM_ALIASES"
```

In contrast to a normal table, it is necessary here to use *INFORMATION_SCHEMA* as a prefix to the appropriate name from the following list:

```
SYSTEM_ALIASES
SYSTEM_ALLTYPEINFO
SYSTEM_BESTROWIDENTIFIER
SYSTEM_CACHEINFO
SYSTEM_CATALOGS
SYSTEM_CHECK_COLUMN_USAGE
SYSTEM_CHECK_CONSTRAINTS
SYSTEM_CHECK_ROUTINE_USAGE
SYSTEM_CHECK_TABLE_USAGE
SYSTEM_CLASSPRIVILEGES
SYSTEM_COLUMNPRIVILEGES
SYSTEM_COLUMNS
SYSTEM_CROSSREFERENCE
SYSTEM_INDEXINFO
SYSTEM_PRIMARYKEYS
SYSTEM_PROCEDURECOLUMNS
SYSTEM_PROCEDURES
SYSTEM_PROPERTIES
```

```
SYSTEM_SCHEMAS
SYSTEM_SEQUENCES
SYSTEM_SESSIONINFO
SYSTEM_SESSIONS
SYSTEM_SUPERTABLES
SYSTEM_SUPERTYPES
SYSTEM_TABLEPRIVILEGES
SYSTEM_TABLES
SYSTEM_TABLETYPES
SYSTEM_TABLE_CONSTRAINTS
SYSTEM_TEXTTABLES
SYSTEM_TRIGGERCOLUMNS
SYSTEM_TRIGGERS
SYSTEM_TYPEINFO
SYSTEM_UDTATTRIBUTES
SYSTEM_UDTS
SYSTEM_USAGE_PRIVILEGES
SYSTEM_USERS
SYSTEM_VERSIONCOLUMNS
SYSTEM_VIEWS
SYSTEM_VIEW_COLUMN_USAGE
SYSTEM_VIEW_ROUTINE_USAGE
SYSTEM_VIEW_TABLE_USAGE
```

Database repair for *.odb files

Regular backing up of data should be standard practice when using a PC. Backup copies are the simplest way to return to an even halfway current state for your data. However, in practice this is often lacking.

In the case of sudden PC crashes, it can happen that open databases (internal HSQLDB databases) can no longer be opened in LibreOffice. Instead, when you attempt to open the database, you are asked for a filter corresponding to the format.

The problem here is that part of the data in an open database is contained in working memory and is only temporarily copied to intermediate storage. Only when the file is closed is the whole database written back into the file and repacked.

To get access again to your data, you may find the following procedure helpful:

1. Create a copy of your database for the steps that follow.
2. Try to open the copy with an archiving program. In the case of *.odb files, we are dealing with a compressed format, a Zip archive. If the file cannot be opened directly, try renaming it from *.odb to *.zip. If that does not open it, your database is past saving.
3. The following folders will always be seen after opening a database file in an archiving program:

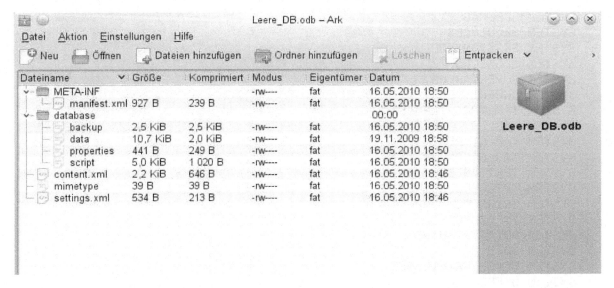

Dateiname		Größe	Komprimiert	Modus	Eigentümer	Datum
∨ 📁	META-INF			-rw----	fat	16.05.2010 18:50
└ 📄	manifest.xml	927 B	239 B	-rw----	fat	16.05.2010 18:50
∨ 📁	database					00:00
├ 📄	backup	2,5 KiB	2,5 KiB	-rw----	fat	16.05.2010 18:50
├ 📄	data	10,7 KiB	2,0 KiB	-rw----	fat	19.11.2009 18:58
├ 📄	properties	441 B	249 B	-rw----	fat	16.05.2010 18:50
└ 📄	script	5,0 KiB	1 020 B	-rw----	fat	16.05.2010 18:50
├ 📄	content.xml	2,2 KiB	646 B	-rw----	fat	16.05.2010 18:46
├ 📄	mimetype	39 B	39 B	-rw----	fat	16.05.2010 18:50
└ 📄	settings.xml	534 B	213 B	-rw----	fat	16.05.2010 18:46

Leere_DB.odb

4. The database file must be decompressed. The most important information, as far as the data is concerned, are in the subfolder `database` in the files `data` and `script`.

5. It may be necessary to look at the `script` file and test it for contradictions. This step can, however, be left for the testing stage. The `script` file contains above all the description of the table structure.

6. Create a new empty database file and open this file with the archiving program.

7. Replace the files `data` and `script` in the new database file with the files unpacked in step 4.

8. Close the archiving program. If it was necessary to rename the file to *.zip before opening it in the archiving program (this depends on your operating system), now rename it again to *.odb.

9. Open the database file in LibreOffice. You should be able to access your tables again.

10. How far your queries, forms, and reports can be recovered in a similar way must be the subject of further testing.

See also: http://forum.openoffice.org/en/forum/viewtopic.php?f=83&t=17125

If, as described in the following pages, you are using external HSQLDB, there may be a further problem with the *.odb file connected with some LibreOffice versions. If external HSQLDB is used, the safest way is through the hsqldb.jar-archive, which is supplied with LibreOffice. If a different archive is used, it can lead to the internal database suddenly becoming inaccessible. This is because LibreOffice 3.x has difficulty distinguishing between internal and external HSQLDB and produces warnings of an incompatibility between versions.

If internal databases can no longer be opened, you must use as your external database the supplied `hsqldb.jar` file. In addition, you must extract from the *.odb file the `database` folder. The properties file in this case has an entry that leads to the above error in LibreOffice:

    version=1.8.1 on line 11

This line should be changed to:

    version=1.8.0

Afterwards the database folder is put back into the *.odb package and the database can once more be opened in LibreOffice.

Connecting a database to an external HSQLDB

Internal HSQLDB is indistinguishable from the external variant. If, as in the following description, the initial access to the database is from the outside, no server function is necessary. You just need the archive program which is supplied with LibreOffice. You will find it on the path under **/program/classes/hsqldb.jar**. The use of this archive is the safest solution, as you then get no version problems.

External HSQLDB is freely available for download at http://hsqldb.org/. When the database is installed, the following steps must be performed in LibreOffice:

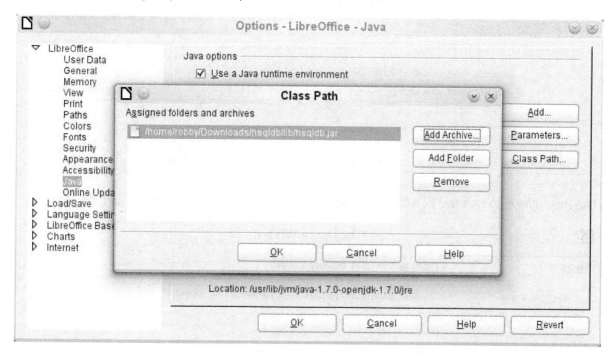

If the database driver does not lie on the Java-Runtime path, it must be entered as a Class Path under **Tools > Options > Java**.

The connection to the external database uses JDBC. The database file should be stored in a particular directory. This directory can be freely chosen. In the following example it is in the home folder. The rest of the directory path and the name of the database are not given here.

It is important, if data in the database are to be written using the GUI, that next to the database name the words **";default_schema=true"** are written.

So:

```
jdbc:hsqldb:file:/home/PathToDatabase/Databasename;default_schema=true
```

In the folder you will find the files:

```
Databasename.backup
Databasename.data
Databasename.properties
Databasename.script
Databasename.log
```

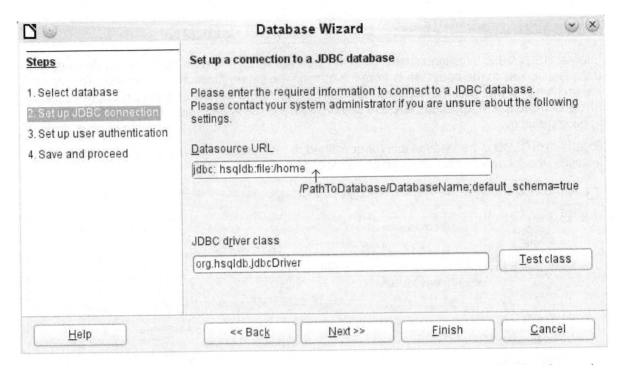

The next step is to give the default user, if nothing in the HSQLDB configuration is to be changed:

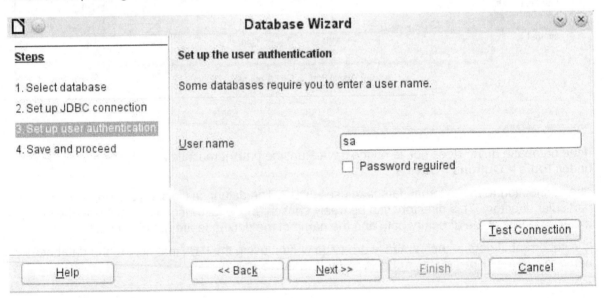

This creates the connection and the database becomes accessible.

| **Caution** ⚠ | If an external database is edited with a version of HSQLDB 2.x, it can no longer be converted into an internal database under LibreOffice. This is because of additional functions which are not present in version 1.8.x. This terminates the invocation in the case of version 1.8.x while the script file of the database is being read in. |
| | In the same way an external database which has once been edited with a version of the second series cannot afterwards be edited with version 1.8.x, which is compatible with LibreOffice. |

Changing the database connection to external HSQLDB

Internal HSQL databases have the disadvantage that data storage involves a compressed archive. Only on compression are all the data finally written. This can more easily lead to data loss than when working with an external database. The following section shows the steps necessary to successfully change an existing database from an *.odb archive to an external version in HSQL.

From a copy of the existing database, extract the `database` directory. Copy the contents into an arbitrary directory as described above. Add the database name to the resultant filenames:

```
Databasename.backup
Databasename.data
Databasename.properties
Databasename.script
Databasename.log
```

Now the `content.xml` file must be extracted from the *.odb archive. Use any simple text editor to find the following lines:

```
<db:connection-data><db:connection-resource
xlink:href="sdbc:embedded:hsqldb"/><db:login db:is-password-
required="false"/></db:connection-data><db:driver-settings/>
```

These lines must be replaced with a connection to an external database, in this case a connection to a database with the name Union, in the `hsqldb_data` directory.

```
<db:connection-data><db:connection-resource
xlink:href="jdbc:hsqldb:file:/home/robby/documents/databases/hsqldb_da
ta/Union;default_schema=true"/><db:login db:user-name="sa" db:is-
password-required="false"/></db:connection-data><db:driver-settings
db:java-driver-class="org.hsqldb.jdbcDriver"/>
```

If, as described above, the basic configuration of HSQLDB was not damaged, the username and the optional password must also agree.

After changing the code, `content.xml` must be put back into the *.odb archive. The `database` directory in the archive is now surplus to requirements. The data will in the future be accessed through the external database.

Changing the database connection for multi-user access

For multi-user access, HSQLDB must be made available over a server. How the installation of the server is carried out varies depending on your operating system. For OpenSuSE, it is only necessary to download the appropriate package and to start the server centrally using YAST (runlevel setting). Users of other operating systems and other Linux distributions can likely find suitable advice on the Internet.

In the home directory on the server (in SuSE, **/var/lib/hsqldb**), you will find, among other things, a directory called `data`, in which the database is to be filed, and a file called `server.properties`, which controls the access to the databases in this directory.

The following lines reproduce the complete contents of this file on my computer. It controls access to two databases, namely the original default database (which can be used as a new database) and the database that was extracted from the *.odb file.

```
# Hsqldb Server cfg file.
# See the Advanced Topics chapter of the Hsqldb User Guide.

server.database.0    file:data/db0
server.dbname.0      firstdb
server.urlid.0       db0-url
```

```
server.database.1    file:data/union
server.dbname.1      union
server.urlid.1       union-url

server.silent        true
server.trace         false

server.port          9001
server.no_system_exit            true
```

The database 0 is addressed with the name firstdb, although the individual files in the data directory begin with db0. I added my own database as Database 1. Here the database name and file begin identically.

The two databases are addressed in the following way:

```
jdbc:hsqldb:hsql://localhost/firstdb;default_schema=true
username sa
password
jdbc:hsqldb:hsql://localhost/union;default_schema=true
username sa
password
```

The suffix **;default_schema=true** to the URL, which is necessary for write access using the graphical user interface of LibreOffice, is permanently included.

If you actually need to work on the server, you will want to consider if the database needs to be password-protected for security reasons.

Now you can connect to the server using LibreOffice.

With this access data, the server can be loaded on its own computer. On a network with other computers, you must give either the host name or the IP address to the server, which in this case is running on my computer.

Example: My computer has the IP 192.168.0.20 and is known on the network by the name lin_serv. Now suppose there is another computer to be entered for connection to the database:

```
jdbc:hsqldb:hsql://192.168.0.20/union;default_schema=true
```

or:

```
jdbc:hsqldb:hsql://lin_serv/union;default_schema=true
```

The database is now connected and we can write into it. Quickly, however, an additional problem appears. The previously automatically generated values are suddenly no longer incremented. For this purpose we need an additional setting.

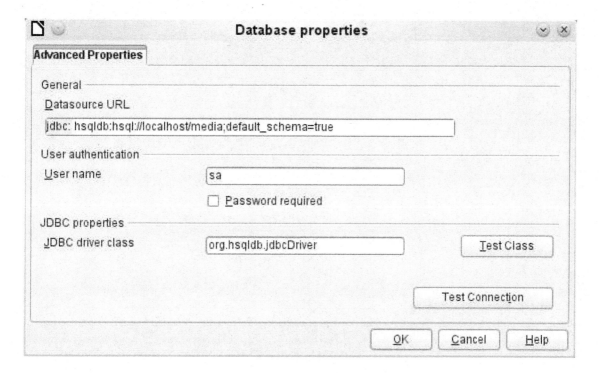

Auto-incrementing values with external HSQLDB

To use autovalues, different procedures for table configuration are needed according to the version of LibreOffice. Common to all of them is the following entry under **Edit > Database > Advance settings**:

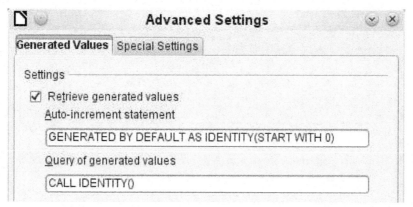

Adding **GENERATED BY DEFAULT AS IDENTITY(START WITH 0)** causes the function of the automatically incrementing values for the primary key to be set. The GUI in LibreOffice takes up this command, but unfortunately prefaces the statement with **NOT NULL**, so that the command sequence for HSQLDB is not readable. Here you must ensure that HSQLDB gets sent the above command so that the corresponding field will contain the primary key.

Note	In LibreOffice the entry of autovalues using the GUI is not possible for this reason. Users of these versions should first create a table with a primary key field that does *not* auto-increment and then enter directly using **Tools > SQL**: ALTER TABLE "Table_name" ALTER COLUMN "ID" INT GENERATED BY DEFAULT AS IDENTITY(START WITH 0) This assumes that the primary key field has the name ID.

CPSIA information can be obtained
at www.ICGtesting.com
Printed in the USA
LVOW03s1803240216

476544LV00025B/540/P